Jerry Bird

The Making of a Skydiving Legend

Jerry Bird

The Making of a Skydiving Legend

Created by Sam Alexander and Raylene West with Jerry Bird
Edited by Linda Collison

Jerry Bird: The Making of a Skydiving Legend is published by Ground Rush Productions, 2025. All Rights Reserved.

Cover and frontispiece created by Chris Johnston with his photograph of Jerry Bird in front of wings painted by Lizzie Jones and historical photograph taken by Carl Boenish.
Book interior design by Mayfly book design.

Names: Bird, Jerry. Alexander, Sam. West, Raylene. Collison, Linda (editor and contributor).

Description: First edition. Steamboat Springs, Ground Rush, 2025. Nonfiction; includes historical images, notes and bibliography.

Identifiers: Library of Congress Control Number: 2025909628
ISBN: 979-8-9852592-5-4 hardback
ISBN: 979-8-9852592-3-0 paperback
ISBN: 979-8-9852592-4-7 e-book

Subjects: Bird, Jerry—Sports & Recreation/Air Sports/Skydiving—Sports & Recreation/History
Biography & Autobiography/Sports—United States—Americas—Canada—Australia—Northern Europe—Social Life & customs—20th century.
Thema Subjects: SMC Air sports and recreation; DNBS Biography: sport; DNBS1 Autobiography: sport; 3MPQ Later 20th century, c 1950–1999

Historical articles and covers first appearing in United States Parachute Association's *Parachutist* Magazine and Australia's *Skydiver* Magazine reprinted with permission.

Compilation copyright © Ground Rush Productions, LLC 2025. All rights reserved.

Ground Rush Productions is an imprint of Fiction House, Ltd.
Steamboat Springs, Colorado.

It's about the people. You can't do RW by yourself.
Jerry Bird

Foreword

It was Jerry Bird who turned sport parachuting into skydiving, and freefalling into human flight. He showed us how to fly together in ways we didn't think were possible. His imagination, leadership, teamwork and perseverance laid the groundwork and built the foundations that would launch Formation Skydiving competition, large formations, and set the pathways for Freeflying, Wingsuiting, Tracking, Angle Flying, and what is still to come. His contributions to the sport are unmatched and we owe him so much regardless of how we love to fly. This book is such an important part of skydiving history. —*Dan Brodsky-Chenfeld*; June 14, 2025

Contents

Foreword vii
Preface xv
Editor's Note xvii
Prologue xix
1. No Star Nights 1
2. Becoming a Skydiver 7
3. Life's a Beech 10
4. It's All Relative 16
    DZ Relatives 18
5. Hollywood Jumps 20
6. 1964 22
    World's First 6-Man 22
7. 1965 24
    Rod Pack's 'Chuteless Jump 24
    First 8-Man Star 25
    Military Service 26
8. 1967 30
    Bob Buquor 30
        Bob Buquor Memorial Star Crest 31
    The Summer of the World's First Ten-Man Star 33
    The First Rumbleseat 10-Man Speed Star Competition 39

9. 1968 43
   Jerry Bird's All Stars 43
10. 1969 46
   First All-Girl 8-Way 47
   Third Annual Rumbleseat Meet 48
      Third Annual Ten-Man Star Meet: A Bird's Eye View 48
   First 10-Way Star Meet Beyond California 51
   1969: RW—Where do we go from here? 52
11. 1970 55
   Stars over Bled 55
      Ray Cottingham: "Meanwhile, High Over Yugoslavia" 58
12. Jerry Bird's All Stars Recall 73
   Sam Alexander 73
   Dick (Rich) Gernand 80
   Donna Wardean 82
   Charlie Wickliffe 83
   Remembering Terry Ward 87
   Carl Boenish 92
   Joe Morgan 95
   Ray Cottingham 100
   Ted Webster 101
   Raylene West 103
13. 1971 105
   Who was D.B. Cooper? 105
14. 1972 111
   World's First 24-Way Star 111
   The Inclusion of RW in U.S. National Competition 112
   The RW Council and RW Underground Newsletter 112
   Jan Works 113
   1972 U.S. Nationals and XI World Parachuting Championships ... 115

15. Sequential RW	119
Jerry Bird's All Stars Scorecard	121
16. Beyond California	123
17. 1972–1976: It Happened at Casa Grande (the Gulch)	125
Mike Larson	125
Skratch Garrison	126
Matt Farmer	127
Jim Captain	127
Jackie Smith	127
Mia Elmsater	128
First All-Girl 16-way	128
BJ Worth	129
18. Columbine Turkey Farm	130
1973 U.S. Nationals	130
1973: Columbine Turkey Farm Wins First World Cup of Relative Work	131
Garry Carter	132
Charmian Cliff: in Bird's words	135
19. Bird and BJ	138
20. 1974: Wings of Orange	146
The Bird Rig	147
21. First Door to Your Right, Then First Star to Your Left	150
22. The Thrill of Victory	154
Mirror Image, 1979	154
U.S. Nationals 1981	155
World Meet 1981	158
Jim Captain	158
23. Utah Daze	161
24. Bird Seminars, Bird Camps, and Coaching Military Teams	170
Bob Sturtivant	173
Rüdiger Wenzel	174
Victor "Lince" Nickolich	175

25. 1977: Smithsonian Air & Space Museum Display 177
26. The 1980s 180
    Boogies, the Bird Machine, and Beth 180
    1984: Jerry Bird Awarded the da Vinci Diploma 184
27. Friends to the Left of Me, Friends to the Right 186
    Dieter Kirsch 186
    Mike "Michigan" Sandberg 188
    Jack Gregory 194
    Dr. Ruth 196
    Steve Woodford 198
    Kung Fu Charlie 199
    Late Jake 203
28. Around the World with Jerry Bird 207
    Venezuela 207
        Jumping Angel Falls 211
        Venezuela 80-Way Formations 217
    Canadian Skies 220
        Bob "Greenman" Smith 220
        William Renfroe 227
    Norway 233
        Busted in Norway 236
    Boogies, Boogies, Boogies! 247
        Iceland Beer Boogie 247
        Stars Down Under 252
        Sweden's Hercules Boogie 255
        Anders Nyqvist 255
        Kjartan Reithaug 256
        Jack Gregory 256
        Party in Paradise 257
        Equinox Boogie 264
        World Boogie in Bali 267

29. Movie Stunt Work	271
Jake Lombard	271
BJ Worth "Filling in for 007"	273
30. Formation Records	282
Early Records	282
Diamond World Record	283
BJ's World Team	285
31. Family Man	289
32. 1990: Skydive City	294
33. Family Matters	297
34. 21st Century Skydiving	302
Cliff Weaver	304
35. Fear	307
36. What Made Jerry Bird Jerry Bird?	311
37. Life After Skydiving	314
JB Bird	316
Coda	321
More Memories & Testimonials	323
About the Creators	335
Acknowledgements	337
Bibliography	341

Preface

In 2018 Jerry Bird called Raylene West and me with a request. Raylene and I had been divorced for many years, but we were still friends and we still shared that friendship with Bird. After a decades-long career as a world-traveling professional skydiver, Jerry wanted to capture and share his stories. He had been trying in vain to write a memoir, but the words just wouldn't flow. As he put it, I'm a storyteller, not a writer. The idea was we would all get together and record those stories. Jerry thought it would take a few days.

Jerry, JB and Rigby with Raylene during one of the Alexander West interview sessions. Sam Alexander, photographer.

Boy, was he wrong. About 15 months and two Florida trips later, we had recorded almost 45 hours of memories, spending countless hours in The Blue Bird, an old school bus that serves as Jerry's office, retreat, storage shed, and mini museum. Jerry is indeed a storyteller and a story maker.

For decades, Jerry Bird was the most recognizable name in skydiving. It didn't matter where you were on this planet, if you encountered a jumper, they'd ask if you knew Jerry Bird. It wasn't just about his skills as a freefall competitor. Jerry was a world-class team leader, organizer, teacher, mentor, an Army Green Beret, and a Hollywood stuntman. Many people all over the world and from all walks of life, including foreign royals and heads of the U.S. Armed Forces have called him friend. His likeness was hung in the Smithsonian's Air and Space Museum, he was one of the first chosen to be in the International Skydiving Museum's Hall of Fame, and his picture is in the Guinness Book Of World Records. Most importantly, over the years thousands of sport skydivers have joined him in freefall and on the ground in friendship.

Dive in and enjoy! —*Sam Alexander*

Editor's Note

This book is a compilation of writings and photographs by teammates, competitors, and friends, interwoven with Jerry Bird's own reminiscences, in his own voice transcribed on the page. It is at once a group biography, a cultural history of the times and a personal memoir of the man whose influence on sport skydiving was phenomenal and is still felt today. During the 1960s, '70s and '80s, when the sport was still young, the name and fame of Jerry Bird spread quickly among skydivers all over the world—not only because he was a champion sport skydiver who introduced freefall star-making to the world, but because he went outside the skygods' eyrie to fly with anyone who wanted to learn from him. Jerry Bird made us all stars. —*Linda Collison*

Prologue

In November of 1974, my friend Jory Pacht and I drove from Laramie, Wyoming to Casa Grande, Arizona—nearly a thousand miles—to jump at the Thanksgiving Turkey Boogie. I was a relatively new skydiver with about 240 jumps over the span of two and a half years (jumps were hard to come by when you lived in Laramie) and I went with the goal of getting my SCR. There were plenty of moderately experienced jumpers who showed up with the same goal, so all I had to do was organize loads until I found seven other more or less capable jumpers.

At the time, the drop zone at Casa Grande was the home of literally the best skydivers in the world, who were mostly busy inventing the sport, but some of them would occasionally deign to jump with a mere mortal like me, and one of those was the legendary Jerry Bird. Jerry had the reputation of being willing to jump with anyone, so after a few dives I felt that I had a group that could be successful, and I asked Jerry to join us, which he did.

The star was building slowly when Jerry docked fifth, and when he did, I lost all interest in everything else. I just stared at him. Oh my God, I'm in a star with Jerry Bird!

But the truth is, Jerry didn't "jump with anyone" entirely out of altruism. Being on one of Jerry's teams was a demanding experience, so his teams suffered from attrition from year to year, and he was always looking for new talent. As I looked at him, I saw him looking around the star, and his face said what he was probably thinking: None of these people can skydive for shit. We did not get an 8-way and I never asked

him on another jump. But I did get my SCR there a couple of jumps later. And Jory got his Night SCR on that trip—on a load with Jerry Bird.
—*Bob Russell SCR #4247*

Bob and Jory weren't the only ones to make the trip to Casa Grande, a small airport in the Arizona desert. From November 1972 until the summer of '77 people came from all over the country and beyond, to jump with the leading freefall skydivers of the time. Bob recalls three guys who showed up with their wives in an RV with Indiana tags. "They were big boys, really big. And they were perfectly willing to lay base for others to swoop in and dock on. They had driven all that way to get their SCRs—and they got them."

Unlike 21st century commercial skydiving operations with their twin engine turboprops, during the 1960s and '70s only a few drop zones had aircraft capable of carrying eight or more people to jump altitude. The experienced skydivers at those DZs were the skydiving elite. They only jumped with certain people—and with a few notable exceptions—they weren't willing to spend valuable freefall time teaching those outside their trusted coterie. Bird was. Always on the lookout for skilled jumpers who wanted to be part of his team, Jerry organized successful "walk-up" formations among skydivers he had just met.

A national and world champion sport skydiver and a military freefall instructor, Jerry is remembered for more than his flying skills. He was organizer, coach, gear designer, teammate, competitor, friend—and he continues to be a friend to countless people of many nationalities. Jerry Bird connected us in freefall.

This book was begun by Jerry's All Star teammate, Sam Alexander, and longtime friend, Raylene West, whose many hours of recorded unrehearsed interviews inspired this sport skydiving bio-memoir and shaped its format. Other interviews were videoed by Ground Rush Productions at Spaceland, Skydive City, Elsinore, and Perris drop zones. The International Skydiving Museum and Hall of Fame posted interviews with Jerry on their website and on YouTube. In this book Jerry's inimitable voice, his way of storytelling, is preserved as an oral history alongside writings, published articles, shared memories, and photographs of his contemporaries.

1

No Star Nights

Jerry Bird left town behind the wheel of his brother's hand-me-down car. It was the summer of '63; John F. Kennedy was President of the United States, a political conflict in Southeast Asia was heating up, and twenty-year-old Jerry was hell-bent for the west coast. Southern California!

Windows rolled down, his blonde hair blew in the hot breeze as he crossed the Fort Steuben Bridge and rolled into Ohio. In the rearview the black smokestacks of Weirton shrank until only their smoke remained visible, a vast haze spreading across the valley. The factory whistle blew, summoning the second shift to work. But that whistle meant nothing to Jerry. He didn't even hear it, radio cranked up playing *Summertime Blues*.[1] Bird was already gone.

In the passenger seat, a buddy rode along and chipped in for gas. The West Coast was where it was happening, that was the scene. All over America radio stations were playing surf music—The Delltones, Jan and Dean, the Beach Boys. Kids who had never seen an ocean knew the names of all the California surf breaks and what it meant to shoot the curl and hang ten.

---

1. Written by Eddie Cochran and his manager Jerry Capehart, "Summertime Blues" was recorded by Eddie Cochran and released in 1958. It has been covered by various bands including The Who at the 1969 Woodstock Festival. In the 1950s, '60s, and '70s music reached and connected young people through radio waves, vinyl records, cassette tapes and live concerts.

From Weirton, West Virginia, to the City of Angels is 2400 miles. Like Todd and Buzz of the television series *Route 66*,[2] they followed the long asphalt trail across America. Unlike Todd and Buzz, Jerry and his companion did not stop in small towns along the way to pick up temporary jobs and get into complicated relationships with women—no, Jerry was saving that for when he got to the promised land. He drove fast, only stopping for gas and to grab something to eat. He felt like he was already late. He had a few semesters of college under his belt, but engineering wasn't what he wanted to do.

Skydiving had not yet crossed his mind. In the summer of 1963, jumping out of airplanes was not what most Americans would consider a sport for everyday people, although it was starting to catch on, popularized by the television series *Ripcord*.[3]

The previous autumn, the United States hosted the 1962 World Cup of Parachuting. Although it was the sixth biennial international meet, this was the first time the U.S. hosted the competition, held in Orange, Massachusetts. He did not know it yet but that summer—the summer of '63—Jerry Bird would jump out of an airplane. That jump would change his life. And he, in turn, would change the sport in ways no one could have foreseen.

Jerry was born in Ellijay, Georgia, on March 6, 1943, to Carolyn Blanche Woodward and John Marion Bird. He was the fourth of six kids. The Birds and the Woodwards had called Georgia home for generations, but when Jerry was three years old his parents broke away and moved to Weirton.

---

2. The television series *Route 66* was created by Stirling Silliphant and Herbert B. Leonard and aired from 1960-1964. Lancer Productions Limited. IMDB. Two foot-loose young men head west and travel around in a Corvette convertible in a version of the Great American Road Trip.

3. *Ripcord*, created by Harry Redmond, Jr. (1961-1963) television series, United Artists Television. IMDB. Two enterprising parachutists have an airplane and lots of adventures chasing criminals and rescuing people. Many pioneer parachutists cite the TV series as inspiring them to jump.

"My father moved us all north, lock, stock, and barrel," he relates in an interview with the producers.[4]

"There had been generations of Birds and Woodwards in Georgia. My mother was from Ellijay and my father's people were from Chickamauga. But my dad followed the opportunity; he was an engineer."

The Bessemer Process—the first that allowed for the inexpensive mass production of steel—involved forcing oxygen into molten iron to oxidate and burn off impurities. Mass-produced steel was in high demand for building ships, trains and rails, aircraft, and high-rise buildings in the first half of the twentieth century. Steel mills cropped up all through the Ohio River Valley, from Western Pennsylvania to Illinois. The mills provided jobs and boosted the local economy.

Weirton's population peaked in 1960, with over 28,000 residents.[5] "Many of the workers were immigrants," Jerry remembers. "A lot of Italians, Greek, Polish, Russians, everybody. We don't care if they don't speak English, we need these workers. A whole mix of people from all over the world and everybody in the town had a job, a job for life, working for the company. My dad was a big shot in the mill. Sometimes, when I was little, he'd take me to work with him. He wore a white hat, and he made oxygen for the furnaces."

"When I was little, we couldn't see the stars in the nighttime sky because the furnaces of the mill turned the darkness into a red glow," wrote Anna Egan Smucker in her 1989 book, *No Star Nights*. Anna also grew up in Weirton, the setting for her memoir, written as a children's book with an environmental message. "The windows in our school were kept closed to try to keep the graphite and smoke out. On really windy days we could hear the dry, dusty sound of grit hitting against the glass . . .

---

4. This chapter and subsequent chapters are based on a series of recorded interviews with Jerry Bird, former teammate Sam Alexander and friend Raylene West: 2018, 2019, 2022 and also recorded interviews with Ground Rush Productions; August 7-8, 2022, as well as many conversations with Jerry Bird.

5. "Weirton's population peaked in 1960" West Virginia Public Broadcasting, "What Happened to Weirton? Part 3 "As Goes the Mill..." https//wvpublic.org/what-happened-to-weirton-part-3-as-goes-the-mill?amp=1

Some days it seemed as though there was a giant lid covering the valley, keeping the smoke in. It was so thick you couldn't see anything clearly."[6]

In Weirton, back then, you couldn't see the stars at night. But out west in California, at Caltech University, a Dutch astronomer and his team had discovered a new star-like source of energy, a quasi-stellar radio source, or *quasar*, as it was dubbed. This discovery by Maartin Schmidt changed astronomy and our understanding of the universe at a time when America was in a space race with the Soviets who had launched the first unmanned satellite in 1957. The new aerial sport of skydiving was also part of the space race and parachutes are an important technology in safe water landings of capsules.

"Weirton was one of the most polluted towns in America—graphite and smoke—the main street cut right through the mill," Jerry recalls. "In the morning they'd come out and sweep the graphite off the street like it was snow. But the Weirton Steel Corporation provided good jobs that paid well. Everybody lived in brick houses and had two cars. If you throw a rock that way it's the Ohio River and Ohio, and if you threw a rock that way it's Pennsylvania. From my dad's farm it was half a mile and you'd be in Ohio and five miles the other way and you'd be in Pennsylvania. A lot of guys were there for life. The mill guys worked hard, and on payday they would go across the river to Steubenville, Ohio to drink. In Steubenville, nobody asked you how old you were. They were glad to take your money."

Like many kids, Jerry enjoyed sports. His father, John Bird, had played minor league baseball; his mother, Blanche, had enjoyed playing basketball. Jerry wanted to be a football or basketball player in the worst way. "I wanted to be Larry Bird, but I was too short, and I can't jump," he jokes. "But I was a state champion in wrestling. The only guy I ever lost to was Bobby Douglas. You've heard of him."

Douglas, from Bellaire, Ohio, downriver from Weirton, West Virginia, went on to become a national freestyle wrestling champion and Olympic medalist before making a lifelong career coaching. Both Bobby

---

6. The heading for Chapter One is borrowed from Anna Eagan Smucker's, No Star Nights, Alfred A. Knopf Books for Young Readers, 1989. The quotations are from that book (pages unnumbered.) Jerry recommended this children's picture book to us.

and Jerry would eventually achieve Hall of Fame status—Bobby Douglas for wrestling and Jerry Bird for skydiving.

"So, there I am, stuck in West Virginia, it's 1963 and I'm California Dreaming[7] before the song even came out."

The Mamas & the Papas hit song summed up the mid-century westward migration; a new gold rush was on, only this time the gold wasn't underground, it was in the air, it was all around. The sunshine, the climate, the youth culture, the lifestyle—kids all over America listened to California songs on the radio and watched Frankie Avalon and Annette Funicello's antics in *Beach Party*[8] at their local cinema. Jan and Dean's "Surf City" was the number one song in the country in July of '63; would-be surfers wanted to go to California to "shoot the curl and check out the parties for a surfer girl."[9]

Americans were on the move, but not everyone was going to California that summer. A quarter of a million people marched on Washington, gathering at the Lincoln Memorial, calling for an end to segregation and racial discrimination. The times, they were a-changin'—but not fast enough for some.[10]

Jerry's brother John was a roller in the steel plant and his brother Richard became a chemical engineer. "My whole family worked for the mill; they had lifetime jobs there. My sisters and two brothers, they never left the nest." But Jerry was ready to fly.

---

7. "California Dreamin." Song written by John Phillips and Michelle Phillips,1963, it was first recorded by Barry McGuire, and in 1965, by the Mamas & the Papas.

8. William Asher, Director. *Beach Party*, a motion picture released in 1963. American International Pictures. IMDB.

9. "Shoot the curl and check out the parties for a surfer girl" Lyrics, "Surf City," written by Brian Wilson, Jan Barry and Dean Torrence, Liberty Records, 1963, it was the first surf song to become a national number one hit. As surfing became a focused and defining lifestyle for some, so did skydiving.

10. "The times they are a-changin" was written and performed by Bob Dylan; it was the title track of his 1964 album. Columbia Records.

They picked up Route 66 in Missouri, then broke down in Joplin, having traveled 850 miles—about a third of the way to California. A passerby towed them to a service station where the mechanic told Jerry the Oldsmobile wasn't worth fixing, but he had a car—a '52 Pontiac Chieftain he would sell him cheap, a car guaranteed to get him to California.

"The floorboards were all rusted out and somebody had cut up pieces of tin from some road signs to cover the holes in the floor. It didn't even have reverse." But Jerry bought it anyway—for twenty-five bucks plus his brother's car in trade. The guys moved their boxes and bags from the broke-down Oldsmobile into the rusted-out Chieftain that only drove forward. And forward they went, through the rest of Missouri and the southeast corner of Kansas, across Oklahoma and the panhandle of Texas, tracking through New Mexico, Arizona, to California at last.

Upon reaching the Golden State, they were amazed to see orange trees, palm trees, Joshua trees, and more blue sky than they had seen all year in the Ohio River Valley. Cruising along the freeways, they came to rest at a friend's pad on Century Boulevard. His road trip companion soon hitched a ride back home, but Jerry and his Chieftain Pontiac stayed in LA. With the friend's help, he found a working transmission at the junkyard and another buddy installed it. Now his car had reverse—but Jerry Bird had no intention of going back.

—*Linda Collison*

2

Becoming a Skydiver

After fleeing the steel town of Weirton, West Virginia, Jerry got a job at Jorgensen Steel and Aluminum Company in Lynwood, California. Employed as a night foreman and laboratory technician, he operated the computers and instruments that heated metals. After cashing his first paycheck, the first thing he bought was a surfboard. After all, that was why he had moved to the West Coast—not to work the graveyard shift in a steel mill but to be outdoors in the sunshine, riding the waves. And meeting girls. Jerry wanted to meet girls.

Working nights left him free to go to the beach during the day. Being fair-skinned with white-blond hair, and unaccustomed to spending much time in the sun, the first day he spent on the beach landed him in the emergency room of a local hospital with severe sunburn over much of his body. Yet as soon as he recovered, he went back—Huntington Beach, Santa Monica, Redondo Beach—with his surfboard.

Jerry was good at a lot of sports, but swimming wasn't one of them. He didn't even really like the water, he admitted later. But he kept going back to the ocean, attracted to the allure of surfing. He wanted to be an athlete, and he wanted to be a part of something. The beach was where it was at—but something in the sky captured his attention.

"One day while I was hanging there, a biplane flew over and a guy gets out of the cockpit and walks out on the wing. He was probably about a thousand feet over the water, and he suddenly does a pull off, gets jerked off the wing, and his parachute opens. There he is, under a full canopy; he does a few oscillations on his way down, and lands on the beach. Everyone was running toward him and yelling, and I thought, that looks exciting. Yeah, I'd like to do that."

His opportunity would soon come.

Jerry wasn't the only young man to flee the Ohio River steel mill towns; there was a whole enclave of emigrants from Weirton who had recently flocked to Southern California. Some guys he knew from his home town had a rock-and-roll band and Jerry would go to the bars and clubs where they were playing, to help support them. One night Jerry met an attractive girl. After a few beers and a little flirting, he asked her to go out with him that Saturday.

She smiled but shook her head. "Sorry, I've already got plans. I'm going skydiving."

"Skydiving? Hey, I want to do that. Take me, will you?"

Sure, that's what they all say, emboldened by a couple of beers. The bars are full of would-be jumpers on Friday night but come Saturday morning, most of them are nowhere to be found.

Saturday morning Jerry was ready. He rode to the drop zone with the girl he met at the bar, and the parachuting instructor, Brian Williams. On the hour and a half drive to the Lancaster drop zone, at the edge of the Mojave Desert, the instructor delivered the first jump course and by the time they got to the airstrip, Jerry knew what to do. Brian put him through the paces: practice exits, canopy control, landings, what to do in case of a parachute malfunction. Then it was time to gear up and go do it.

Jerry arched as he left the airplane, as Brian had taught him. His parachute opened less than three seconds later, sitting him upright in the harness, and he felt the adrenalin coursing through his body and the elation of being alive, 2000 feet over the California desert. After hearing the engine's drone on the climb to altitude and the noisy prop blast from the open door, the quietude seemed to sparkle in the desert air. Guiding his canopy to the landing area, Bird landed safely after a two-minute ride, the mushroom-shaped 'chute settling down behind him.

"That was great!" Williams said, "You're a natural, Jerrybird."[11]

The blonde, sunburned kid from West Virginia glowed in the warmth of his instructor's praise.

"Now let's get packed up so we can go again."

"What? You mean you do this more than once?"

Williams grinned, his eyes dancing. "Oh, yeah. It's like sex. The more you do it, the more fun it is."

Jerry made three jumps that weekend. That was all it took; he was hooked.

—*Linda Collison*

Brian Williams and Jerry Bird.

---

11. Many years later, the skydiving innovator Skratch Garrison mused, "When I met Bird everybody called him JERRYbird, smooshing his two names together and accenting the first syllable and I still think about him that way."

3

Life's a Beech

"A golden era of skydiving was the mid-sixties in Southern California"
—Jerry Bird

"Hey Bird, you owe a case of beer."

If there was one shared tradition the pioneer parachutists shared with the new generation of skydivers, it was beer drinking. Early on, it became the unwritten rule that any jumper doing something for the first time was obliged to buy a case of 24 for the DZ. New student jumpers ensured a steady supply of drop zone suds.

Jerry Bird recalls being sent to buy his first case of beer:

"We're out in the middle of nowhere, there's no stores close by. Bill Stage, one of the regulars, throws me his car keys and says, go get the beer. I go, which car is yours and he goes, that Corvette. I'm thinking wow, this guy doesn't even know me, and he trusts me with his 'vette! Oh, this guy has got a different attitude than what I grew up with, I like that. You can't do relative work by yourself, it's a group thing and there is a lot of trust involved. We all trust each other with our lives."

After that first weekend, Jerry was invited to Brian Williams's house, as an initiate into the jump instructor's Music Appreciation, Wine Sipping, and Parachute Packing Society. Brian had the first hi-fi system Jerry had ever seen.

Williams was held in high regard by the younger jumpers, and served as a role model, not just in skydiving but in the finer attributes of culture.

Jerry described his instructor as a complete skydiver. "He did demo jumps, he wore smoke. Bob Buquor, Dave Keaggy and Bob Higley were his partners. They did all kinds of camera jumps. They'd done wing-walking acts," he said. Like the one that had so impressed him that day on the beach.

Brian enjoyed teaching and encouraged new students to bring more people into the sport. He was a hands-on instructor who taught by demonstrating in freefall—one of the few teachers to do so at the time. Southern California had quite a few good skydivers, but not many of them wanted to take on newbies and teach them how to fly. Jumps were too precious to waste on "turkeys," as inexperienced and ungainly freefallers were sometimes called. The good skydivers tended to jump together exclusively, and the turkeys referred to them as skygods, only partly in jest. Turkeys too, wanted to be skygods.

In those days, the more experienced jumpers who taught students generally followed the military methods they had been taught, modifying them as they saw fit.

"You made static line jumps at first," Jerry said. "But there were no rules that said you had to make three or five, or seven. You could move on whenever your instructor thought you were safe to do a clear and pull. After I had two static line jumps and a clear and pull, Brian said, Let's do a freefall. I'll teach you in the air."

A clear and pull means you jump without a static line—you deploy your own 'chute by pulling the ripcord—but you do it as soon as you are clear of the plane. In less than five seconds you have an open parachute above you and your freefall is over. Provided, of course, the parachute doesn't malfunction.

In the 21st century, most skydivers have never made a static line jump or landed under a round parachute. Most make their first freefall on their first jump—either in tandem with the tandem master or with two AFF jumpmasters holding onto their harness.

"By the time I had 12 or 13 jumps, I could fall stable. I could dock on another person, I could track away. By the time I had about 17 jumps and there was a star load going up, Brian told me I could get on it."

Brian was my mentor; he taught me the basics of freefall. He also taught me a lot about the basics of life. Brian Williams was one of the main influences in my life" —*Jerry Bird*

Those first jumps with Brian were at the Lancaster drop zone, northeast of Los Angeles, on the edge of the Mojave Desert where it was windy much of the time. In March 1964, the operators, Chuck and Pep Hill, left Lancaster for a field near Arvin, some sixty miles northwest, just south of Bakersfield. Drop zones, in those days, were moveable feasts; often, the landing area was a farmer's field lying fallow for the year. Arvin's DZ was a shack and a few packing tables on a flat and dusty field. Chuck and Pep Hill's barebones operation attracted jumpers like Lee Hunt, Lyle Cameron, Don Molitor, and Bob Buquor.

"Brian introduced me to these guys," Jerry relates in an interview with Sam and Raylene. "They already had their D license. They were doing Hollywood stunt work. Some of the jumpers were making movies or working on the TV series *Ripcord*. Bob Buquor and Lyle Cameron were cameramen and these guys were jumping with professional equipment, like 16mm Nikon button-operated automatic cameras. At that time there were a lot of experienced people jumping at Arvin and my goal was to be on these loads. Pep ran a segregated manifest and if you were not up to snuff, she put you on Load B because Load A was what they called a Good Guy load. You had to get a nod from Brian or Bob to get on that load or the lady at manifest went, No, no, no, you do not have the experience to be on a Good Guy load."

Both Williams and Buquor soon gave Bird the nod, and then he was a Good Guy too, learning to fly with the best of them.

These Arvin jumpers and some other West Coast groups developed a reputation of being rebels, of not always following the Basic Safety Regulations established by the Parachute Club of America, (soon to reorganize as the United States Parachute Association) which some of them scorned. The Arvin gang rather liked their outlaw image and didn't see the need to pay membership dues and abide by what they felt were arbitrary guidelines for their safety. They saw no need to conform to the requirements for the organization's licenses, most of which were based on the number of jumps and landing accuracy skills and had nothing to do with freefall relative work.

The story goes that when Arvin closed and the Arvin gang showed up at Taft, Lyle Cameron said in good-natured smack-talk, "Uh oh, here come the bad guys," to which Bill Newell quipped, "No, we're the good guys," and Terry Ward added, "The Arvin Good Guys." The name stuck.[12]

The Arvin Good Guys were a fluid group with no written roster. Like a rock band, they jammed, drawing from a certain set of talent, depending upon who was available that weekend. Like rock stars, many hardcore skydivers displayed oversized egos and bold personalities, and they hung together in tight circles. But Bird didn't jump exclusively with the Arvin clique. In the early '60s there were other good skydivers doing relative work at other California DZs:

> *You'll find 'em jumping at Arvin, Oceanside, and Elsinore*
> *Bakersfield and Old River, and up in Livermore*
> *From Monterey to San Diego and way out east of L.A.*
> *Everybody's skydivin' Califor-nigh-ay*

Like "Surfin' USA," the 1963 Beach Boys song that memorializes the surf breaks, a song could've been made from the numerous California skydiving clubs and drop zones in the same era.[13]

California had open land, year-round sunshine, and an abundance of superannuated World War II-era aircraft, like twin engine Beechcraft, for sale. Skydivers all over America were experimenting with relative work but mostly jumping out of single engine Cessnas—the workhorse of

---

12. Lyle Cameron, "Letters," *Parachutist* Magazine, February 1998, 8.
13. Song "Surfin' USA" attributed to both Brian Wilson and Chuck Berry ("Sweet Little Sixteen"). Capitol Records, 1963.

Mom & Pop parachuting operations. Great little jump planes, yes—but limited in the number of skydivers they could carry at one time. Twin Beeches—radial engine D-18s—could carry twice as many; DC-3s, triple that. These aircraft were relatively inexpensive in the 1960s, and for a couple of decades they were skydiving starships, flying jumpers to 11,000 or 12,000 feet above the ground so they could dive out and fly together.

There were about 20 regular skydivers, according to Bill Newell, jumping at Arvin in the spring of 1964. Some of these regulars jumped at other clubs and drop zones too, and occasionally jumpers from other places showed up. In August of 1964, pilots Walt Mercer, with his 1947 Howard, and Dave Keaggy, with his Cessna 195, moved the Arvin drop zone about a mile west. Newell described the new DZ as a "tumbleweed-infested bone yard of animal skeletons, a dirt runway and a landing area adjacent to high-voltage lines and the highway." Meanwhile, another sub-group developed at Old River, a "wide spot in the road with two bars" just three miles away. The Latins jumped here as well."[14]

Every drop zone, every club, had its favorite meeting place—often the closest tavern, pub, or roadhouse. The Rumbleseat Bar was THE clubhouse for Southern California skydivers. From Elsinore, Oceanside, Arvin, Taft, Old River, Bakersfield and beyond, they congregated.

Over the years there were several Rumbleseat taverns, said Dennis Henley. The first one was in Hollywood. When it closed, Frank Carpenter and Willy McDonald opened up the Rumbleseat Bar/ParaScuba Club in Hermosa Beach, to which Dennis belonged. Later, there was a Rumbleseat Bar near the Elsinore operation.[15]

---

14. Bill Newell, "The Rise and Demise of the Arvin Good Guys," *Parachutist* Magazine, October 2004, 34 –37.

15. Dennis Henley, "That was the Rumbleseat ParaScubaClub," Facebook Old School Skydivers group, December 25, 2024.

The Hermosa Beach Rumbleseat tavern was Southern California's quintessential skydiving clubhouse where jumpers congregated midweek to watch films from their dives the previous weekend. This was before the availability of video and instant replay. The camera fliers shot 16mm film and 35mm stills and developed it after the weekend's jumping, to project on a big screen at the Rumbleseat for all to see and learn from.
—*Linda Collison*

4

It's All Relative

"Relative is easy to understand, but I've often wondered how the word Work got in there." —*Skratch*[16]

"Relative Work is the intentional maneuvering of two or more skydivers in close proximity to one another during freefall," wrote Dan Poynter in *The Skydiver's Handbook*, Seventh Revised Editon.[17] "Rapid precision freefall relative work is fun, fast, and exciting; there is something to learn and enjoy on every jump. Relative work is an activity that requires teamwork; it is a coordinated balancing act requiring maximum effort from each and every participant. The preparation is great while the flying time is short, and anyone in the air can blow the jump by taking out the entire formation. When successful, relative work is an incomparable joy to be shared by all. Whereas relative work was once a hit-or-miss affair between two jumpers, it is now an exact aerodynamic choreographed performance . . .

Relative work (RW) was born in 1958 when Lyle Hoffman and James Pearson made the first baton pass over Vancouver, BC. Later that year, Steve Snyder and Charlie Hillard made the first baton pass in the U.S.

---

16. Skratch is his chosen name, spelled with a *k* and no quotation marks. Skratch is a skydiving philosopher, or a philosophic skydiver who was an early creator of sequential relative work and "sky dance" dives. He and Clarice Garrison were on the Arvin Good Guys team that won the first Rumbleseat Meet in 1967.

17. Relative work. Dan Poynter began an independent publishing imprint Para Publishing in 1978 with the first edition of Parachuting: The Skydiver's Handbook. The quote comes from the seventh edition, 1998 revised, 206–207.

In subsequent years, the stick was abandoned but small *star* formations were being accomplished routinely. Size was usually held to four, the capacity of most jump planes . . ." —*Dan Poynter* and *Mike Turoff*

At first, stars were identified by the number of participants. A 4-person star was called a 4-man, even if a woman was one or more of the four. Man was not a sexist term. Like the term "mankind," it was inclusive, a synecdoche commonly used in the mid-20th century, implying "human." Most mid-century skydiving women weren't offended by the terminology but were proud to be on a 4-man—or any man—star.

Soon, "all-girl" stars[18] began to form as more "girls" learned RW and the gender neutral term "way" replaced "man." Although there were, and are, great skydivers who happen to be female, the percentage of female skydivers has always been around 15 percent.[19]

Relative work skydiving is an equal opportunity sport. Gravity doesn't care about sex or gender and the sky is an open playing field; the proof is in the completed star.

Andy Keech had this to say in his photographic work-of-art book trilogy, *Skies Call*:

Andy Keech

"The world of the relative worker is a group involvement. He feels the comradeship of team effort, the loyalty to a charismatic leader, the desperation to avoid letting the team down. We have seen the team, drunk with success, walking in with arms full of parachutes, voices raised over

---

18. Female skydivers of the era often referred to themselves as girls when speaking of RW formations, as in an all-girl star. In 1977, RW terminology was officially changed to the gender neutral "way" instead of "man" or "girl" by the FAI RW Subcommittee because a French all-female team named Pink Panthers refused to be called a 4-man team in competition, according to Eilif Ness, FAI RW Subcommittee Chair. From his blog https://eilifness.no/?p=615 accessed 18 June, 2025.

19. The percentage of skydiving women at the competition level and the professional level is higher, possibly 40% according to USPA statistics. USPA.org.

each other in instant replay of the event they shared a few minutes before. We have never seen a stylist in a similar euphoria over turning 6.7 seconds. It is all so serious, as if we would spoil the purity of competition if it was enjoyed."[20] —*Andy Keech*

DZ Relatives

In Bird's words

"Skratch and Clarice Garrison came to Southern California from North Carolina back in the 60's and they were doing freefall. Clarice was on the first winning Rumbleseat 10-way Arvin team. When one of Clarice's sisters, Diane Mason, came to California for the summer, we started dating. Skratch had a red-headed sister named Luena. All three women were very good skydivers.

Clarice smiling for the cameraman, Arthur Tucker. Cover of *Parachutist*, April 1973.

---

20. Andy Keech, Skies Call Vol. 1, independently published and printed in England and the U.S. in 1974. The books became collectors items and Keech's succinct poem is often quoted when asked why they skydive: *Man small, Why fall? Skies call, That's all*. Two more volumes followed in 1979 and 1981. The photographs capture the intensity, the focus, the wide range of emotions and the many possibilities of skydiving.

Carl Boenish graduated from USC with a degree in Engineering. Skratch's skydiving sister Luena shared a house with Diane and me, and Carl used to come to my house to date Luena. Skratch was married to Clarice and I married Diane.

Eventually, we went our separate ways. Carl met a different girlfriend and later got married. Diane and I divorced. Skratch and Clarice divorced. Later, we all married other skydivers."
—*Jerry Bird*

Diane and Jerry at Elsinore. Photo by Sam Alexander.

5

Hollywood Jumps

"We all wanted to be in the movies." —Jerry Bird

The first movie solely about parachuting, *A Sport is Born*, was a mini documentary about the new sport of skydiving. Made in 1960, this ten-minute film featured the first air-to-air freefall footage, shot by Lew Sanborn. *A Sport is Born* served to introduce the Parachute Center at Orange, Massachusetts as the world's first purpose built commercial parachute school and showcased to the world the new recreation of parachuting—a sport not restricted to the military but something adventurous civilians—men and women—might enjoy. The short movie, shot in color on 35-millimeter film, was nominated for an Academy Award in 1961.[21]

Meanwhile, Bob Sinclair began his Hollywood career in Southern California. Bob had first jumped with the 13th and 82nd Airborne Divisions, then continued jumping as a civilian in 1947. He jumped in Alaska from 1949 to 1960, mostly exhibition jumps, and he was a charter member of the Fairbanks Parachute Club, formed in the early 1950s. In 1960, Sinclair migrated south to Glendale, California, to do stunt jumping and aerial camera filming for the *Ripcord* series with creators Dave Burt and Jim Hall. He spent the next 15 years jumping for Hollywood and training actors and actresses like Julie "Catwoman" Newmar, talk show host Johnny Carson, and the *Ripcord* stars Paul Burk, Ken Curtis, and

---

21. *A Sport is Born*, directed by Richard Winik, U.S.: Paramount Pictures, 1960. Lewis Sandborn is credited as "Cast" (IMDB). He is known to skydivers as D-1, the first parachutist rated "expert."

Larry Pennell. Bob was one of the respected "old schoolers" Jerry Bird looked up to when he started jumping.

Bob Buquor, who had come to Southern California from Texas, made his first jump at Elsinore in 1958, learned to fly camera, and got work in the film industry. When he wasn't working for Hollywood, Buquor was shooting pictures of the sport skydivers, especially the Arvin gang. He photographed Arvin's first 4-man: Mitch Poteet, Don Henderson, Lou Paproski, and Andy Keech.

Jerry Bird joked that he was too short to double for any Hollywood heartthrob, but he admitted to practicing fancy work with pistols, in hopes of landing a gig as an extra on a Western. "We all wanted to be in the movies."

—*Linda Collison*

6

1964

World's First 6-Man

On September 6, 1964, Bob Buquor photographed the world's first 6-man star over Arvin; two months later the shot was featured on the cover of *Sky Diver* Magazine. That same month Los Angeles skydiver Inge Onnes wrote an article in *Sky Diver* Magazine, quoted in part here:

Inge Onnes:

"Bob Buquor, who became bored with still photography, unorganized mass jumps, etc., started filming multi-man stars. He had a 3-man, so Bob organized a 4-man, which came off on the second try. The 5-man was the next challenge which took considerably more jumps to accomplish. The 5-man was eventually accomplished and Bob then planned for the 6-man star.

The first attempt, which failed, was due to one of the jumpers coming in a little too hot and breaking up the initial foundation of the star. When this happened, some of the jumpers fell below and were never able to get together again.

On the second attempt, before boarding the planes, the jumpers briefed the pilots regarding close formation flying. The jump altitude was to be 12,000 feet, with a wave off at 3,000. Dave Keaggy, flying a Cessna 195, and Walt Mercer, flying a Howard, kept in constant communication on the Unicom during the jump run. Even then it took two passes to get the desired formation. After exiting, Bob Thompson and Richard

Economy were the first to hook up. Then Jon DePoorter came in to form a three-man star. Bob started shooting when the 3-man star was formed. As more jumpers filled out the star, Bob had to continually change his position in order to keep the jumpers framed.

Once the 3-man star was formed, the fourth, fifth and sixth man had to break open the circle in order to form the planned 6-man star. The initial 3-man star provided a stable platform for the other jumpers to work in on. Don Henderson came in as the fourth man, Mitchel Poteet as the fifth. Then it became a real struggle as Louis Paproski reached and reached, and finally at 7,000 feet, completed the 6-man star. The star was held for twenty seconds. The biggest problem encountered while filming the six-man star was maintaining a rate of descent equivalent to that of the other jumpers.

This just opens the door, of course, for step-by-step progress to a maximum 80-man star out of a Lockheed Constellation," Onnes mused. "By the time Bob accomplishes that 80-man, there will probably be a C-124 available to work towards a 200-man star."[22]

That, and more, would come to pass . . .

---

22. Inge Onnes, "Six Man Star," *Sky Diver* Magazine, November 1964, 29.

7

1965

Rod Pack's 'Chuteless Jump

In Bird's words

"I witnessed the first 'chuteless jump at Arvin, California, January, 1965.

Rod Pack would jump without wearing a parachute and Bob Allen would carry a front-mount reserve for him. They would fly together and Bob would hand the reserve to Rod to snap on to his harness during freefall. Rod was a stuntman, and they wanted to do this jump as a stunt to promote his career.

At that time, Rod Pack was separated from his wife, and she was dating Bob Allen. They were all friends. This was a situation where you really needed to trust your friend.

I remember Rod saying that he would normally be wearing a rig that weighed 20 pounds. Bob would be wearing a 20-pound rig plus be carrying the extra reserve. Should Rod wear 20 pounds of weight so they would match in the air? He thought about it for a long time, and I don't remember what he ended up doing exactly, but I know he didn't wear all those weights because the last thing he wanted to do was go low. They also changed the order of exit. Like, I'll jump first, and you follow.

No, you jump first with the reserve in your hands and I'll follow.

The third member of this group was Bob Buquor. We all said that with or without the camera, he was the best RW jumper. Not only did he wear the camera, but he could stay still while filming you, or dive to the right place and do the job. In addition to filming the jump, Bob would also be their backup. He would wear a 32-foot parachute, Low Po's they called them, which was larger than the average parachute. (I jumped a 28-foot regular parachute, military surplus.) They put a riser with a snap hook onto Bob Buquor's harness so that if Bob Allen and Rod were unable to make the reserve pass, Bob Buquor would hook up with Rod, snap on the D-ring, and they would ride down together under Buquor's parachute.

Rod and Bob Allen made the hook up. The reserve was a T-7A front mount with two snaps to snap onto the D-rings. When he snapped the first snap on, the reserve opened, probably because Rod accidentally pulled the reserve in the process. Those reserves have a cross connector between the risers that doesn't let them be separated, so Rod rode down under a parachute and survived without getting hurt. That was pretty amazing.

Under FAA rules, a pilot in command is not allowed to have anybody jump out of his airplane without a parachute. When the FAA found out about the stunt, they went after the pilot. The pilot said, I'm sorry, you can't suspend my pilot's license—I don't have one." —*Jerry Bird*

First 8-Man Star

On October 17, 1965, the world's first 8-man star was born over Arvin. The jumpers exited from a Howard and a Cessna 195 flying in formation at 12,500 feet. They flew together to form a star at 5,500 above the desert. These star makers were Gary Young, Al Paradowski, Bill Newell, Mitch Poteet, Bill Stage, Jim Dann, Don Henderson, Brian Williams, and with Bob Buquor who photographed it. The Associated Press ran the pictures nationwide. While Rod Pack's jump was notoriously daring almost beyond belief, the 8-way hook-up in freefall presented skydiving as a sport to do on a Sunday afternoon with seven of your closest friends.

Jerry Bird was not on the world's first 8-man star, though he would organize and be part of many more record-breaking formations to follow.

On the day the first 8-man star was formed, Jerry Bird was in Germany with the Army's 10th Special Forces. The United States' involvement in Vietnam's war was heating up fast—a war that would affect a generation of young American men and women.

Military Service

Skydiving was born of freelance pilots and their daring performers—"barnstormers"—and the early 20th century military leaders who recognized the beneficial uses of parachutes in aviation warfare. Parachutes could save a pilot's life and parachutes could drop spies, soldiers, equipment and supplies behind enemy lines.

The development and mass production of military parachuting equipment became an early part of the 20th century arms race. Many sport skydivers who started jumping in the 1950s and early 1960s made their first jumps while serving in the armed forces. In the United States, the 82nd Airborne Division and the 101st Airborne Division gave many young men their first jump training.

Jerry Bird started as a sport skydiver but soon joined the army. Things were heating up in Southeast Asia.

In Bird's words

"At that time, you had a number in the draft. I was no longer a college student, so I turned down an Air Force ROTC commission because it was a six-year thing, and said, I'll take my chances on the draft. Well, I ended up with a low number and no sooner than I got the draft notice, my buddies urged me to join the Army. So, I had a weird thing that I was drafted—that's a two-year thing—but I joined with a one-year extension so I could get to go to school rather than go to basic infantry and be sent to Vietnam.

I scored really well on all the aptitude tests so they sent me to the Russian language school in Monterey and that started another adventure. But the military wasn't really good for me, you know, kill or be killed and here I am, a hippie—peace, love, Hari Krishna, and everything. I was still jumping in Southern California while I was up in Monterey, at Fort Ord, and people didn't even know I was in the army. At the language school, you didn't have to have a haircut. You dressed in civilian clothes, went to school every day. You didn't salute anybody. They wanted you to learn Russian. Period." —*Jerry Bird*

After completing language school, it was Airborne jump school at Fort Benning, then it was time for Bird to gear up and go.

In Bird's words

"Once upon a time in a faraway universe, I boarded a troop ship, the U.S. Patch, named after a World War II General. I'm going through the North Sea to Bremerhaven, Germany, on a ship that was built to carry a thousand people at most, but we probably had 3000 troops on it. There were people from the Air Force and the Army. For most of the trip across the ocean, I set up camp in a lifeboat. It was better out there than it was below deck.

We arrived at Bremerhaven, which is on the north side of Germany. They lined everybody up by companies. The Navy chiefs had the most spectacular uniforms. The rest of us looked like we had been beaten in an alley. Our uniforms were all rumpled but theirs looked like they just came from the cleaners. We were on shore and one of the chiefs was instructing us to line up and do this and do that. Just then some seagulls flew over and littered him with droppings from his hat to his feet while he's standing there in front of us. A thousand guys couldn't help but laugh at this.

There were guys going to the 707-canteen rebuilding camp and there were sergeants and trucks there to pick them up. I was standing there by myself, the last guy, and nobody's called my name yet. Hey, how about me? Where am I going? They go, Oh yea, you're going to Bavaria. That's on the other side of Germany. We don't have any trucks going there. Here's a train ticket. Here's some food. Here's some Deutsche Marks. Catch a train. You have three days to get there.

I had been in jump school and language school. I could speak some Spanish, I could speak some Russian, I could speak English, but I didn't speak any German. But what good fun. I could buy beer on the train. When we stopped at a station, there'd be somebody there selling Wienerschnitzel or Bratwurst. I lollygagged my way through Germany and by the time I got down to Bavaria, I knew how to order beer (bier, bitte) and a few other things.

The train took me right to where I was going. I ended up in a place where the Seventh Army of Europe had their NCO Academy at Flint Kaserne in Bad Tölz, Germany, which was also the headquarters of the 10th Special Forces, which was the group I was assigned to. I had already been California dreaming and all that stuff and had made jumps in the Army and I was a skydiver. I'd been to military jump school and this place had a jump club. I showed up, signed in, gave them my orders, and was told that since I just arrived from the States, I was in quarantine for the next three days. There was a transient room down the hall where I could hang out over the weekend. The chow hall was downstairs, but I couldn't go off post without a pass. So, here I am, a California kid sitting in this room by myself on a Saturday night.

Along come these NCOs and they go, Hey new guy, who are you? You're not going out? I told them I had just arrived and was in the quarantine unit. They said nobody ever checks that. I go, I'm supposed to get a pass to go out of the gate. They said, You're one of us. Put on your civilian clothes and get in the car. We're going to the Hofbräuhaus Munich. It's Oktoberfest.

We got to the Hofbräuhaus where women would come up carrying ten huge mugs of beer to serve our table. We drank until the appropriate time, middle of the night, and then we decided we'd better go back to the base.

It was early morning and we were driving fast. We had just crossed a bridge and there was an early morning bus that stopped there. As we started to pass it, here comes a little European car that we hit head on.

Welcome to Germany. It was my first real day, and I went with the police to jail. Later that day, I met a guy by the name of Chilly Willy who was the First Sergeant of Headquarters Company of the 10th Special Forces Group. I remember someone later telling me that he was the meanest first sergeant in the U.S. Army. He was not happy to meet me that day. But in the great American way he said, Troop, you're in trouble. What was your rank? Well, it's lesser now.

And then he grabbed me by the ear and said, Come with me, we're out of here. I just saved your ass. Those other two guys are in trouble and now you're in trouble with me. You're confined to barracks and on extra duty for the next 30 days, and you are reduced in rank.

But I met some great people over there. I won the PFT Mile as an athlete. I was on the Trojan Parachute Team with Harry Belton who was well known up in Fort Bragg because at one time he was the non-commissioned officer in charge of the JFK Special Warfare Center, which is the Green Beret Headquarters. He maybe retired as the second highest enlisted man in the U.S. Army, and he was my friend. We made the first 3-way freefall in Europe jumping out of an H-34. We were the Trojan Sport Parachute Team for the 10th Special Forces Group. It was an honor to serve with those people and to jump with the Tenth Group."
—*Jerry Bird*

While Jerry was deployed, back home the sport skydivers were having fun without him and the camera fliers were capturing their skydives on film. The world's first 8-man was made in 1965 while Bird was in Germany.

8

1967

Bob Buquor

In Bird's words

"Bob Buquor was one of my buddies. He was handsome and he was famous. He had been the cameraman for TV shows. After the 'chuteless jump, he got a job on a movie called *Don't Make Waves* with Tony Curtis, Claudia Cardinale and Sharon Tate.[23] They jumped at Malibu. Bob wore all of his camera equipment, including a battery belt around his waist that must have weighed at least 30 lbs. They would make the jumps in the morning when it was less windy.

Skydiver Lee Hunt was a stunt man and he was playing the part of a reporter. All he wore was a harness and under his shirt, he had a reserve without any container, just the risers that snapped onto the harness with the reserve stuffed under his shirt. When it came time to pull, they made sure the spot was out over the water because he was only jumping one rig, a little round reserve. Lee Hunt would purposely land in the water and there was a boat there to pick him up. Bob was jumping a Para-Commander and would open first so he was able to run in and land on the beach and keep his cameras dry.

One day the shoot was delayed until the afternoon. They essentially went out and did the same thing, spotted over Malibu Bay, and jumped,

---

23. Alexander Mackendrick, director. *Don't Make Waves*, 1967, Filmways Pictures, distributed by MGM, is a romantic comedy of the 1960s California beach movie era. IMDB.

but on that day the wind was blowing from the land. Bob was pushed backwards and landed in the water. The pickup boat saw the round reserve and picked up Lee Hunt, not realizing that Bob was not going to make it to the shore. Bob was a great swimmer, but he had no room to wear a life vest. By 2000 feet, when he realized he would not make it to land, he should have taken the camera off and thrown it away. But because he was a company man, he didn't do that. He didn't jettison the batteries either. The camera was attached to his helmet. He took it off and held it in his hand upside down by the strap.

He landed in about 30 feet of water. It was late in the day because the jump was delayed, and they couldn't find Bob. The next day the scuba divers searched the area where he landed and found him sitting on the bottom of the sea with the camera in his hand. When he hit the water, the camera or something sharp on his helmet, hit him in his face and cut him through his cheek, his eye, his forehead, and probably knocked him unconscious. Bob drowned. I was a pall bearer at his funeral."

Post Script: "Bob Buquor was not his real name, his sister told me at the funeral. He had come west for a new start, took a name from a tombstone and changed the spelling. B-u-q-u-o-r." —*Jerry Bird*

Bob Buquor Memorial Star Crest

Pat and Jan Works

"Bill Newell founded the Star Crest in 1967. The purpose was to award everybody who had been in an 8-man at that time (about 20 people), and from then on out, some kind of recognition for it. He named the Star Crest after Bob Buquor, one of the first promoters of star-making."[24]

---

24. Pat and Jan Works, *Parachuting: United We Fall*, RWunderground Publishing Co., 1978, 191.

SCR patch, courtesy of Rachel Newell.

"The SCR [Star Crest Recipient] candidate must free fly the exit (no grips) and must participate in a freefall formation involving eight or more skydivers held together for a minimum of five seconds. The SCS [Star Crest Soloist] candidate must dock eighth or later and remain in the formation for a minimum of five seconds.".[25]

Although Bird was deployed in Germany when the first 8-man was made, he earned SCR #11 upon his return.

Phil Mayfield

The Star Crest Awards quickly became the standard for measuring one's freefall skills. If you were good enough to be in a formation with at least seven others, after leaving the aircraft separately (not already holding on to each other), and holding the formation stable for at least five seconds, you earned the right to wear the coveted SCR patch and were assigned a number—a chronological reference to when you earned it. Other awards

---

25. https://www.starcrestskydivingawards.com/home. Bill Newell. "Bob Buquor Memorial Star Crest." *Parachutist*. Dec. 1968, pp. 24 –25.

were later developed, recognizing those who entered the formation eighth or later, doing it at night, flying through a hula-hoop first (my favorite), doing head-down formations, and more. —*Phil Mayfield*; SCR 374, SCS 36, BASE 2, El Cap 256.

Bill Newell, creator of The Bob Buquor Memorial Star Crest Awards, faithfully administered the program for 45 years. His daughter, Rachael Newell Machado, and her husband John Machado have taken over the awards program since Newell's passing in 2012. The Star Crest Awards are ongoing for 21st century skydivers with many more categories.

The Summer of the World's First Ten-Man Star

There's something happening here . . .[26]

The summer of 1967 was called the "Summer of Love" by the organizers of the West Coast counterculture event. Hippies, trippers, free spirits and disaffected young people gathered in San Francisco's Golden Gate Park and the Haight-Ashbury district to "turn on, tune in, and drop out," as American psychologist Timothy Leary famously said, referring to his experimentation of psychedelics to expand consciousness.[27] The Summer of Love actually began in the winter of '67 with the Human Be-In, held in Golden Gate Park on January 14.

Meanwhile, in Southern California, a different sort of aerial "Be-In" was happening; More and more skydivers were getting high, dropping out and coming together in freefall at terminal velocity . . .

---

26. There's something happening here, lyrics in the song "For What It's Worth" written by Stephen Stills and released in 1967 by Buffalo Springfield, about protests and demonstrations in the U.S.

27. The slogan, "turn on, tune in and drop out" Leary, advocate of psychedelic drug use, attributes to Canadian philosopher Marshall McLuhan. Timothy Leary, *Flashbacks*, 1983, p. 253. "It was a naive romantic time," wrote Leary in his autobiography. "We were excited by the notion that we humans could fly." Pg. 42.

Brian Williams

July 2, 1967

"Things just didn't seem to be working out," Bird's mentor Brian Williams wrote. "With the closing of the Arvin DZ and moving to Old River for a while, and then over to Bakersfield. Buquor drowned while shooting some film for a movie about this time and threw us all into a state of shock. With Buquor gone, we just didn't have that extra spark.

Bit by bit, we found ourselves jumping at the Taft, California, DZ which was operated by my longtime friend, Art Armstrong. Old Art indicated to us that he would be very glad to have us rebels jump at his place providing we deployed our rags in relatively thin air ("anything you say Art"). When our regular pilot, Walt Mercer, and his cherry twin Beech started flying out of Taft, all the old gang started jumping there.

About this time, while quaffing a few beers at the Rumbleseat Skydiving Bar in Hermosa Beach one night, Luis Melendez grabbed hold of Jerry Bird, one of our outstanding jumpers, and says: 'Jerry, I have just bought myself a keen camera and I have just invented a new jumpsuit so I can fall fast or slow and I know you guys need a cameraman, so why don't we try for a 10-man star?' So, Jerry says: 'Hey man, sounds like a winner, why not?'" —*Brian Williams* [28]

In Bird's words

"Luis Melendez, Jr. was a friend of mine and had magazine connections. We had a plan this weekend to try and break the record and make a 10-way star. When I went through all the names, I had 12 people, and we were only going to take 10 because we had a cameraman, so that filled the airplane. So, when the first 10-way star was made, we had 11 people, and we left one person on the ground and went up and made a 10-way star.

Since we had done it once, we wanted to do it again. I thought, I am the one who cut this guy and left him on the ground, so this time he can take my slot. And they went up and did a second 10-way star. We made two jumps and made both stars." —*Jerry Bird*

---

28. Brian Williams, "World's First Ten-Man Star," *Parachutist*, October 1967, 11–17.

Brian Williams

"Now, let me tell you about this Melendez cat. For one thing, he is an artist—you know, brushes and oils and all that jazz, and when he is taking pictures of a star, he waits until the composition, lighting, jumpers' expressions, etc., are just right before he shoots. WOW, what a perfectionist, but he was getting a lot of pictures of stars—7, 8, and 9-man, that is.

Around this time, we heard rumors that the jumpers in Elsinore (California), were getting pretty sharp doing 6 and 7-man stars and were bragging that they would be the first group to make the 10-man star. My God, the audacity of those guys! Really though, I think when we realized we had competition on our hands it gave us that little something extra we needed. So, on July 2, 1967, after starting off with a rather disappointing jump and the sun just about melting the galvanizing off the roof of the hangar and the jumpers dragging around with their tongues hanging out, we were only too glad when we were again at 12,500 and on jump run.

Just as the first man started to exit the Beech, someone bumped into the camera sight and Luis Melendez shouted, 'Don't Jump!' We had to go around for another run while Luis adjusted his sight. This delay was fortunate for Terry Ward, who had been having problems with his lunch and he was feeling much better as we made our second run. This time it was a good run and we unloaded out of the Beech plenty fast.

The first two men to hook up were Gary Young and John Rinard, followed by Clark Fischer, Jim Dann, Jerry Bird, myself, and Paul Gorman (Paul had less than 100 jumps at the time.). Luis Melendez left the plane squeezed in between Jim Dann and Jerry Bird. Everyone hooked up super smooth and they hooked up in the order of exit. WOW, we finally did it, the WORLD'S FIRST TEN-MAN STAR!"[29] —*Brian Williams*

Luis Melendez

"Tall Paul Gorman had come close to closing a 10-man on prior jumps. On this dive the Arvin Good Guys put this 9-man together early. Paul needed to be aggressive for this one. As Paul approaches the perfectly

---

29. Williams, "World's First Ten-Man Star," *Parachutist*, October 1967, 11–17.

flying and stable circle of his buddies in a not-too-much-of-a hurry attitude, I am, in my head, screaming GET IT GET IT GET IT! For a moment I had forgotten what I was there for, then I realized I had been back sliding away from the guys. I managed to get back into position, and I was lucky to record this event in our history." —*Luis Melendez*[30]

Brian Williams

"To top it off, the same identical crew did it again the following weekend. I might explain here that there are many more jumpers in the old gang who have been in these stars, but we just can't get everyone in a twin Beech.

About a month later, Carl Boenish, who, by the way, is a better than excellent cameraman, showed some pictures he had taken of a 10-man star. It was just beautiful, but who were they? It seems that those ungrateful upstarts at Elsinore had made a 10-man star while Carl was on the scene with his 'Brownie. They tied us but didn't better us. Besides, we really don't dig being tied . . .

Just last Sunday, September 10, 1967, with Bob Allen and his 16mm movie camera along, Clarice Garrison hooked up with 10 of us fellows to make the world's first 11-man star—whoops—10 man and a girl star. If this isn't enough, we had two more jumpers just inches away from hooking up—one of whom was Art's young son Rich, age 16, with only 36 jumps to his credit. How about that!

Well anyway, as I say, we are on the make for a 12-man star now and we really don't expect too much action from that Elsinore gang, I don't think???"[31] —*Brian Williams*

Ray Cottingham

Ray was part of the Elsinore Group at that time. "We were definitely competing against each other. But there wasn't any animosity; we were

---

30. Luis Melendez, Jr. Facebook profile; photos. Accessed February 1, 2025.

31. Brian Williams, "World's First Ten-Man Star," *Parachutist* Magazine, October 1967, 11–17.

all friends. We used to meet every week at the Rumbleseat."³² —*Ray Cottingham*

Luis Melendez

"I made Jerry Bird famous," the aerial photographer quipped in an in-person interview with Ground Rush more than fifty years later.³³ Melendez's photograph was the cover shot of the September 1967 issue of *Parachutist* Magazine. His photo essay titled "Go and Make a Falling Star" featuring a series of his freefall pictures of the world's first 10-man star was featured in *Esquire*'s July 1968 issue—the same legendary issue included an interview with James Baldwin, a profile of Susan Sontag, and articles by Allen Ginsberg and Timothy Leary.³⁴ 1960s legends, all.

First 10-Man Star completed July 2, 1967, over Taft. Luis Melendez, photographer. *Parachutist* Magazine, September 1967.

---

32. Larry Jaffe, "Southern California, 1963–1970: The Stars are Born, Part I," *Parachutist* Magazine, November 1987, 21.
33. Ground Rush interview with Luis Melendez in Apache Junction, April 2022.
34. *Esquire* Magazine. July 1, 1968, 66–67. Back issues available on line by subscription.

The men who made the first 10-man star. Standing (L to R): Brian Williams, Gary Young, Bill Stage, Jerry Bird, Clark Fischer, Paul Gorman and John Rinard. Kneeling (L to R): Jim Dann, Terry Ward and Bill Newell. Luis Melendez, photographer. *Parachutist* Magazine, October 1967.

Luis Melendez with SCR patch (#149) on his sleeve.

The world record had been set and within a few weeks duplicated by two groups of sport skydivers. Suddenly, there were enough skydivers good enough to make 10-way stars a competition and the Speed Star was born.

The First Rumbleseat 10-Man Speed Star Competition

A Brief History of the 10-Man Star Competition: How It Started,

from *Parachuting: United We Fall*, edited by Pat and Jan Works.[35]

Garth Taggart

"10-Man Star Competition started the very same way as many famous and infamous deeds throughout history: a drunken, boastful argument between two gentlemen. I can remember that argument vividly. (Hell, I started it.)

It was on a Wednesday evening in 1967 at the Rumbleseat Tavern. Every Relative Work jumper in Los Angeles was there to view movies of recently made 10-man stars.

Two different teams, the "Arvin Good Guys" and "The Group" from Elsinore shared the world's 10-man star record at that time.

Bob Allen, Arvin's photographer, and myself, a member of "The Group" were discussing the two teams' ability to make the 10-man again. Bob said "The Group's" 10-man star was luck, but Arvin could do it again anytime.

I just couldn't let a statement like that go unchallenged. The discussion turned into a lengthy argument, which ended with a $5.00 wager between Bob and me.

It was decided that the two teams would jump, attempting a 10-man star to settle the bet.

---

35. Garth Taggart, "A Brief History of Ten-Man Star Competition, How it Started," *Parachuting: United We Fall*, edited by Pat and Jan Works., Fullerton, CA; RW underground Publishing Company, 1978, 190–191.

The next day I commenced drafting the first set of rules for the jump. This original draft was modified extensively by a rules committee consisting of Skratch Garrison, Carl Boenish and Jerry Bird." —*Garth Taggart*

In Bird's words

"That's when the thing with Garth Taggart, Skratch Garrison and me, when it became Us vs Them and we started the Rumbleseat Meet. Frank Carpenter's Rumbleseat Bar put up the great big trophy and said, OK, now we're going to make the rules. And that was the beginning of the Rumbleseat 10-way Speed Star competition, and it was held at Taft.

There were three teams: Ours [the Taft Team], Dirty Ed's Team, or the Elsinore Valley Rats, and the third team called themselves the River Rats. Somewhere between Arvin and Taft was a place called Old River where some people jumped. A lot of these guys we later called the Latin Skydivers. The team on the trophy was the team called The Taft Team, captained by Jerry Bird. We had the first female competitor to jump with us and win a competition—Clarice Garrison."
—*Jerry Bird*[36]

Garth Taggart

"Arvin made the only 10-man of the meet—two perfect back-to-back 10-man stars. The rest of this story is recorded in the pages of Skydiver Magazine and USPA *Parachutist* Magazine.

Yes, I lost the $5.00 but I have seen a new dimension in parachuting gain international acceptance." —*Garth Taggart*[37]

Norm Heaton, then United States Parachute Association's (USPA) Executive Director and co-editor of *Parachutist* magazine, wrote an enthusiastic postscript following Brian Williams' article, "World's First Ten-Man Star." Competitive in the old-school discipline of landing accuracy, Heaton reveals his awe and respect for freefall relative work:

---

36. Alexander-West interviews with Jerry Bird.
37. Garth Taggart, "A Brief History of Ten-Man Star Competition, How it Started," 191.

Clarice accepts the trophy for the Arvin Team—the first awarded—from Frank Carpenter, sponsor of the annual Rumbleseat Meet.

Norm Heaton gets excited about RW

"This editor is concrete, final, and living proof that these guys are great! The biggest hookup I've ever experienced in my jumping career has been a 4-man (3-man star with someone hanging onto a boot). On September 17th I was asked if I wanted to make a Beech load with them. (This is almost like being asked to be on the U.S. Team.) I informed them of my not-too-great relative work ability (I even mess up kiss passes) and they said that was okay, that they'd use me as 'pin man' (the first one out).

I went out of the Beech and waited. Soon I was joined by John Rinard. Then another, and another, and another, and another, and yet another. We missed an 8-man by scant inches. . . . None were overly impressed when I landed in the pea gravel, kicking up the dead center disc; but mumbled something about "getting him off that competition kick."

"It's absolutely a fantastic experience watching these guys (and gals) work in the air," Heaton said. "It's precision that is indescribably and practically unbelievable until you see it for yourself..."[38] —*Norm Heaton*

Norm Heaton would soon earn SCR #51.

---

38. Norman Heaton (editor), "World's First 10-Man Star" postscript, *Parachutist Magazine*, October 1967, 12.

9

1968

Jerry Bird's All Stars

"I advised this young wimp 10 years after the start of RW competition: Look Jerry Bird, if you want guys to jump your way, you find nine guys just off static line and train them the way you want." —*Lyle Cameron*[39]

In Bird's words

"I had the less experienced people because the other guys didn't want to listen to me telling them how to do RW. So, I made up my team with new jumpers and girls." —*Jerry Bird*

By 1968, the former Special Forces Green Beret had formed his own competitive speed star team made up of skydivers from various drop zones. As All Star teammate Sam Alexander writes, "Jerry had an uncanny ability to recognize talent, the instinct for seeing how all the pieces of the puzzle fit together, and an aptitude for bringing out the best in a former rag-tag group of jumpers. We trained to win, we expected to win, and we won. When Jerry set out to establish a new record, he planned it, he organized it, and he executed it."

---

39. Lyle Cameron, "Letters," *Parachutist* Magazine, February 1988, 8.

Jerry had what many call a photographic memory. After a sixty second freefall with others, Bird could accurately recall who was where at what altitude. He observed the dynamics of the formation as it built, or did not build. His recall was spot on, as proven by the camera in freefall. Long before other athletes started using video replay to improve their performances, California skydivers were using film—and Jerry Bird's critiques.

Not everyone took kindly to his post dive debriefs. The SoCal cliques were happy to jump with Jerry—he was good—but they didn't want him taking over. Relative workers were cool. They had strong egos, many prided themselves on their innate body-flying abilities. To them, skydiving was not a sport to be practiced: you were either good or you weren't. It was as if body flight was a God-given gift. Jerry Bird, however, was into practice jumps—as if relative work was a competitive team sport or something—which it was rapidly becoming. But practicing was too much like what the old guard who competed in style and accuracy had to do. The cool kids didn't want to practice—least of all under the leadership of Jerry Bird, who had started jumping after they had. He was good, sure—Brian Williams had discovered him—but who was this transplant from West Virginia to tell them how to build a star?

Bill Newell

"Jerry was an Arvin Good Guy from the very beginning and was well liked, but his aspirations to organize and manage our team were met with skepticism by some and grated on others. By now, the Good Guys knew who they were and didn't want an individual taking credit for the team's performance. Bird was savvy in organizational skills and a shrewd politician but not the hottest or most experienced skydiver on our team. When Jerry got married [to Diane Mason] and took a two-week honeymoon during team practice, Ron Richards replaced him as team captain [of the Good Guys.]

"To make matters worse for us, Terry Ward switched to Bird's team," Newell admitted in the article. "Finally, the long-anticipated third annual Rumbleseat Meet at Taft arrived in November 1969. Jerry Bird's team beat us by one second over four rounds. Bird's team members were Dick Gernand, Russ Benefiel, Diane Bird, Jerry Bird, Bob Feuling, Terry Ward, Sam Alexander, Rich Armstrong, Donna Wardean, and Doyle Talbot."[40]

All Star Sam Alexander

There is a fun side story to this. We might have won by even less than one second; one of the Arvin guys complained that our team had won by—and he clapped his hands together like a snare drum—*this* much. To which, Jerry went around for the rest of the day, and several occasions after that, leaning in toward the other team members, and saying, "we won by (mimicking the clapping sound) *this* much." He loved to rub it in!

Rumbleseat perpetual trophy.

---

40. Bill Newell, "The Rise and Demise of the Arvin Good Guys," *Parachutist* Magazine, December 2004, 49.

10

1969

Come Together[41]

Psychedelic cover of *Parachutist* December. 1969.
Designed by Carolyn Gruber, USPA office manager.

---

41. "Come Together" is the title of a song written by John Lennon for Timothy Leary's gubernatorial campaign against Ronald Reagan and released by the Beatles in 1969 as the first track on Abbey Road. Leary wrote, "The next day John asked what he could do to help my campaign for governor. "Write a campaign song," I replied. "Okay, said John, "What's the theme?" "Our campaign slogan is Come together, join the party. Great title," said John. He grabbed his guitar and started improvising. *Come together right now . . ."* Timothy Leary, *Flashbacks*. Tarcher/Putnam, 1983, 1990. Come together describes the goal of relative work skydiving in the 1960s and '70s.

Brian Williams

"For many, it was a great time in which to be living. People were enjoying the music of the Beatles, Tijuana Brass, The Doors, The Mamas and the Papas, Pink Floyd, Led Zepplin, The Beach Boys, and many others. It was *The Age of Aquarius.*

It was hip to read underground newspapers, go to underground parties, and listen to underground music. Flower Power, Free Love, and the psychedelic experience were in vogue. For many, it was a rough and frightening time in which to be living . . . There was the war in Vietnam where so many lives were lost. Kids who had never heard of Vietnam were drafted into the services and sent there, never to return.

Many Americans of all colors were involved in the Civil Rights Movement. There was rioting in Los Angeles where scores of buildings were burned to the ground . . . There were people who got caught up in the drug culture. It was the decade of change." —*Brian Williams* writing as Pat Dunbar, in the preface to *A Dark Night*.[42]

First All-Girl 8-Way

Eight women build the first all-female star formation and earn their Women's Star Crest Recipient awards at Skydive Elsinore in California in 1969. Photo by Ray Cottingham.

First all-female 8-way star over Elsinore in 1969. Participants: Patty Croceito, Linda Padgett, Diane Bird, Ann Gardiner, Sheila Scott, Jean Schultz, Luena Garrison, Laura Mackenzie. Ray Cottingham, photographer.

---

42. Pat Dunbar (pen name of skydiver Brian Williams), *A Dark Night* (creative nonfiction), independently published, 2003.

Pat and Jan Works

"The first 8-girl star (it was exceptionally *not* organized by J.B.) was built at the end of July 1969, at Elsinore. The girls taking part were:

Jean Schultz, Laura MacKenzie, Ann Gardiner, Diane Bird, Luena Garrison, Linda Padgett, Patty Croceito and Sheila Scott."[43]

Third Annual Rumbleseat Meet

Jerry Bird describes the third annual Rumbleseat Meet in an article published in *Parachutist* (January 1970), reprinted in part here.

Third Annual Ten-Man Star Meet: A Bird's Eye View

written by Jerry Bird

"Relative Work continues to grow in California. The World Championships of Relative Work were held at Taft, California (Art Armstrong's DZ) on October 11 and 12 [1969]. The event was the Third Annual 10-Man Star Meet. Every year the meet gets bigger and better. The first year there were only three teams, last year six teams, and this year eleven teams—110 competitors. Not bad for a mere relative work meet in Southern California. Maybe someday we will get relative work of this size on a national level.

Saturday started with beautiful weather, clear and windless. Everyone went through an equipment check similar to the one at the Nationals. The team captains, pilots and judges had a brief meeting and discussed rules, jump run direction, etc. ... We had FOUR—check that—four Twin Beechcraft to fly the teams. We had four judges with telemeters and stop watches to judge; each judge had two assistants to record times and the size of the star. The judges were Skratch Garrison, Art Armstrong, "Tag" Taggart and Bill Pyle.

---

43. Pat and Jan Works, *Parachuting: United We Fall*, Chapter 6, Fullerton, CA; RWunderground Publishing Co., 1978, 199.

The Old River Rats opened the meet with an 8-man, pretty good for anywhere except Southern California. . . . Our first jump [Jerry Bird's All Stars] was a bit hairy; the star opened at a 9-man but they got it back together and I came in to make it a 10-man in 47 seconds. Four other teams made 10-mans in the first round: Calistoga, Arvin, Elsinore, and Lakeside. The Calistoga Love Birds made the fastest star in the first round with a beautifully executed star in 41 seconds flat. The surprise of the first round, and of the meet, was the Lakeside team. They had made their first 10-man star only one week earlier in practice and now they made their second 10-man.

The second round started with five teams still in contention for first place. . . . We kept the pressure on the other teams by making another 10-man, this one in 46.5 seconds, the fastest in this round. Lakeside kept pace by making another 10-man (quite a feat for a group just starting.) Calistoga failed to make their 10-man. Because of a badly spinning star, the last two jumpers couldn't enter the formation. Elsinore (Linda Padgett's team) and Arvin also kept up the pace by making their 10-man. The second round and the first day of competition ended with four teams still in contention for first place.

The meet directors, Gary Young and Dick Gernand, had a party planned at the hangar Saturday night. Everyone gathered to drink the free beer and to watch the movies shown by Carl Boenish and John Randall. It was a beautiful night—everyone telling jump stories, renewing old friendships, and making new friends, the common bond of the sport bringing everyone into a close knit group. For me, this is one of the highlights of any meet—I met many of the jumpers from the Bay area and from Lakeside for the first time. After much spreading of good faith, we said good night and retired to face the challenge of the second day of competition.

The third round ended with only three of the eleven teams still in contention for first place: Jerry Bird's All Stars, Linda Padgett's Elsinore Team, and the Arvin Good Guys.

We responded to the pressure in the last round by making the fastest star in the meet—a 39.5 second 10-man. This was the fastest 10-man made in any of the three annual star meets. Also, this was our team's 14th consecutive 10-man star—a record in itself. . . . We had such a big lead (in seconds) on Elsinore that it would be virtually impossible for them to make a 10-man fast enough to beat us. They needed approximately a 29 second star to win. Giving it all they had they broke at a 6-man and were out of the running. The Arvin team made their 10-man but it was not fast enough to unseat us. We had won the meet.

In the victory ceremonies that followed, Gary Young presented the Calistoga Love Birds with a fifth of booze each for their third place finish. The Arvin Good Guys received nice silver trophies for second place. Our team received individual golden trophies for first place, plus the perpetual trophy donated by the Rumbleseat Para-Scuba Club. This trophy is symbolic of supremacy in relative work and was first awarded to the Taft Team in 1967 and Dirty Ed's Team in 1968. I accepted the trophy for our team (this being the second time I have captained the winning team.) Terry Ward and I were on the Taft Team that won in 1967, and Russ Benefiel was a member of the Elsinore team that won in 1968—two years in a row for Russ.

In retrospect, our team was quite unique; our members hand-picked from different drop zones and grouped as a team for only one purpose—to win. Russ Benefiel is an Elsinore regular but chose to jump with us. Bob Feuling is primarily an accuracy jumper (he was leading the Nationals at Marana this year after eight jumps). Bob lives near San Diego and we were practicing at Taft, a round trip of over 500 miles. We had desire!

We also had two girls on our team: Donna Wardean and my wife, Diane Bird. Donna formerly jumped with the Arvin group but she also had the desire to win so she joined our group. Diane hasn't reached 200 jumps yet but is one of the best relative work jumpers anywhere. She was in the 8-girl star and the 16-man star at Elsinore earlier this year—both records for relative work. (Russ and I were also in the 16-star.)

Terry Ward and I are holdovers from the winning team of 1967. We have been making 10-mans together since the first one in July 1967. Everyone on the team made some personal sacrifices for our team. Dick Gernand and Sam Alexander gave up more prestigious places in the exit order to make our pins, a spot unfamiliar to them. As it turned out, we had the fastest pins of all the teams. Doyle Talbot began as our alternate but later gained his spot on the team. Richard Armstrong, our youngest team member, competed in the Nationals at Marana. "Slick" Armstrong, like Feuling, is an outstanding style and accuracy man as well as an excellent relative worker.

I would like to thank all the competitors for coming and making this the great meet it was. It will continue to grow and next year we hope to have teams from outside of California make an appearance. Taft fielded five teams this year, Elsinore two (Larry Perkins' staff team was there), Lakeside one, and three from the Bay area." —*Jerry Bird*

About the Author: Jerry Bird began his parachuting career in California in 1963 and since that time has accumulated 550 sport jumps. While in the U.S. Army, Jerry attended jump school at Fort Benning Georgia (1965) and served with the 10th Special Forces in Germany. A native of West Virginia, Jerry attended West Virginia University, majoring in Electrical Engineering. He now makes his home in Southern California and is employed by Security Pacific Optimization Services as a computer operator. The 26-year-old Bird participated in the first 10-way baton pass and was in the first 9, 10, 11, 12, 13, 14 and 16-man stars.[44]

First 10-Way Star Meet Beyond California

November 1969

Bill Newell

"That November [1969] Skratch Garrison, Garth Taggart and I were invited to judge the first 10-way star meet to be held outside of California at Zephyrhills, Florida. There were three teams—from Florida, Texas, and a pick-up team from California. The team from Tampa won, with the Texans in second. Skydivers from out of state finally beat California jumpers. [In 2025 Dennis Henley SCR #216 argues that the pick-up team from California came in second.]

---

44. Jerry Bird, "Third Annual Ten-Man Star Meet: A Bird's Eye View," *Parachutist* Magazine, January 1970, 20–21.

Early 4-way sequential RW over Taft, 1969. Diane Bird, Jerry Bird, Sam Alexander, Frank Venegas. Carl Boenish, photographer.

In December at Taft, Jerry organized an integrated 18-way star attempt with about half the participants from Elsinore. The 18-way completed.

This marked a turning point, though—a gradual changing of the guard. Jerry Bird was on a roll, while the Good Guys were losing momentum. Bird was on his way to becoming the most influential organizer of formation and competition relative work for years to come."[45] —*Bill Newell*

1969: RW—Where do we go from here?

1969: The USPA Competition Committee asked Skratch Garrison for his proposal to add Relative Work events to the U.S. Nationals. A condensed version of his proposal was published in the December 1969 edition of *Parachutist* for all members to consider.[46]

---

45. Bill Newell, "The Rise and Demise of the Arvin Good Guys," *Parachutist* Magazine, December 2004, 51.

46. Willard Skratch Garrison, "Relative Work at the Nationals," *Parachutist* Magazine, December 1969, 27–30.

Curt Curtis

USPA National Director, James F. "Curt" Curtis III, wrote "An Administrative History of Relative Work," published in *Parachutist*,[47] quoted in part, here:

"Relative work, like every other event in parachuting or any other sport (the World Series, the Stanley Cup, the super bowl, tennis, golf, basketball), has an administrative history. None of these sports, events, or grand finales happened overnight. They are the result of hard work by many people in the administrative end of all sports as well as by the athletes themselves.

The SCR is formally recognized by the USPA and is known by every other national parachuting organization in the world. As a result of the SCR and the inherent popularity of RW itself, it became apparent that something must be done. This something was a problem. What? Many relative workers did not want to see RW become competitive for fear it would take the fun out of RW. Others did. Goals were needed if something was to be accomplished. A direction was needed. The concept of *where do we go from here?* was discussed by the USPA BOD at the January 1969 meeting in Washington D.C. A motion was passed that the 1970 Nationals would include a relative work event. It was decided that four would be the magic number, as four-place aircraft were readily available throughout the country and the event must be a national event by virtue of the title of the Championships.

The Competition Committee was to have a set of rules (Part 52) for presentation to the BOD at the June/July meeting. Skratch Garison, Jim West, Bill Ottley, Mike Schultz, and others worked together to write the rules. From these rules came the basic concept of sequential RW. The event was never accepted with great enthusiasm, but it was a start.

The next significant step on the RW scene resulted from the energies of Ted Webster. Ted took the bull by the horns and announced the Webster Sweepstakes as a method of determining a team to display RW to the world in Bled, Yugoslavia, in 1970. His timing was perfect, for in

---

47. James F. "Curt" Curtis III, "An Administrative History of Relative Work," *Parachutist* Magazine, March 1973, 2–14.

January of 1970 at the CIP meeting in France, the new CIP President, Chuck MacCrone, admonished the CIP for its failure to recognize RW as an aspect of the sport itself. Until this time, the majority feeling, led by the Czechs, was that RW had its place in the Baton Pass with Accuracy event." —*James "Curt" Curtis*

11

1970

Stars over Bled

"I want to turn the World on to Relative Work" —*Ted Webster*, team sponsor.

1970: Bled, Slovenia, the site of the 10th World Parachuting Championships. The official U.S. Parachute Team, led by Michael E. Schultz, was made up of 12 men and women who were national champions in the individual disciplines of accuracy, style, and combination—the only disciplines recognized at sanctioned competitions.

The United States Parachute Association sponsored the official team, and after some convincing, agreed to allow the self-named, privately sponsored United States Freefall Exhibition Team (USFET) to be under their banner. Featuring both teams on the January 1971 cover of their publication is evidence of USPA's recognition of freefall Relative Work as a competitive branch of parachuting.

"The prime objective," Team Leader Ron Bluff said, "is to show through exhibitions at Bled, before an international assemblage of parachutists that relative work has come of age, that it is being done by responsible people, that the recognition we're demanding for our kind of parachuting is justified."[48]

---

48. Ray Cottingham, "Meanwhile, High Over Yugoslavia," *Parachutist* Magazine, January 1971, 20.

The U.S. Parachute Team and the first U.S. Freefall Exhibition Team. Lowell Bachman, photographer. *Parachutist* cover, January 1971.

Several team members share their memories of being on the first United States Freefall Exhibition Team, captained by Jerry Bird.

Sam Alexander

I was on Jerry Bird's All Stars and we won the Webster meet like we won almost all of the meets that we entered. Not everyone on the All Stars could go to Bled; some of the people had to stay home and work. I almost had to quit my job to go, but I was not going to miss that one!

Ted chartered the seats on a charter flight to Frankfurt and we took the Marrakech Express, I think, from Frankfurt to Bled overnight. Ted put us up in a hotel in Bled for the three weeks that the world meet went on. We made exhibition jumps every day for the World Championships. It was a wonderful time, it was a great experience, it was so exciting. The purpose of that trip was to introduce relative work to the world, to show the skydiving universe what could be done with relative work because it really wasn't going on in Europe or Asian countries particularly.

We were the exhibition team there and we were very popular. On many of the jumps we would take someone from another country or one of the dignitaries in the international association with us and put them in a big star for the first time in their lives, and after having that experience, their enthusiasm was through the roof. I mean, you share it, you spread it, they see it's possible. Once you've done it, you can do it again. —*Sam Alexander*

Donna Wardean

I was drafted onto Jerry Bird's team, and we won the Ted Webster meet. Then we became part of the U.S. Team as the Freefall Exhibition Team. Ted Webster, who had sponsored that meet, sponsored our trip to Yugoslavia out of his pocket. Our train rides, our hotel—everything that we needed, wherever we needed while we were in Bled Yugoslavia for the world championships, 1970.

While we were there we jumped in the opening ceremonies. We jumped in-between the style and the accuracy events for all the other nations that were there in the world championships. We would take team

captains up in the air with us and we would build a star around them. Now they weren't just seeing it in a magazine as they had been, or in the movies. Now we've got them right there with us and honestly, I could see there the history—the future—change in their eyes. It was like, oh my god this is the best thing in the world! Well, look at the sport. Look what has become of it! We took a lot of team captains—as many as we could—into freefall out of the big AN-2s—what a great airplane. I'm so proud to have been a part of the beginning of all this.
—Donna Wardean

In Bird's words

"So, we have Carl Boenish and Ray Cottingham as our cameramen, and we've got the matching jumpsuits. Ted Webster then made a proclamation. He said everybody can bring their wife or girlfriend and he paid for the whole trip for everybody. You couldn't buy a beer, you couldn't pay for a dinner and so we traveled, we put on demo jumps and we were out of the country for 20-something days and Ted Webster paid for it all.

There wasn't anybody in Europe doing RW much at that time and then we're at this world meet for style and accuracy, so we would pick the world champion female Russian jumper and she'd come, and we'd put her in a 10-way—put her in the base—and we'd make a 10-way with her. Part of the Ted Webster goal was to turn the world on to skydiving. There were 30 or 40 countries represented there. We gave away pictures, we showed movies. That was 1970 and that got me to quit my job because I didn't have any vacation time, so I said I am now a full-time skydiver, and I never went back to a regular job." —*Jerry Bird*

Ray Cottingham: "Meanwhile, High Over Yugoslavia"

Team member Ray Cottingham wrote the definitive article about the first United States Freefall Exhibition Team at the World Meet in Bled which *Parachutist* published in January 1971. "Meanwhile, High Over

Yugoslavia" is reproduced in part here, with permission of *Parachutist* Magazine:[49]

... Conception was a deliberate yet unobtrusive act that took place in the Fall of 1969. While at a party Ted Webster made a casual remark that he would like to attend the World Meet and demonstrate relative work. Further discussion brought about the realization that to demonstrate relative work at its present level would be impossible—the jumpers necessary would not be at the World Meet. Continued discussion, triggered primarily by Ron Bluff, resulted in a proposal by Ted to sponsor a team to the 10th World Parachuting Championships at Bled, Yugoslavia. The initial plan was to select a representative group of 12 jumpers; to this plan Ron applied himself. The jumpers selected were from both centers of mass relative work. Jerry Bird, captain of the 1969 first place team at the annual 10-Man Star Championships, selected six jumpers from the Taft DZ, while Ron selected six jumpers from the Elsinore DZ.

Because of the widespread growth of relative work it was decided that a competition was necessary. This fact became quite apparent with Ron and Jerry's selection of only 12 jumpers. At about this time, the first of the year, the rumor became fact—there would be a 10-man star competition with the first prize being an expense paid trip to the 10th World Parachuting Championships. Prenatal growth continued as the many organizational problems were confronted. In retrospect Ted commented: 'We were fighting a general disinterest and disbelief.' Initial contacts with USPA were discouraging—there had already been an 8-man star made over Hoppstädten, Germany, by the 1969 U.S. Parachute Team.'

At our request, the fine efforts of Norm Heaton and Chuck MacCrone, President of the International Parachuting Committee of the FAI were utilized at the CIP meeting in Paris (in early February) to obtain permission for a team to jump at the World Meet and demonstrate relative work. Growth continued under Ted and Ron's guidance as details of the trip and competition were finalized. At this stage it became possible to

---

49. Ray Cottingham,. "Meanwhile, High Over Yugoslavia," *Parachutist* Magazine, January 1971, 20–33.

advertise the upcoming "Sweepstakes 70" at a national level through *Sky Diver* and *Parachutist* magazines (May-June and March issues, respectively.) To further herald the upcoming event Ron Bluff called upon the talents of Earl Newman to create a souvenir poster—a black light poster at that. Attesting to their popularity, a large quantity were stolen at Plattsburgh during the Nationals.

Earl Newman designed the poster, based on Luis Melendez's photograph.

Paralleling growth at the contestant level was also taking place. The jumpers originally selected by Ron and Jerry joined together as the All Stars, captained by Jerry Bird. This team was ultimately to be the victors at "Sweepstakes '70." An early belief that the best team, not necessarily the best individual jumpers, would win, resulted in many practice jumps. Our team captain comments: 'When this group of jumpers were brought together, they were a loose group of competent relative workers. As we practiced and the meet drew closer, the group became a team. We didn't go for speed, but to make stars consistently with complete confidence in our ability to do so.'

Our team jumpsuits, red, white, and blue Ward-Vene originals, were donated by Terry Ward and Frank Venegas. Through the efforts of Donna Wardean and team members came our team name (United States Freefall Exhibition Team), our team patch, 10-man star patch and name tags. Stan Troeller saw to it that we had red metal flake helmets with each jumper's name on his helmet. Dick Gernand called upon Galpin Ford to sponsor our team jackets and new jump boots. The boots were received at cost from Parachutes Incorporated through Eddie Brown. Dick also contacted Para-Gear and obtained blue gear bags at dealer cost. Diane Bird and others were actively involved in contacting possible sponsors.

Once created, Ted did not desert the team. He paid for two practice jumps per week. We were no longer a 10-man star team but rather a 12-man exhibition team. We practiced so that we could demonstrate all aspects of relative work, including the 4-man relative events used at the U.S. Nationals. Ted also provided a team photographer, Carl Boenish, who recorded most of our practice jumps on film. Our Team Captain remarks, 'After winning the meet, we now focused our attention on turning the best 10-man star team in the world into the best exhibition team. We did this because we wanted to show all phases of relative work at the World Meet.'

Jerry Bird felt the image and acceptance of the team would be enhanced if we were the undisputed large star record holders. To this end he organized, from the Southern California relative work jumpers, to include all fourteen team members, several record attempts filmed by the Team Photographer. The results were World Record 20 and 21-Man Stars!

As our preparations progressed a great misgiving developed. Attempts to promote our purpose were blocked and rumors were the word of the day. Our greatest concern was whether we would be accepted by the United States Parachute Team. The USPT was training at Marana; Ted called Paul Tag and received permission for the USFET to jump in and meet the USPT. On Saturday, August 8, twelve members of the Exhibition Team flew to Marana. A day of talking and jumping with the USPT developed a comradeship that left us optimistic and provided fuel for continued preparation. Preparation to promote a professional image abroad as well as "turn the world on to relative work."

Probably the most significant outside donation to the team came through the efforts of Ron Bluff and Max Kelly. A paid demo jump at Ontario Raceway was arranged through Tommy Walker Productions. The advertising for the speedway referred to the speedway as the "Big O." Ron proposed a 24-man load, confident of the support of the Southern California relative workers, during opening ceremonies on Time Trial Day. Although our "Big O" was only a 15-man star, the demo jump was a great success ("Ontario Demo Jump" *Sky Diving*, Nov-Dec. 1970). A thank you to the jumpers and ground crew came in the form of an outdoor steak barbecue that evening.

On the afternoon of September 1, we departed L.A. International Airport aboard an Atlantis flight to Frankfurt, Germany. It was at this time we were introduced to Carl Boenish's camera crew of four Hollywood professionals from Major Independent Film Studios, Inc. We had one and a half tons of equipment to ship—about 1300 lbs. of parachute gear and 1600 lbs. of camera equipment. The services of DAX Air Freight, through Stan Troeller, Tommy Charles, and Mike Benson were appreciated.

The flight over was quite enjoyable as the reality of the trip took hold. We were accompanied by other jumpers who joined the group, nucleused by the Exhibition Team, which was to grow both in numbers and stature as it sought to "turn the world on to relative work."

"Upon arriving in Frankfurt we rushed to the station, only to find that our train had left before the airplane landed. Lyle Cameron came to the aid and made new arrangements. A night in Frankfurt gave everyone a rest, well, nearly everyone, before catching an early morning train to

Munich, to Jesenice, [formerly] Yugoslavia. Our late evening arrival on the 3rd was met with bus transportation to Bled and a meal at the Hostel Sloboda, our address for the next 17 days.

Bled church and castle. Ray Cottingham, photographer.

That first early morning view of Bled was breathtaking. The fairytale setting never ceased to awe us during our short stay. The morning was free, so several early risers set out sightseeing. A sunny path led to the old Castle of Bled, towering atop a sheer rock above the lake. From the terrace of the castle a panorama of the surrounding country unfolded. Our wandering led from the castle museum to the lake shore and through the lakeside tourist shops of Bled.

The day was not idled away as Ted and Jerry were in contact with the U.S.P.T. (United States Parachute Team) and made a trip out to the Lesce-Bled sport airfield of the Alpine Flying Center (about 3 miles). It was here that the 10th Jubilee-World Parachuting Championships were to take place. They succeeded in arranging a jump for the next day, the day before opening ceremonies. At the same time, in Bled, Ron Bluff was to make a chance acquaintance with two Yugoslavian sisters, Vika and

Lesce Bled Airfield. Sam Alexander, photographer.

Moitza Yezlnik, who spoke English and were working at the meet. Also, Carl and his camera crew were busy setting up equipment and making necessary contacts.

Our first jump on Friday was a 12-man star attempt with Carl and Ted filming from the outside. We exited at 4,000 meters from two AN-2s at the far end of the runway, due to clouds. This was our first hint of weather and communication problems—the Russian pilots did not speak English, nor did we speak Russian, and they were, we were to find out, definitely captains of their ships.

Saturday morning looked as if it were going to be a nice day for opening ceremonies. Suited up and sitting at the manifest area, we watched the clouds move in with long faces. As we waited, five AN-2s unloaded jumpers from all countries. We stood in awe as sixty-some-odd canopies dropped down—Jim Wilson, SCR-141, at the bottom of the stack, came in for the first unofficial dead center of the meet.

We went up to form a 12-man star with everyone wearing smoke but had to turn in on a low (9500 ft.) jump run. Stan gave the signal, I turned on the cameras, popped my smoke and sat in the door. Just as I exited, the two AN-2s in formation hit a cloud. We dropped out of the clouds linked in a 6-man star with Ted filming. The other aircraft, blind, did not exit and later landed without the other seven jumpers exiting. Stan's spot was good, for we landed in front of the reviewing delegation.

All Stars Joe Morgan and Stan Troeller exiting AN-2, 2nd, and 3rd.
Ray Cottingham, photographer.

Everyone was disappointed, especially those in the AN-2 that had landed. We had failed—tempers flared, and our first team argument followed. The following morning a more rational analysis of the jump was made. Our areas of difficulty were exposed and solutions proposed. Probably most significant was an even more attention demanding point—our arrival seemed to have come as a surprise, even though we had received permission to attend the meet and jump. No preparations for our arrival had been made, with the exception of an old star picture of another (competitive) group being posted throughout Bled. We did not have a tent to store our jump gear in, nor did we have passes necessary to enter the contestant area.

"Tremendous preparations were made for the competition by the Yugoslavian organizers. However, each area of responsibility, judges, organizing committee, and competition committee were nearly autonomous, and it was nearly impossible to find out just who was who without an interpreter.

It was necessary for us to establish our own liaison with Yugoslavians in spite of the fact that the leadership of the U.S. Team was supposed, we thought, to work with us to this end," said Ron Bluff (pg. 27).

It was obvious that we were on our own. We would have to provide our own liaison, but without the initial advantage of being recognized as a team. Our first positive move was to formalize our team leadership and assign responsibilities. Ted Webster was Team Sponsor, Ron Bluff was Team Leader, and Jerry Bird was Team Captain. Also, Mike Milts was made lead aircraft captain and Jerry Bird was trail aircraft captain—communications were simplified, and authority was recognized.

We were also aware of the necessary social/fun outlet and to this end Hal and Nancy Hurley worked. They obtained information on tours, places to visit, and organized several trips. The first was a short excursion to Ljubljana, that afternoon.

At this moment, the biggest job fell upon the head of the Team Leader. That fortunate meeting of Vika and Moitza paid off. Through them I was able to meet Franc Mirnik, the Chief of the Competition Management. It was through him and Janez Brezar, a member of the Competition Management and in charge of the airport service, that the liaison for the Star Team was developed. From these gentlemen we received almost preferential treatment as to aircraft and the trouble they went to on our behalf. Neither ever said 'we'll let you have this or that airplane,' rather 'how many airplanes do you need, one, two, or three?'

Mirnik made the statement that we were the most professional team at the meet and that it was his pleasure to work with us, for which we were most grateful.

Ultimately, through our team leadership, we were each to make 10-12 jumps demonstrating relative work. Early in the competition we jumped at the noon break; later, we were forced to jump at the close of the day's competition. It seems a protest, that we were wind dummies for the USPT, was filed by Soviet General Lisov. Most of our jumps were made from low altitudes due to late afternoon clouds and exhibited 4 to 6-man relative work. At the request of the Panel of International Judges we demonstrated a 4-man relative work event (star and caterpillar) used at the U.S. Nationals.

Whenever we were able to make a high jump, we invited jumpers from other countries along. We wanted to bring their hearts, minds, and bodies into the star—total experience. Our first guest was Janez Brezar who participated in a 10-man star with the USFET. Later that afternoon he was presented with a team photo and an 8-man star patch, which he proudly wore throughout the remainder of the meet. Claude Gillard, President of the Australian Parachute Federation and an experienced relative jumper, joined us for his first 8-man star. He got to watch our cameraman, Carl Boenish, come in 8th, filming all the way. Sadaharu Ohta of the Japanese team made his first hookup as a 5-man star with the USFET and Japanese jumper Chi Aoki was included in a 9-man. [In Japan, maximum jump altitude is 3,500 feet, which doesn't allow much freefall time.]

Two Japanese Team members jumped with us. Chi Aoki watched a 9-man star build around him and Sadaharu Ohta was equally thrilled as his first hookup was a 5-man star (out of five jumpers, the star was made high and flown for about 30 seconds.) Hal Hurley found the 5-man star with Sadaharu to be his most memorable jump of the meet. An impromptu jump put Soviet jumper Ossiupov in a 6-man star. A jump was scheduled with Gene Tkatschenko, USSR, past Men's World Overall Champion; however, for unclear reasons neither he nor any other Soviet jumper was allowed to jump with us. [Sam Alexander recalls: This was cold war time. The Russians were strictly chaperoned and after the first day or so, were forbidden to hang with the Americans. Of course, that made the attraction between the teams unmanageable, and some of the Russians would climb out of the window of their hotel at night to party with our guys. The Russians were the life of the party.]

On one jump Bill Edwards (SCR-56) and Jim Wilson (SCR-141), both of Elsinore, joined Dara Krstic of Yugoslavia in a 7-star with the Exhibition Team. Dara placed 9th overall at the World Meet.

All of our jumps and most of our activities were recorded on film. The professional talents of Carl Boenish and his four-man ground crew were everywhere evident. Supplementing Carl's freefall footage was that shot by amateur freefall photographers Ted Webster, Sam Alexander, Ron Bluff, Max Kelly, and Ray Cottingham.

Not all our time was spent at the airport; several days were set aside for excursions. In addition to the local attractions, team members visited Austria, Trieste and Venice, Italy, and toured the Dalmatian Coast of Yugoslavia. The beauty and history of each place visited was appreciated, but best remembered were the remarkable and friendly people we were to meet.

Ted explains, "The real value, what I got out of it, was our contact with jumpers, not spectators, to involve them." Yes, we involved them by involving ourselves. To simply watch—no, to become involved in this fantastic struggle for seconds and centimeters was inevitable. We shared the competition with many teams, but most of all with the U.S. Parachute Team. The USPT girls never ceased to amaze me; they were always there when the team jumped—at the tent, at the manifest, at the airplanes and back at the target. Many a conversation and friendship started out with a trade—jackets, patches, pins coins, pictures, etc. Our most popular trade items were team pictures and team patches. Dick Gernand noted that he had the most fun trading with the Russians.

Many, never to be forgotten, experiences are looked back upon. Our furtherance of international relations—a hand walking contest at the local discotheque—Ted Webster vs. a member of the Dutch Team. Ted's only comments, "the place was terrifyingly packed... I won that contest hands down." Stan [Troeller] and Donna's [Wardean] gift of a miniature parachutist's canopy on a chain by one of the local filigree jewelers. Bronco, head waiter at the Hostel Slobota, who must have had an adrenaline problem as he rushed about providing exceptional service. An evening meal in the eerie-like restaurant of the medieval Castle of Bled. The airport café where the Yugoslav national drink, Turska kava (Turkish coffee), slivovka (plum brandy) and pivo (beer) were ordered... discussions with a roomful of Yugoslavian students... The interest and constructive concern and support of Jacques Istel and Chuck

MacCrone . . . A silver medal for second place accuracy, earned by Bill Edwards, when he, Nancy Black and Jim Wilson went south to a local Yugoslavian meet at Zagreb. Several evenings of films submitted by many countries—Boenish's "Sky Capers" and "Masters of the Sky" and a delightful film of musical antics performed by the Soviet girls were popular. But, most of all, the many hours spent with those jumpers we were turning on to relative work.

USFET All Stars building a star over Bled. Ray Cottingham, photographer.

Our final day in Yugoslavia was Sunday, September 20—closing ceremonies and an exhibition jump competition in which the USFET placed third. The winner, of course, was the Russian trapeze act. No one could dispute its spectator appeal, the object of the judges' decision. We once again attempted a 13-man star (Ron Bluff was with us on this attempt) with everyone wearing smoke. Just before turning in on jump run at 12,500 ft. the pilots dropped us down below the clouds for an 8,000 foot jump run. The trail aircraft captain made the decision we would go for a 10-man star—the last three jumpers from his aircraft did not exit. A perfect 9-man star resulted, but the spot, because of clouds, left us at the

Completed star over Bled. Ray Cottingham, photographer.

Bronze medal awarded Jerry Bird's All Stars USFET, for their RW demonstration.

far end of the runway. Dick Gernand separated from his Para-Wing for our one malfunction in Yugoslavia.

Within the hour we completed our goodbyes and loaded the chartered bus for Frankfurt and home. Staying behind were Ron, Max and Carl, later joined in Switzerland by Ted, who accompanied us to Frankfurt. Onboard the departing bus Ron presented each team member with a bronze medal. This medal was presented to each participant at the 10th World Parachuting Championships. Later that evening at the formal Awards Banquet, Ron was presented with the Star Team's 3rd place prize in the exhibition jump competition. He also set a precedent by presenting to the heads of the Organizing and Management Committees, Chief Judge, General Lisov and Chuck MacCrone, large, mounted color pictures of the world's first 20-man star.

The photos caused mild sensation, first time a team had presented gifts in appreciation of the hospitality and co-op received ... The team leaders from each country also received lovely crystal goblets. Very important and dear to those of us on the Star Team were these tokens, crystal, and medals, for they indicated most certainly that we were accepted as a team and will be in the future. In this context, we were delighted to be invited to the next World Meet and to Portoroz for the Adriatic Cup Meet. Friendly invitations were also made by the Turks, the Russians, the Austrians, and the Japanese, to come, stay, jump, but most of all to demonstrate and teach. Yes, the world was ready for us and for relative work.

Epilogue: Ted Webster was presented with a bronze plaque at his birthday dinner in December. The plaque was engraved with the USFET patch, team member's names and the inscription, "In appreciation for the opportunity to participate in the advancement of relative work in World Competition."

In retrospect, our purpose was simple. Turn the world on to relative work. Were we successful?

Czech Team Leader, Ivo Skoták, asked me if he could ask a few questions about relative work, our team, and our goals. He had two pages of questions. They were intelligent efforts to learn how we go about organizing a 10-man or larger star, from base man and pin to how and why the third, fourth, etc. jumpers make their approach. From the nature of his questions I would not be too surprised to hear of a 10-man in Czechoslovakia. —*Ray Cottingham*

Brno 10/12/70
Hi Ron,
  Many Greetings from "the other part of the world!"
  Your colour free-fall pictures have a great success among parachutists in Czechoslowakia!
  I send you some pictures from Bled on which your team is acting.
  I am expecting your new material about star jumping and new color

pictures with great interest, because the same interest have our magazines and I would like to make through your material a good propaganda for star-jumping in Czechoslowakia too.

Thank you very much beforehand!

Ron, please, give my best regards to all members of your team!
Your Czech jump friend,
Skoták Ivo
Bendlova 1
BRNO 14
CZECHOSLOWAKIA

"I feel that this team reached and surpassed all the goals we set at the beginning. We formed the team for one purpose—to win the Webster Sweepstakes. We did. The team purpose at the World Meet was to demonstrate relative work. This we did and in doing so the jumpers from around the world were turned on to our thing—Relative Work." —*Jerry Bird*, Team Captain.

In 2022, The Skydiving Hall of Fame recognized the entire 1970 U.S. Freefall Exhibition Team for its contribution to the sport with the Pioneers of Excellence Award.

Donna, Ray, Sam and Jerry accept the International Skydiving Hall of Fame's Pioneers of Excellence recognition for the first United States Freefall Exhibition Team. Randy Forbes, photographer

12

Jerry Bird's All Stars Recall: 1968-1972

Sam Alexander

My Jerry Bird story began when I spotted a small, spring-loaded parachute in the front window of an Army surplus store when I was 10 years old. I paid $1.00 for it, and after removing the spring and attaching a toy paratrooper, I spent countless hours throwing it and watching it unfurl and float to the ground. I never knew what that chute was designed to be used for; it wasn't a pilot chute but was about the same size.

Fast forward eleven years: As a junior at Michigan State University, while on a class field trip I overheard a classmate discussing his skydiving experiences. Bob Olson was a former Green Beret who served in Vietnam and was a member of the U.S. Army parachute demonstration team. His stories captivated me, and as our group prepared to leave, I caught his attention and asked, "Can I try that?" He asked me to meet him at his apartment the following day, where he showed me how to perform a PLF, parachute landing fall, and arch my back when leaving an airplane.

The following morning, we gathered at the drop zone in Marshall, Michigan, where he taught me how to pack a main parachute. After I finished packing, he asked if it had been packed correctly, and when I meekly responded, "Yes," he replied, "Okay, then put it on, and let's go!"

Gulp.

A few minutes later, sitting on the floor of the club's Cessna 180, I promised God that if He let me survive, I would never do this again.

God kept His part of the bargain, but I didn't. I'll never forget the sense of relief and awe I felt at line stretch, looking down to see the ground over 2,500 feet below. I kept checking all the suspension points—the connectors at the risers, Capewells, harness straps, etc.—wondering if everything was secure enough. I was, and still am, afraid of heights. Olson asked if I was ready for a second jump, but I wasn't—that was enough for one day. But the next day I came back to try it again.

About a year after I made my first jump, the Arvin Good Guys achieved the first 10-Man star on July 2, 1967. When Olson told me about it he said, "When you get back to California, go to Taft; that's where everything is happening." So, right after I graduated, that's where I headed. Of course, at that time I had no idea what was really happening in freefall, what the Arvin group had actually accomplished, or what it might have to do with me.

Taft was an inviting place; everyone was captivated by what was unfolding during that time, and I felt drawn to the scene like a moth to a porch light. Jumpers like Skratch and Clarice Garrison were approachable and willing to jump and share their knowledge and experience with newcomers.

Everyone was curious, and jumping to have fun, and experimentation was the order of the day. The sky felt like a playground where anything was possible—relative work, hula hoops, batons, umbrellas (seriously, but only once!), and even chasing a freefalling grapefruit (to no avail). I was still scared all the time when I was jumping, but stronger forces kept bringing me back: Freefall is an indescribably amazing feeling, and being a skydiver set me apart at my office job and made me feel special. Also, it was the first time in my life that I felt like I was really good at something. I knew I was getting better and better at this, and I took a lot of pride in my growing skills and in the confidence that I was building.

Ever since my brother gave me a 35mm SLR camera when I was in high school, I have carried a camera everywhere. It's rare for me not to capture pictures of everything around me. When I first saw pictures of jumpers in freefall, I had to try it for myself, and after a few clumsy attempts with a handheld, I mounted a 35mm camera with a cable release on my helmet. Voila—with a camera on my head, I was welcomed on pretty much any load I wanted, and now I had an abundance of new skydiving pals!

I became friends with Bob Allen, known for his famous "Rod Pack jump without a parachute," and he was regularly shooting and showing 16mm films at the Rumbleseat Tavern or the Taft Hanger. One day he asked me if I wanted to carry his camera on an RW load with some of the "Good Guys." He didn't have to ask twice—I filmed a 9-man and was instantly hooked! As a sad footnote, on that jump, Allen Walters, one of the original Good Guys, had a line over (Mae West), then tangled his reserve with the half-separated main, and was killed. A somber rest of the weekend for all of us.

My first job after college paid me $450 per month, and I allocated a budget of $50 each weekend for skydiving, which covered about six jumps, meals, and gas. During those days, we often slept in tents near the peas or on packing tables in the hangar. Occasionally, a group would splurge and rent a room at the Taft motel for about $5 each. We would draw straws to determine who got the beds and who had to sleep on the floor.

As my RW and camera skills grew, I was invited on more and more loads with "good guys," and I was getting to jump and drink beer with names that I read about in *Parachutist* and *Skydiver* Magazine—Skratch Garrison, Lyle Cameron, Gary Young, Terry Ward, John Rinard, Carl Boenish, Jerry Bird, Bob Allen, etc. When Carl Boenish asked me to carry a camera for point-of-view film, I eagerly accepted, and I carried a Boenish rig on countless jumps after that. I loved being a part of that and seeing my film on the screen!"

When I met Jerry, I had no idea he was destined for greatness or that I would be embarking on the adventure of a lifetime. At that time, it was all about having fun. And in those days, the most fun a jumper could have was getting together in freefall, and for all of us, that meant making stars.

Jerry was one of the Good Guys at the first Rumbleseat meet in 1967, and I was on a pick-up team. I had never even been in an 8-man star; our

Taft team never made a practice jump and were very happy to achieve a 6-man and a 7-man star in that meet.

A few months later, the Arvin group invited me to fill in for someone who couldn't make it for a "round robin" jump from Elsinore to Oceanside and back to Elsinore. On January 13, 1968, I participated in my first 10-man over Oceanside, California, making me SCR #62.

Over the next year, I became good friends with Jerry and his new wife, Diane. By the summer of 1968, the rumor was that Jerry was done with the Good Guys—he wanted to lead a team, but the Arvin bunch didn't want a coach; they wanted to keep doing what they had always done. When Jerry approached me and Dick Gernand about forming a new team, we were all in! We were short on time though—our first practice jump took place just before the 1968 Rumbleseat meet, and we only scored 38 points over the 4-jump contest. But things would change before the next meet!

During the summer of 1969, Jerry handed out practice schedules and we began working in earnest as a team. By November we had made 10-man stars on 17 out of 18 jumps, and Jerry dubbed us the "All Stars." Our practice jumps had not gone unnoticed; we were regarded as the team to beat by the day of the contest. We won, but the outcome was close, and we learned from it and were determined to keep improving.

That 1969 Rumbleseat meet was the real beginning for the All Stars—we dominated the sport for the next 4 years!

Creating and keeping a formal schedule, practice and discipline represented the difference between professional and sandlot. From the beginning, it was obvious that Jerry had the ability to recognize talent, the instinct for seeing how all the puzzle pieces fit together, and an aptitude for bringing out the best in a former rag-tag group of jumpers. Like a professional team, we trained to win, we began to expect to win, and, after that first big victory, we did win, over and over again. Jerry wanted jumpers who were talented, dedicated, and disciplined on his team. He regularly tweaked the exit order to test people in different positions and to see how to optimize results. For instance, in our first team practice jump I exited base with Dick Gernand as pin (not optimal). Whatever the exit order (and I went from first to 9th, to settle in at 5th or 6th, my

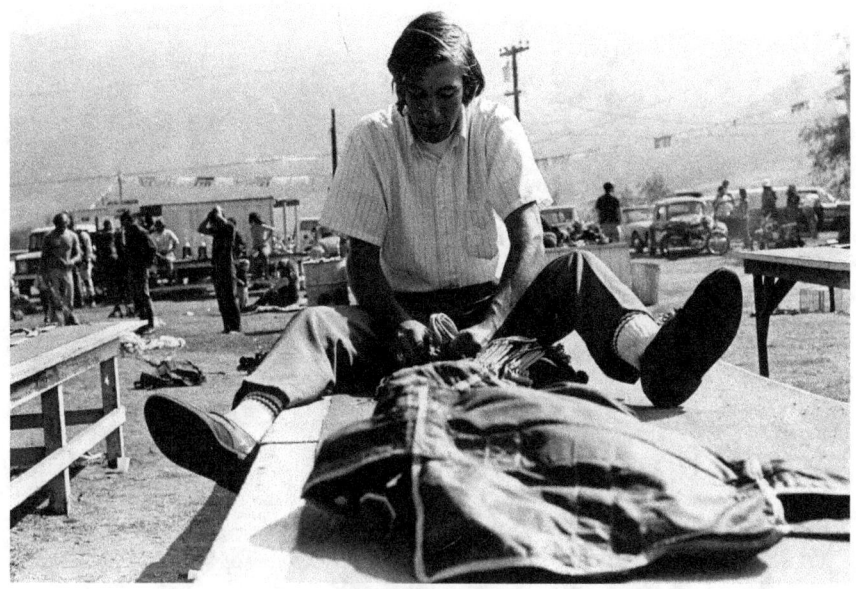
Bullet Bob Feuling. Photo by Sam Alexander.

goal was the same: never shake or break a star and always enter before the jumper behind me. As Jerry would say: "Fly to the slot, not through it." To Jerry, I was a "utility" player—not the best or fastest in any specific position, but dependable to step in with confidence wherever needed.

During practice weekends and at any skydiving event, Jerry joined loads with other jumpers, scouting for talent and ideas. He was the team recruiter, leader, organizer, and coach. When he set out to establish a new record, he planned, organized, and executed the process carefully. I think that every time we attempted to set a record, we succeeded.

The five years of All Stars were fun, exciting, intoxicating (in various ways), and habit-forming. My mom complained that I was obsessed, and I never admitted it to her, but she was right. I went to work from Monday to Friday, but every weekend was about being an All Star. When my employer told me I couldn't take time off to be part of the U.S. Freefall Exhibition Team at the World Championships in Bled, Yugoslavia in 1970, I told them to replace me if they didn't like it—I was not going to miss that opportunity! They caved.

Jerry Bird's All Stars Bob Feuling and Sam Alexander; Elsinore 1970. Photo by Raylene West.

On my second day in Bled I met Raylene West. She had hitchhiked from the Bay Area to the East Coast, then flew to Amsterdam and rode trains and buses to watch the All-Stars and the World Meet. After returning to the States, Raylene moved to Southern California. We got married the following year and we invited Jerry to live with us when we moved into a new house. Jerry stayed there for the next 2 years, and we were immersed in skydiving and Jerry Bird stories pretty much every day.

That leads me to more of the Bird legend. His talents went beyond skydiving: Jerry was a star athlete in high school and excelled at almost everything he attempted throughout his life, including athletics, puzzles, and various fun sports. For instance, hand-eye coordination and reflexes. On a warm summer night, flies buzzed around our living room, and Jerry said, "Watch this," then simultaneously snatched two flies out of the air,

JERRY BIRD'S ALL STARS RECALL: 1968-1972

Sam Alexander at Bled. Carl Boenish, photographer.

one in each hand. It was unbelievable, and I dared him to do it again. He said "OK," then he did it again. Many years later while Raylene and I were interviewing Jerry for this book, Jerry stepped outside his Blue Bird bus with a bottle cap and a Daisy Red Ryder carbine action BB gun (yeah, the same one that Ralphie used)[50]. With the gun hanging from one hand at his hip, he flipped the bottle cap about 15 feet away, then swooped the gun up in one motion and shot the bottle cap. I asked him to do it again, and he said, "You were watching—I just did it."

By early 1973, Jerry had been living with Raylene and me for over two years. When he decided to leave California, it effectively ended the team that had just won the 1972 national championships and set another world record. I had just under 950 jumps at that point, and I knew that things would never get better than that. After five-plus years, setting too many records to remember and winning every skydive competition we entered (except one), and dominating the newly minted sport of relative work, I was done. Carl Boenish had been urging me to try his new sport of hang gliding, and I decided to give it a try.

I never made another jump. —*Sam Alexander*

Dick (Rich) Gernand

My first exposure to skydiving was in May 1967 at a drop zone in Lancaster, Calif., a hot, dry desert area of Los Angeles and the San Fernando Valley. I went to make a jump based on a friend's "dare." Actually, I made two that day. Little did I realize that was the beginning of a very exciting and dedicated period of my life.

A few weeks later, it was suggested that I go to a drop zone in Taft, CA. There I met the owner Art Armstrong, and jumpers Sam Alexander, Gary Young, Don Choura, and a whole bunch of others. Being the new kid on the block I tried to learn as much as I could, as fast as I could from the "experienced" guys.

---

50. *A Christmas Story*, directed by Bob Clark. Ralphie Parker, played by Peter Billingsley, is the character who wants a Red Ryder BB gun for Christmas. MGM, 1983 (IMDB).

Sam Alexander and I hit it off and he became my mentor and friend for the next five years. He remains a great friend to this day.

My first exposure with Jerry Bird was a 4th of July exhibition jump into a local college. No issues and a big success. I was slowly learning who this Jerry Bird guy was and was duly impressed.

Fast forward to the "big day" when Sam came up to me and said he and Jerry Bird were organizing a team for a 10-man star meet in Taft and was I interested. I couldn't say YES fast enough. That was the beginning of my time with Jerry Bird, Jerry Bird's All Stars and the U.S Freefall Exhibition Team.

Jerry is everything you have read about him and more. The master planner, no guff, just get it done type of personality. Plan and execute which involved early arrival at the DZ, dirt dives, and a lot of planning. There was a real team spirit as we developed into a hard-core group, all with Jerry's guidance. I had a family and good job and occasionally (but rarely) needed to be other than at the drop zone. I do not recall Jerry ever getting angry or distant. He would say "just let me know if you will be here" (the drop zone) "to jump with the team." I seldom missed a weekend. I'm not sure how long his list was of capable replacements, but every practice load had a waiting list of anxious competitors wanting to jump with the All Stars. I loved every minute of it.

The World Meet in Bled, Yugoslavia, 1970, in which our participation was promoted by Jerry, was the highlight for all of us. However, as time went on family, jobs and other personal issues took a toll on a lot of us. Even then, Jerry continued promoting the team and we became more noticeable around the country as the Jerry Birds All Stars Team Supreme.

I continued to make exhibition jumps at air shows, music concerts and colleges as well as fun jumps at Elsinore, Taft and other DZ's. but could not maintain the pace (time and expense) Jerry Bird's All Stars and USEFT needed. A couple of years after Bled I finally made peace with myself and reluctantly hung it up.

I had no regrets. Kudos to Jerry Bird and Sam Alexander as they supplied unconditional support during my years on the team. It was fun while it lasted but I quickly realized it requires TOTAL emotional and physical commitment. It amazes me that Jerry has maintained the pace needed.

Dick Gernand at Taft.

Fast forward (again) to today and I am totally amazed that 50-plus years later most everything that is skydiving and available to see in movies, on-line and at the drop zones is a result of those earlier efforts by Jerry Bird and the All Star team. At the time we were good, but no comparison to what is happening in the air today. —*Rich Gernand*

Donna Wardean

I took up skydiving on May 16, 1966, at Arvin, California, the true cradle of relative work, which is now called Formation Flying. On my first jump there were twelve other guys who went higher in the Beech after I got out. On that jump they did the world's first 10-man baton pass [Al Paradowski, Bill Stage, Don Bradley, Jim Dann, Bob Buquor, Alan Walters, Jerry Bird, Tommy Owens, Joe McKinney, and Terry Ward] These men were my mentors; these were the people I learned from.

There were women before me and there were women after me and there were women at other drop zones. They had a really hard time and men kind of talked down to them. When the first Formation Flying competitions came about, relative work was so young that there weren't enough girls to have girls against girls, boys against boys, so I fought and fought and fought to jump with the boys. I probably drank way too much beer, inserted myself into many conversations, some of which I was not welcome, in order to fight for talent-based teams for meritocracy. I'm proud to have pushed and pushed for that so when the first RW competition came about in Taft, the teams were made up of guys and girls. Arvin Good Guys brought in Skratch and Clarice. I came in 9th on one of their 8-ways. Got my SCR 26 on that jump. It was my first world record.

I was part of Jerry Bird's first All Stars. I knew him from the very beginning, back in Arvin and in Taft. I coined the name, The All Stars. I remember saying, We are all stars and we are making all of our stars, so let's be the All Stars. I was lucky to be one of his ALL STARS.
—*Donna Wardean*

Donna Wardean at Bled. Ray Cottingham, photographer.

Charlie Wickliffe

From a very young age, I was attracted to high-risk activities, and I was interested in skydiving for as long as I can remember. When I was in my mid-teens, I watched some early skydiving in a dry wash in San Marcos, CA, close to my home. The jumpers were equipped with the standard gear of that era: Sears coveralls, combat boots, modified military gear, and aircraft altimeters on their chest-mounted reserves. I knew then and there that I was going to be a skydiver.

At age nineteen, I enlisted in the US Army, wanting to go airborne. Unfortunately, at my physical, a cocky corporal medic sporting his new airborne wings, declared me eligible for enlistment, but not airborne duty due to having orthopedic hardware in my left ankle as the result of an injury two years previously. It was a tremendous disappointment.

Not to be deterred, five months into my enlistment, I found a small club close to my duty station, in a swampy area in Ocean Springs, Mississippi, right on the Gulf of Mexico, and I made my first two jumps in April 1966. My instructor was the most experienced member of the club, having about 25 jumps . . . It seemed like a lot to me at the time. I made two static line jumps there.

The Army reassigned me to various duty stations during the next few months, eventually assigning me to the 3rd Armored Division outside of Frankfurt, German, and I couldn't make another jump for a year. With some research, I found the Aerobats SPC on the Army base in Schweinfurt, just an hour or two away by train. They required an Army doctor's medical approval, which I passed with no issue. With the Aerobats, I was able to make ten jumps, getting through the static line and early freefall progression. Eventually, winter weather set in and in December 1967 I was reassigned to my tour of duty in Vietnam.

In November of 1968, I returned from my tour of duty in Vietnam and was separated from the Army. After not having jumped in two years, I wasn't sure if I was going to continue jumping or not. I had been exposed to the anxiety of static line jumps, but none of the elation of freefall. With the encouragement of an army friend whom I had introduced to jumping in Germany, I decided to give it another shot, so I went to Elsinore, just an hour from my hometown, and resumed jumping with jump number 13.

Prior to military service, I had begun racing motorcycles, and that was my priority when I returned from Vietnam. So, for nine months, I was getting into jumping while I was racing motorcycles. With assistance and sponsorship from my local Kawasaki dealer, we won the AFM Pacific Coast Championship for our class! Also, in that time I had also made quite a few more jumps, and by then I was hooked, and skydiving became my priority!

Within that first year after Vietnam, I met many new people and made many new friends in the sport. As I progressed, I jumped with a couple of ragtag 10-man star teams in local (Southern California) 10-man star competitions.

Within a year, I was invited on higher quality jumps and became acquainted with Jerry Bird. Eventually, I was invited on the 20-man star record jumps at Elsinore. Half of the participants on that record jump were members of Bird's previous year's team, which, with financing from Ted Webster, had gone to the World Meet in Yugoslavia to do RW exhibition jumps.

I felt that my performance on the 20-man star had opened doors for me. With a few hundred jumps now under my belt, and having made a favorable impression, JB asked me to make some jumps with a new team that he was building, which I considered quite an honor. It was the dawn of a new chapter in my skydiving career!

For two years, we—Jerry Bird's All Stars—dominated 10-man star competitions in the West. Most of the competitions then were done from a small door Twin Beech, which was considered a large jump aircraft at that time, late 60's and early 70's. There was a learning curve jumping with the best of the best, during which I devised a personal, and perhaps unconventional technique for getting to the star in the least amount of time.

Jerry had me exiting tenth on the team. No one was using floaters then. I don't think anyone had even considered the idea at that time, and besides, the small-door Twin Beech did not really lend itself to such a concept. Ten-man exits from a small door Beech took close to four seconds; anything less was considered very quick.

My theory, exiting tenth, was that my priority was to accelerate as much and as quickly as possible, considering that the base, with a four second head start, was still distancing itself from me for the first few seconds after my exit. My technique was to take a quick glimpse of the base as I went through the doorway and immediately get into a straight, head down vertical dive. I found that if I held the vertical dive for about the same duration as the exit, it would put me at about a 45-degree angle to the base, when I would transition from a vertical dive to a steep delta position aiming straight at the base. Transitioning from the vertical dive to a delta gave me a tremendous boost of forward speed toward the building star. It didn't provide the delicate type of dock needed in larger formations, but it saved time, which was the whole point in 10-man competition. The team knew I was coming and had bullet-proof grips.

Always one step ahead, when Jerry Bird learned that the first 10-Man Star National Championships was a looming reality, with DC-3s as the jump aircraft, he immediately found a DC-3 for us to practice our team jumps. It was then that we began to use floaters. The memories are a little hazy, but I think we were putting three people outside of the aircraft. Obviously, our exits were much quicker than from a small door Beech, and the difference was reflected in our 10-man completion times.

I don't think any other teams were using floaters previously, but when we arrived in Tahlequah for the '72 Nationals, and began our preliminary practice jumps, the other teams, seeing our procedure, immediately began to emulate our team exits.

The six competition jumps proceeded without a hitch and we won the first 10-Man Star National Championships with a comfortable margin. One of our jumps produced the first sub-20-second star—a 19.6, which was somewhat demoralizing to our competition. Obviously, we were all elated, and this was a significant milestone in my life, not to mention my skydiving career.

The real bonus of our victory was the invitation by USPA to return to Tahlequah in August to put on RW exhibition jumps at the World Parachuting Championships of Style & Accuracy! So, we spent the time after the Nationals practicing the formations and transitions that we would perform at the world meet.

Without the pressure of competition, our demos at the world meet were pure fun. It was glorious! We all wore smoke on every jump, as I recall, which made the jumps look impressive from the ground.

On some of our jumps, we had the opportunity to take some of the foreign competitors up with us, many of whom had hundreds or thousands of style & accuracy jumps but had done little RW and had never been in the air with more than a couple of people. One jump I particularly remember was taking the French Women's Champion up to build a 12-way star, and I made a point of docking beside her to surprise her with a kiss pass at breakup. I suppose you could call that an authentic French kiss!

I have always been somewhat amused by Jerry Bird's motivation in organizing the record attempts. One of our main rivals during that era of 10-man competition was another Elsinore team by the name of the Flying Farkle Family, which included some very competitive jumpers. They were determined and tried in vain to beat us in local competition, however they were not invited by USPA to compete in the 1972 Nationals.

Around the time that we had returned from doing the demo jumps at the World Meet, a group of jumpers in New Zealand announced that they would be holding the first World 10-Man Star Championships—unofficial, of course, since there was no such FAI event. The Flying Farkle Family's motivation and "revenge" was to travel to New Zealand and, hopefully, win the event.

Meanwhile, our team, after having spent so much time away from friends, family, and work, decided we were not interested in traveling to New Zealand to compete in this unofficial competition. Jerry Bird was aware that they would be very competitive and have an excellent chance of winning. Not to be outdone, Bird organized the 24-way record dives to coincide with the absence of the Flying Farkle Family.

As it turned out, the Flying Farkle Family did win the New Zealand meet, only to discover on their return home that their unofficial title had been overshadowed by the new record star, which was considerably more meaningful in that era.

As you know, the 24-way record was lauded in the skydiving world, including the writeup in *Parachutist* and *Life* Magazine, and our appearance on *I've Got a Secret* TV show.

This was simply another perfect example of Jerry Bird's cunning and genius! —*C. Wickliffe*

Remembering Terry Ward

Skydiving is as much about the personalities as it is about body flight. Every California jumper from those days seems to have known Terry Ward. He might be called an outlaw—but he had a lot of friends.

Rt. 2, Box 501
Elsinore, Calif.
July 29, 1969

Gentlemen:

The following were grounded at Elsinore 7/27/69 indefinately for intentional low openings:

    Terry L. Ward
    Doyle M. Talbot.

    SKYLARK AVIATION
    Larry L. Perkins.

Terry Ward and Doyle Talbot are grounded – SKYLARK

*

JERRY BIRD'S ALL STARS RECALL: 1968-1972

In Bird's words

"Terry Ward was on my Jerry Birds All Stars in 1969 and went 10th on our team when we won the Rumble Seat Meet. So, we were 10-way champions with Terry in as our 10th man. I offered him a slot on the team that went to Bled, Yugoslavia, but Terry wanted to stay with his old crowd, the Arvin group.

Art Armstrong and his family ran the Taft drop zone. When Terry flew up, drove up, or rode his motorcycle, he would usually go into Art's office before he jumped and empty his pockets, so to speak. He would give Art's wife his wallet and car keys and a big wad of money with a rubber band around it. She would put it in the desk and when Terry was done for the day, she would give it back. Terry wasn't extravagant, but he always paid his way and everything.

Terry would get grounded all the time for pulling low—around 1000 feet. There were other people that did that too. Bill Newell was a pull-low guy, and it would excite the crowd. Nobody got hurt doing that, but they would get grounded. Terry, for some reason, got in trouble with Norm Heaton, who ran the PCA [Parachute Club of America] at the time, and was at Taft on official business one weekend. Terry flew in with somebody in a smaller airplane and he was out on the flight line. Somebody said to Norm, If you're looking for Terry to reprimand, he's over there. Norm walks over there and starts talking to Terry. Terry's real polite; he says, Yeah, yeah, yeah while he's getting his gear out of the plane. He's got two kit bags and Norm is a nice guy so Terry picked up the bag with his rig in it and said, Norman, can you give me a hand with the other bag? The airplane was parked about 50 yards away from the hanger, so Norm walked over with Terry, and they dumped the kit bags on the floor of the hanger. They finished their conversation and Terry probably got reprimanded. Later Terry said, Hey, I've got to thank Norm. He just carried 200,000 amphetamines for me in the kit bag.

Terry's place at Topanga Beach was 24 hours of sex, drugs, rock and roll. He knew everybody. His house had an open-door policy, and he always made sure his guests were accommodated. In the middle of his table, he had a Lazy Susan that had one of everything on it. Take your choice. This was Timothy Leary days in California.[51] I didn't do that type of thing, but there was always lots of LSD and stuff.

Terry did a lot of things—and big time. Once he was flying back east and somebody called in a bomb threat on the airplane he was on, so now they searched Terry's luggage. He had, like, fifty thousand dollars, ten thousand pills, a machine gun, some hand grenades, and some dynamite.

Well, Terry ended up going to prison in Terminal Island, which is in San Pedro, California. Later, while he was doing time there, we get a letter from him. He says, Hey, I got it set up for you to come and do a talk here. So, Donna Warden, me, and Sam Alexander go to Terminal Island and meet Terry at the gate, He's got the warden with him. We no sooner go inside, and Terry whispers to us, does anybody need any drugs?

I want to get out, you know, so we do our show on stage and show Carl Boenish's films and everything and later I get a letter of appreciation from the Terminal Island Federal Prison, Terry Ward, President. The warden says he's got his run of the place. He got along with everybody; he did his time and then he went on his way, and he never stopped doing what he was doing. Terry Ward was one of my best friends.

In that era, 60's and early 70's, we only had a few Beechcraft pilots. We had Walt Mercer who flew D-18 Beechcraft. In Elsinore, there was the Perkins family and some of them flew a Beechcraft. Spike Yarder flew out of Van Nuys Airport and many times we'd get on his airplane, fly up to Taft and jump from 15,000 feet. Spike was one of the few multi-engine Beechcraft-qualified pilots and he was blind in his right eye.

Spike probably flew thousands of loads of skydivers. Beechcraft normally carry 10 people, but it really depends on the weight of the people. If there are several girls on the load, it can carry more. If the fuel tank is low, then the pilot might carry 12 people. One weekend at Taft, the Beech was loaded and ready to go, with Spike as the pilot. A student who

---

51. Timoth Leary, clinical psychologist at Harvard University and leader in the experimental use of psychedelics for consciousness raising and mind expansion.

weighed over 200 pounds was added to the load and they put him in the rear of the airplane because that was the only place he fit. There were probably people standing up so when Spike turned to look over his right shoulder, he couldn't see because he was blind in that eye. He asked, Are we good? Everybody forward? How many do we have? A pilot knows the most important thing is that if you are on the ground and something is not right, you stay on the ground.

On this particular load, I think that the plane was overloaded, and the weight was not balanced. Spike lost an engine on takeoff, the airplane crashed, overturned and melted into a puddle of aluminum. The most common thing that happens when a Twin loses an engine is that the pilot lands it upside down. It's possible that even without the extra person or the unbalanced weight, losing the engine would still have been fatal. But my pilot, Mike Schultz, and Walt Mercer would never have let that airplane go upside down, we've lost engines before. The pilot has to immediately cut the other engine and put it back on the ground. When the engine quits at 14,000 feet in the air, any rookie can handle it.

Terry Ward was on the plane that day and died along with 13 other souls. A lot of people knew what Terry Ward was, but he was a good guy and no matter how drugged out he was, he always rode his motorcycle, at times with his Pit Bull, Macho, riding with him. They would say, like the guy, Scotty Carbone, He's going to die living that type of life. Well, unfortunately, Terry died at Taft in an airplane that lost an engine on takeoff. It turned upside down and crashed, killing everybody.

Terry was one of those guys who you either loved or hated. Most of the people who knew him really well, loved him. He died a tragic death, but in life, he was a live wire. Back in the '60s, *Look* Magazine took a picture of the five houses on the beach where Terry lived. In the picture, Terry's house was just covered with people. I'm one of those 50 people or so who were up on the roof. Going to Terry's house was just like going to a smaller version of Woodstock. Yeah. Terry Ward was one of my great buddies." —*Jerry Bird*

Carl Boenish

Carl Boenish, 1972. Randy Forbes, photographer.
"Late spring or early summer 1972, at the very first Richmond Boogie, I had about 60 jumps and had JUST made my first camera helmet. Carl himself removed the counterweight bolted to the back of it and fitted a thing called a "chin strap!" This all happened minutes before I took this shot!" —*Randy Forbes*

In Bird's words

"As soon as Carl graduated from USC, he was hired to be the cameraman for the movie *Gypsy Moths*. After he graduated, he was ready to take a job with Hughes Aircraft, but he made enough money doing *Gypsy Moths* that he was able to start his own business and become a professional cameraman. Carl went on to make a short movie about skydiving called "Sky Capers." It was set to music, and it was the first skydiving movie of its type.

Carl used a 16-millimeter movie camera, and he always had extra cameras. He would teach someone to shoot a skydiving formation from the ground with a long lens and get one of our teammates, Sam Alexander, to wear a helmet camera and show his point of view. Sometimes it was, wear a camera on your belly, or mounted backwards on your helmet—he was always looking for a different shot.

Carl Boenish in freefall. Ray Cottingham, photographer.
Published in *Parachutist*, September 1972.

Carl was a perfectionist. He could solder and make a switch or fabricate the wiring on a skydiving rig. I made a lot of jumps with Carl, and never once did he say that his camera didn't work or something broke or he didn't get the shot. His equipment always worked, he knew where the sun was, how far away to be, what angle to shoot from, what he wanted to highlight and what background he wanted. He was a technician, an artist, and a true professional.

Then Carl wanted us to jump with smoke. We didn't know anything about jumping with M-18 smoke grenades, but Carl built brackets that fit around your toe and had a wooden block that went under to create a heat shield, and it had a bungee that went around your boot. He taught us how to ditch it if you needed to. There was a line running down to the pin. First you jumped from the plane, then you activated your smoke bomb. He showed us how to use them, and we jumped with smoke at the World Meet as a demo team. Nobody got hurt or burned up their canopy. Carl did the engineering. He taped the line to your leg, so you just had to reach down and pull it to activate the smoke. It worked every time.

Boenish smoke bracket.

Carl became the All Stars' personal cameraman and made our team popular. Every time we went to set a new record back in those days, from the 16-way, the 20-way, the Webster Sweepstakes Meet, to Europe, Carl was our cameramen. When we jumped at Perris Valley and set the 24-man record that was in *Life* Magazine, Carl was our cameraman. He came to Zephyrhills with us in the '70s where they held 10-way, 16-way, 20 and 40-way competitions. Our team would enter every event, and Carl would film us and give cameras to people on our team to wear on those jumps.

He made the second skydiving movie called *Masters of the Sky* and our team was one of the featured teams in the movie. Sam Alexander from Jerry' Bird's All Stars did some of the photography. These were skydiving movies that people around the world could buy. Carl was one of the best cameramen in the world at that time, using 16-millimeter film. He used a Newton Ring Sight, motorized Nikons, Hasselblads and 35-millimeter cameras. He made posters of Jerry Bird's All Stars.

Shortly after we filmed at Angel Falls, Carl went to Europe and was killed BASE jumping." —*Jerry Bird*

Joe Morgan

Reprinted from *Parachuting: United We Fall*, edited by Pat and Jan Works, RWUnderground Publishing, 192–197.

Recollections of Summer of `70 . . . Southern California-style

Relative work and life in Southern California—the summer of Ted Webster's 10-man Sweepstakes Meet.

Gear was heavy. The standard relative work rig was a Para-Commander in a Pioneer 3-pin with a 26" Navy or Security conical (the only sport reserve available). We had three hogbacks on our team. It was generally felt at the time that they were okay for big guys, but conventional was better for most people. I had the lightest rig on the DZ, a step-in with rocket jet fittings instead of Capewells, 26' Navy, Pioneer 28' 1.6 main. It weighed about 27 lbs.

Jumpsuits had turned the corner. Although they didn't look that different except for color, it was hard for someone with a Pioneer jumpsuit to keep up with a bunch of people in Ward-Vene suits.

We had Beeches and could put almost any number up by flying formation with the Cessna or Howards. Relative work, of course, was not near the size it is today [1979]. Max Kelly and I had the highest SCR numbers on our team; he's 235, I'm 183. The numbers were up to about 500 or so at that time. There had only been a handful of stars eight or bigger outside California.

Ted Webster's Sweepstakes was the biggest RW meet ever. Of course, competition had only been going on since 1967. Ron Bluff, who ended up as "team leader" (a weird title for a weird job), Jerry Bird and Ted Webster (who was putting up the bucks) evolved a plan at the end of 1969 to demonstrate RW at the World Meet in Bled, Yugoslavia, the following September. A team was picked, half from Taft, half from Elsinore, as a representative group from Southern California.

However, the hideous long and agonizing howl that arose from those not lucky enough to be picked changed the best-laid plans of Bird and men. A competition was forced by the incessant demands for fair play, so instead of practicing all the things we'd daydreamt about—formations, etc.—we began practicing for 10-man speed stars. All the people who'd done the yelling were already far behind; while they scrambled teams together, we practiced.

Looking back through my logs, I find that what I remembered as a long and arduous training period was remarkably relaxed considering the stakes involved. The All-Stars only made thirty jumps in the two-and-a-half months before that 1970 meet. In contrast, "Terminal Chaos" made the same number of jumps in the two and a half weeks before the 1977 Nationals.

Also in looking back, I found that half the fun jumps we were making then were formations, mostly snowflakes, but we built the first Murphy—an 8-man with me in backwards—that summer, too. How did we get side-tracked to circles? The very competition we wanted did the trick, I believe.

Hal Hurley and Ron Bluff picked the Elsinore people: me, Max Kelly, Mike Milts, Ray Cottingham and Stan Troeller. Jerry Bird was Captain, and he picked the Taft people: Donna Wardean, Sam Alexander, Dick Gernand, plus Bob Feuling from San Diego and Russ Benefiel from Elsinore. It was a compatible group; we meshed at once into a team.

Personally, it was a weird situation. Our main competition was the Arvin Good Guys, and I lived at the beach in Malibu with two of them. The only other team with a chance was Dirty Ed's, and I was going with his ex-wife, a situation he considered intolerable. I had no trouble getting up for the meet.

It was pretty funny at the beach. We were practicing at Elsinore, and the Arvin team at Taft. I'd usually get home first. I'd be slumped in the living room relaxing from the weekend when they'd come in. Ron Richards, the Arvin team captain, would be the first in the house.

"How'd you guys do?" I'd ask.

"Great! How 'bout you guys?"

"Oh, OK. Tens in the thirties..."

"Well, shit! We're doin' *that* good!" He'd smirk and go off to his room.

Then Terry would come in, and I'd ask him how they were doing. "Fine. We're working on some stuff, but it's looking good."

Then Debby, Terry's lady friend, would come in. While Terry fiddled around the kitchen opening wine, I'd ease up to Debby and quietly ask how they did. "Terrible! They funneled two and had someone low on one jump!" It was all I could do to keep from cracking up.

We were confident—so much so that with the meet set for the 18th of July, Jerry gave us the 4th of July weekend off! (Can you imagine that happening today?)

While we were gone the psychological warfare escalated. Webster put out word that wives would also be allowed to go. A couple of the Arvin guys got married. None of *us* went that far, rightly figuring that Ted would let us take our old ladies.

Then Jerry Bird started the rumor that we had already gone down and gotten our passports. When Terry and Ron confronted me about that, I just smiled my best Sphinx grin and said nothing. Richards almost went into shock.

The morning of the meet Jerry Bird handed out little orange buttons that said

Better because we want to be.

He'd picked them up from Hertz or Avis or somebody, and we all wore them, ladies' auxiliary included, so they were everywhere. It was the kind of thing that made Ron Richards physically ill, which was exactly what Jerry wanted.

Ron did have something up his sleeve, however. There had been whispers and stuff about some Arvin secret weapon, and to Ron Richards goes the credit for changing the first part of RW forever. He had invented the floater.

Brian Williams in 1970—a little bitty, good-looking dude, SCR #8. (If you had totaled the SCR numbers of the Arvin team, it would have been under a hundred!) Brian had a big foam-filled jumpsuit and launched *in front* of the base/pin. He came in about eighth, if I remember right. It was startling to us, but not really scary as we got to watch them Friday. Their time was not as good as ours. (It did take a couple of years to work the kinks out of the idea.)

The morning of the meet the floater tactic and Dirty Ed's team's week of practice made Hurley nervous, but he's the only one I recall feeling that way. The rest of us were cocky. We were the first to jump and had a 32. Bird said to turn it up a bit.

Dirty Ed's team overamped and took themselves out. On the way to a sub-30 they broke into a line and took about 45 seconds to close it. They had no chance after that, and bit themselves to death like sharks in a feeding frenzy fixing the blame (the second most important part of relative work).

Arvin had about a 37 or so, if I recall right. Still a chance, theoretically, but we got faster (averaging about 30 seconds) and they dropped eight to ten seconds a dive on us, so the meet was never in doubt. We just cruised along doing our thing and let the other guys break up chasing us. It's Jerry Bird's favorite tactic and it has served him remarkably well over the years. We got a blue ribbon—and jumpsuits, helmets, 20 practice jumps, kitbags, boots, jackets, patches, and a free trip, all expenses paid, to Yugoslavia (with our girlfriends).

The weekend after that we jumped into team training for the style and accuracy people being held that year at Marana, Arizona, site of the '68 and '69 Nationals. We made a 10-man with smoke from fifteen-grand. I remember we were *extremely* dingy from hypoxia—Sam Alexander went base and it took us 15 seconds to get him to go. I rolled lazily through the prop blast jerking on my smoke lanyard—everyone was kind of drifting for the first 15 seconds or so. We thought it was sloppy, but it was the first star most people on the ground had seen, so demo-wise the jump was a success.

We also took a load up in one of the Cessna 207's they were using for training and made a nice six of six. Mike Schultz was on the load, along with Clayton Schoepple (overall champ that year) and Gloria Porter (women's accuracy champ and a real fox). It was Gloria's first star bigger than a two-man, and she had almost a thousand jumps. That would be hard to imagine today.

The next weekend we broke the 20-man barrier. It was a barrier—we'd been working on it for six months. The first one was clean and smooth, breaking for altitude. We backed it up with a 21. In the pictures, half the jumpsuits are team red-white-blues.

A few more practice jumps and we departed for Europe as the first United States Freefall Exhibition Team.

Yugoslavia in September has weather rather resembling the Midwest—clear in the morning, clouds forming in the afternoon. Consequently, we had constant cloud problems and made many low altitude (4000 ft.) four and six-man dives. The altitude meant that we just had to take it off the bottom, so me and Stan and Max took it to the streets. The people running the meet didn't hassle us, figuring we were professionals and did this for a living.

The best one was when the organizers approached Bird and asked us to demonstrate the four-man-back loop formation then being proposed for RW competition. Jerry looked up at the clouds and picked me, Max, Stan and Dick Gernand. Dick's only problem was that he was jumping an old Irwin Deatha-Two-Paranoid, the forerunner of the Paradactyl. It was not the ideal low pull rig.

We got about six-grand, built the four-man quickly, then made a discovery that has haunted sequential since—namely, caterpillars are hard to build. We got it about 1500 ft. and Dick's eyes were bugged out six inches as he opened about 1200. I was open about half that.

At the closing ceremonies we could only get eight-five. The clouds were broken, spotting would have been a snap, but the Russian pilots would not go above the deck (as a matter of fact, they did go above it but came down!) which really infuriated us. Stanley dumped his smoke in the door, then Mike and I, then Ron, and Donna, standing up right next to the pilots, popped hers, too. The airplane was emanating a solid red cloud of smoke and Russian expletives as we exited. We landed, got on the bus, and hauled ass.

It's funny, looking back now. If you'd asked those people on that bus if they'd do it again, they'd have reassured you they were going to keep jumping. Five years later when the next USFET was formed, only me, Max and Ray were left from the original, and only five of the twelve were still jumping. At least, they're all still alive." —*Joe Morgan*[52]

Ray Cottingham

An engineer by profession, Ray Cottingham is also a highly accomplished aerial photographer and cinematographer whose involvement with skydiving has continued for over fifty years. Known for his expertise, dependability, and generosity, Cottingham has worked on many major motion pictures, including *Point Break* (1991), *Terminal Velocity* (1994), and *Operation Dumbo Drop* (1995), and *Honeymoon in Vegas* (1992), for which he dressed as one of the Flying Elvises and jumped a camera on his helmet, landing at night on the Las Vegas strip.

Ray made his first static line jump in 1960 with the 82nd Airborne and did some photography. He continued sport jumping in the mid-'60s, starting at Lake Elsinore, where he credits Kevin Donnelly and Carl Boenish with helping him develop freefall photography skills and opportunities. Ray was on Jerry Bird's All Stars as the first U.S. Freefall Exhibition Team, along with Carl Boenish, and continued skydiving and

---

52. Joe Morgan, Pat and Jan Works, eds. *Parachuting: United We Fall*, RWUnderground Publishing Company, 1979, Chapter 6, 192–197.

camera flying for decades. In 2018, Ray Cottingham was inducted into the International Skydiving Museum Hall of Fame.

Ray Cottingham, from his own collection.

Ted Webster

Webster was one of the Elsinore skydivers who had participated in a 10-way shortly after the Good Guys did it first. Webster, Bird, and various other jumpers wanted to sell the world parachuting community on freefall relative work. Ted Webster had two things most skydivers lacked: A deep commitment to bring freefall star-building as a competitive sport to the world's attention—and the money to make it happen. The best forum for doing so was the World Championships of Style and Accuracy scheduled for September 1970, in Bled, Yugoslavia.[53]

In Bird's words

"Ted really was in large part responsible for the way relative work spread to the world because he said, I will put up the money.

Ted Webster was a young jumper and was good friends with Carl Boenish. He wanted to demonstrate RW to the world and show how much fun it was. At first, he was going to pick 10 people and say, Hey, you're my group, but it was suggested that there be a competition. There were no national RW championships at the time, but we had the Rumble Seat 10-man Speed Star, which was the biggest championship meet. Ted decided to hold his own meet, and the winning team would travel to Yugoslavia for the World Meet and do RW demonstration jumping introducing to the world what we were doing in Southern California. So, Ted held a meet called the Webster Sweepstakes in 1970 at Elsinore, California.

Ted Webster came from a well-to-do family. He was the grandson of Edwin S. Webster of Stone & Webster Engineering, one of the largest builders of power plants, hydroelectric dams and other big utility projects in the world. Ted personally sponsored the winning team to go to Yugoslavia for the 1970 skydiving World Championships. This was a big event at that time in our lives—a free trip around the world. Ted jumped with the team, The Flying Farkle Family, which went to New Zealand in 1971 and won the World Cup.

There were four or five good teams from around Elsinore and Taft. There was Jerry Bird's All Stars, the Flying Farkle Family, the A-1 Downers and the Arvin Good Guys. Any one of those teams could usually beat teams from any other state or country. But in Southern California, all of those

---

53. Larry Jaffe, "Southern California, 1963–1970: The Stars are Born Part II," *Parachutist* Magazine, December 1987, 19.

teams were competitive. Jerry Bird's All Stars won nine out of ten of those events. For the meet, we jumped out of a small door Beechcraft and during that competition, we won with a 32 second average and we were the first team to break 30 seconds on a 10-way jump by doing one at 29.5 seconds during that competition.

So, Jerry Bird's All Stars won the free trip to Yugoslavia. Ted was such a generous guy that he paid for spouses and girlfriends to go on the trip also. We had a whole production crew including cameramen, Carl Boenish and Ray Cottingham, and we became the first USFET—United States Freefall Exhibition Team.

Because of Ted, relative work was introduced to the world of skydiving." —*Jerry Bird*

Raylene West

Raylene at Elsinore. Photo by Sam Alexander.

I was a young skydiver at the Elsinore drop zone in the early '70s. I knew who Jerry was, but he was on a totally different level than I was. He was in the stratosphere, and I was hoping to survive each jump. I knew some of Jerry Bird's All-Stars so when they went to Bled, Yugoslavia for the world meet, I tagged along. Back at Elsinore, Jerry would sometimes let me follow his team out on practice jumps so I could time them.

When Sam Alexander and I got married in Las Vegas, Jerry was our best man, and after our wedding, we invited him to move in with us. When we got home from work, the three of us would sit on the floor and play games. One very popular game was to race the clock while putting a three-dimensional wood puzzle together. It was a very competitive atmosphere, and we'd each practice for hours to get the upper hand. We cut a hatch into the closet floor and built a secret room in the basement with a waterbed and black walls covered with black light posters. You could access it by climbing down the ladder from the closet or entering the basement through the backyard. It was a great party room and sometimes we'd hide there so guests would have to search to find where everyone was.

I loved going to the US Nationals and World meets in Tahlequah and I was one of the All Stars biggest supporters. When Jerry moved to Colorado, Sam and I quit skydiving and started hang gliding. I lost touch with Jerry but did not forget him. Through the years when I happened to meet other skydivers, I always asked them if they knew Jerry Bird, and every single one of them did.

Fast forward 40 years to the Hall of Fame weekend at Eloy and there was Jerry. He looked the same, he talked the same, and it was like no time had passed by. He arranged for us to fly in the wind tunnel, and MC-ed the event banquet. Our friendship continued as if no time had passed.

Sam and I met with Jerry at Zephyrhills several times as we wanted to hear his stories. We sat in his bus, the Blue Bird, and he told story after story, which we recorded. His bus is a mini skydiving museum. I felt so privileged to hear Jerry's stories and later transcribe them for posterity. He has lived a remarkable life and contributed so much to the sport of skydiving. —*Raylene West*

13

1971

Who was D.B. Cooper?

FBI Notice

D. B. Cooper was his name. Allegedly. He hijacked a Boeing 727, Northwest Orient Airlines Flight 305, from Portland to Seattle the night before Thanksgiving, 1971, telling a flight attendant he had a bomb and requesting $200,000 in a knapsack and two parachute rigs.

Flight 305 circled Puget Sound, giving the police department and FBI time to assemble the ransom money and the parachutes. Once the rigs and the cash—ten thousand unmarked twenty dollar bills—came on board, the passengers were released, the aircraft refueled, and the hijacker instructed the pilot to fly to Mexico City.

About thirty minutes after take-off, the hijacker donned the gear, took the money, opened the aft door, deployed the staircase and disappeared into the dark and stormy night somewhere over the forests of Washington state.

Nearly a decade later, some of the money was found along the Columbia River near Vancouver. For 45 years after the hijacking, the FBI kept the investigation open but never reached any definite conclusions as to the skyjacker's identity. A legend has developed around D.B. Cooper with books, magazine articles, documentaries, movies and podcasts rehashing the story, speculating on Cooper's identity and whereabouts. Few, if any, experienced skydivers of that era were consulted.

Jerry's mentor Brian Williams wrote his own fictionalized version about the hijacking under the pseudonym Pat Dunbar. Titled *A Dark Night* and independently published in 2003, it is definitely an entertaining book with references to actual skydivers.

In Bird's words

"On November 24, 1971, DB Cooper jumped out of a Boeing 727 with $200,000 and has not been seen since. I have a theory about his fate based on personal experience.

I jumped the DB Cooper jet—a 727—twice and have two plaques giving me a DB Cooper award We were doing boogies in Quincy, Illinois where they brought in a jet to jump from for the first time. They used the DB Cooper-type jet. There were 800-1000 jumpers and when the jet first flew in, the captain walked to the door, looked out at the crowd and said, Bird, is that you? He was a pilot I had known a long time ago and was flying for the aviation company that flew the jet in.

We were out in the middle of the corn fields and the sky was clear. We were making our first jump and there were three different guys spotting. You couldn't hang out the back. It's down the steps and you're out of there. The spotter in the back has to give signals to somebody else who signals to somebody a hundred feet away and they have to relay to the pilot which way or turn, how much, etc. So, basically the pilot is going to line it up and you guys say when to go. I think the first load missed the airport by two miles. The jet was flying and they slowed it down to maybe 150 to 200 mph.

Because of the jet blast, when you hit the door you might lose your goggles. Some people had their tennis shoes blown right off their feet. Some helmets and cameras were blown off. If your rig is not cinched tight it's blown sideways.

DB Cooper had one jump out the 727, almost 50 years ago, and technology wasn't what it is today. Skydivers were not as experienced as they are today. The average jumper had a couple of hundred jumps. When I made jumps from the 727 I had 10,000 jumps.

In the effort to solve the mystery of DB Cooper, some skydivers tried to duplicate the jump to see if he could have survived. The problem was, they were wearing Para Commanders and a piggyback rig so they still had something to hang the money bag on the front. I go, Great. You jumped over Elsinore out of a Twin Otter in the daytime over the drop zone. Faking flipping and flopping to see what happens with the money bag on the front, is not a very good simulation of what DB Cooper did. It was raining the night of DB Cooper's jump and as an experienced jumper, I've occasionally jumped in the rain. A raindrop is shaped like a teardrop. When you are falling from above, you're hitting the sharp end of them. They are like little torpedoes. They sting so bad it is like somebody is shooting you in the face with a BB gun. Jumpers in freefall while it was raining would quit doing RW and put their hands in front of their face or roll over on their back to protect themselves. Sometimes after they landed, they would take off their jumpsuit and it would look like they were covered with bee stings. There were red marks all up and down their body and legs and face. That's how much it hurts.

DB Cooper was wearing a business suit and a pair of penny loafers. He wasn't wearing gloves or a helmet or goggles. He was wearing a pair of sunglasses. He jumped at night with no spot over the mountains in a thunder and rain storm. He had a choice of rigs to use. There was a regular World War II equipment rig and I believe there was a Para Commander but the rig he chose was a Navy NB6 that Brian Williams and I wore as our freefall rigs. This rig originally came with no D-rings on it, so you had to have it specially modified in order to hang something on the front, the reserve in this case. This rig had a cross pull which means the ripcord was on the left-hand side facing into your chest. If you are an experienced skydiver, you should have your ripcord over on the right hand side. This was going to be a one-time jump with him jumping an NB6 where the muscle memory is to go to your right side. He chose the NB6 rig which is a reserve canopy with no steering line or modification. It is meant to save a pilot, oscillate and land on the ground. It is World War II vintage equipment.

If you were to take a board and write Happy Birthday Mom and jump from the airplane holding that miniature airfoil, it would fly you all over the sky. Try taking a briefcase in one hand. That would put you in a foot down position and you'd probably helicopter with it spinning. If two jumpers carry a banner by sticking their hands in a loop and one guy lets go, it will wrap around your arm and now it'd be like you have a cutaway parachute dangling off of you. Carrying extraneous stuff in the air is exponentially dangerous. My understanding is that the $200,000 was in bank bags. He would have had to tie the container full of the money onto his front somehow. The reserve has to be secured by snapping it on, then you have huge straps that go around to your main backpack that you snap on and cinch down as tight as you can. If you've ever seen somebody that forgot to hook on the back straps of their front mount reserve, this thing is flapping, it'll beat you to death in the face or it might just deploy. I don't think DB Cooper was stable when he hit the air stream. Anyone jumping out of a plane like that today can hardly get stable. If he were wearing goggles or a helmet or hat, those would be gone. He wasn't wearing gloves. His shoes were gone. If he wore a suit jacket, it would have inflated or flapped behind him, filling full of air. The front packet with the money was probably as big as a regular reserve and would have to be tied to something. Did he tie it to the ripcord handle? Or did the money bag cover up the rip cord handle?

Now he hits the jet blast and rain drops start hitting him in the face and he's tumbling. It's very possible that he never found the rip cord. That bag was hitting him in the face, he was in the rain, with no spot, in the dark over the mountains in a thunderstorm. I read one time that some people thought he landed next to his jeep and drove away. Now that would have been the greatest accuracy jump ever made. More likely, the money blew out of the pack. That's why they found some of the money or packages of it. If it were taped up, it would fall like a brick and land somewhere but wouldn't be eaten by animals. The NB6 harness did not have a canopy release on it. So, if he survived the rain that was hitting him in the face, found the rip cord and pulled and he was lucky enough not to land in that great big lake up there, he probably landed in a tree because he jumped over a forest. He was in a harness that had no release mechanism, so unless he had a knife and a rope, he had no way of extricating himself from a tree.

If he did manage to deploy and land, he was probably injured and barefoot. Did any branches tear out his eyes or did he break an arm or leg? Parachutes rot after a few months in the sun. I think that if he did make it to the ground, the animals ate his body and the parachute rotted. If he did pull and survived the jump and landing, how did he get out of there with no shoes?

I knew a skydiver named Max Freeman who looked like the person in the FBI sketch. He might have had something to do with the airlines. He always got us these free plane tickets—handwritten tickets. Through the years whenever anybody asked me if I knew who DB Cooper was, I said Max Freeman. Of course, that was probably not his real name. I'm not the only one who thought this. [Pirate, a friend of Jerry's who jumped with the James Gang, said that Max Freeman was never seen again after November 1971. He remembers seeing embroidered patches—Where's Max?—in Elsinore, after the hijacking made the news.][54]

Max ran with a wild bunch. I had met some of these guys like Chris Ranson and Greg Nugent—these two were the wildest of the wild. They went around the world on other people's credit cards or fake airline tickets. They would show up somewhere and I'd say, Hi, nice to see you guys. Nice car. And they would say, Yeah, we stole it in Ohio. One time they showed up in Elsinore with a twin engine airplane that they had

---

54. Where's Max? Telephone conversation with Pirate and Jerry Bird May 28, 2025.

"found." One of the guys had five hours of flight time and the other had ten hours. Jim Heydorn, a pilot who could fly anything said, Let me show you guys how to save your life. He took them up and showed them the basics of flying the airplane. They didn't even know how to use half the instruments.

They came to the Turkey Meets in Zephyrhills. Chris, Greg, Tony Fredin and DB Cooper—I mean Max Freeman. Zephyrhills was having bad weather and it was foggy when they flew in and they always had a bottle of something. This time it could've been LSD. They decided it'd be a good idea at midnight, in the fog, to make a jump. So, they had to choose who was going to fly. They made the jump and of course they pulled low and of course they were in an altered state. Tony did a "no pull" and bounced on the runway. The rest of them pulled at 600 to 1,000 feet in the fog (in more ways than one). They left Tony on the ground, got their stuff, got on the airplane and flew away.

The airplane was stolen—none of them had a pilot's license. They went on their merry way. Both of them spent time in prison over the years. They were serious criminals. Max Freeman was involved with those guys. They thought it was a hoot to live on the edge.

Max was a middle-of-the road jumper. He was a part time weekend skydiver and was not a jumper who could make a reliable 4-man. He was not good enough to jump on our team, but he was everybody's friend. He gave us T-shirts when we went to Europe in '70. He had a silkscreen company. In fact he and Terry Ward might have been involved. T-shirts fit in boxes and other things fit in boxes.

If I had been in that airplane, I would've chosen a Para Commander, a steerable canopy, over the NB6. Or at least a harness that had D-rings on the front of it so I had something to snap on to. When the experienced skydivers re-created that jump, they didn't use the equipment that he used, they didn't jump at night, and they didn't jump out of a 727. They wore goggles and helmets. DB was tumbling out of control going 200 miles an hour out of a jet in a rain storm at night. I don't know for sure what happened, but I think DB Cooper died on that jump." —*Jerry Bird*

14

1972

World's First 24-Way Star

Where: Perris Valley, California
When: January 16, 1972
Aircraft: DZ owner Jerry Karman provided two Beech D-18s, and a Cessna 206 for the videographers.
The skydivers: Bud Krueger, Al Krueger, Joe Faulk, Bob Skinner, Dennis Trepanier, Gary Quick, Mike Roberts, Bob Westover, Stanley Troeller, Pete Grueber, Hal Hurley, Bill Stage, Donna Wardean, Patti Wilson, Bob Feuling, Bill Coven, Rich Piccirilli, Charlie Wickliffe, Jerry Bird (organizer), Ron Haun, Stan Brown, Steve Fielding, Warren Frazier, Sam Alexander (POV camera). Ray Cottingham and Carl Boenish were the camera fliers who recorded the event. Weeks later, Carl Boenish's photograph of the 24-way was published in *Life* Magazine. Jerry and the team then made a televised appearance as guest contestants on the nationally syndicated television game show, *I've Got a Secret*, released July 7, 1972.[55] The 24-way star was also included in the 1974 Guiness Book of World Records.

---

55. "I've Got a Secret," directed by Marc Breslow, Season 1, Episode 3, July 7, 1972 (IMDB). Alan Alda was the celebrity guest contestant. Jerry Bird is credited as a contestant playing himself. https://www.youtube.com/watch?v=j1mvAT-xOJk.

First 24-way over Perris Valley, 1972. Carl Boenish, photographer.

The Inclusion of RW in U.S. National Competition

The first U.S. Freefall Exhibition Team turned the world on to the possibilities of relative work at the World Meet in Bled. Skratch Garrison's proposal had been well received by the USPA board, who were largely receptive. Move over, Style & Accuracy!

The RW Council and *RW Underground* Newsletter

Pat and Jan Works

"The Relative Work Council is a loosely knit group of active relative workers who are banding together to see that better things happen for RW more quickly. Some 42 relative workers at the Nationals, representing both 4-man and 10-man RW, agreed there was a need. The RW Council will act to supplement rather than supplant USPA. The Competition

Committee recognizes the Council as an advisor to the Committee. All RW Council members must be active in RW and should be a member of a 4-man or 10-man team. In addition, Council members must be SCR.

This newsletter [*RWUnderground*] serves as the communications media for the Council and interested parties."[56]

Jan Works

Pat and I started the newsletter in 1972 and published the last issue in June 1976. We typed its pages—bought a used IBM Selectric and already had an Underwood typewriter—and sometimes used other typewriters (surreptitiously while at our jobs) to produce stories and then pasted everything together before photocopying. Illustrations were clipped out of *The Fabulous Furry Freak Brothers* and other underground comic books of that time. We bought a mimeograph label addressing system and when it was time to mail an issue we recruited our drop zone friends to help assemble, staple, address, fold, and apply stamps. We made a party out of it. We sold subscriptions to finance the postage and photocopying.
—*Jan Works*

The *RW Underground* Newsletter went to over 1,120 relative workers worldwide. Members included USPA's Competition Committee, the FAI, CIP, and relative work teams and leaders from France, the U.K., Australia, New Zealand, South Africa, Germany, Holland, Sweden, Finland, Norway, Belgium, Canada, Texas, and more.

---

56. Pat and Jan Works, *Parachuting: United We Fall*, RWunderground Publishing Company, 1978, 211.

JERRY BIRD

Newsletter of the RW Council
No. 4
Fall 1972

Ribbit·Mumble·Mumble·Wolf-Wolf·and·Extra·Innings·News by everybody • Published by CRAZY PAT SCS-1 and little People + Bukibet

THE KEN DOBELL MEMORIAL 10-MAN MEET, OTAY VALLEY, SAN DIEGO. This usually sunny valley turned dark for the Saturday start of the annual Ken Dobell 10-Man Star Meet October 14. Three Twin Beeches, a DC-3 and 11 competition teams sat on the ground and waited for blue. Sunday cleared enough for four good rounds. Ten of the 11 teams entered were from So. Calif.; one from Arizona.

It was a fast meet. Teams placing one thru four made all ten-mans and AVERAGED 28 seconds or less. National champions Jerry Bird's All-Stars took first with an average of 24.9; the Flying Farkle Family (revised) were runners-up with 27.0; a new team, NWLF, 3rd, and Arizona, 4th. Fastest star was out of the DC-3 by the All-Stars. . .18.8 seconds.

MISSOULA $$MONEY$$ 10-MAN MEET, MONTANA. Ten crisp $100 bills with a 10-man stamped imprint went to Jerry Bird's All-Stars for their first place win at the money meet of the year. Friday and Saturday the weatherman presented crappy weather. Eight teams from all over the Northwest USA, Calif.and Canada drooled over 3 sanitary D-18's and 2 DC-3's and waited for clear weather which came 11:00 am Sunday to blast off 4 rounds. All-Stars won with a 24.5-second average followed by Seattle with 28.5 seconds.

The first and second place teams both credit sequential, multiple-maneuver RW for their success. J.Bird said, "DC-3 exits make subterminal RW skill a must. Subterminal work gives you ability to cope with traffic jams and to establish a pattern for building the star in a smooth manner... You learn to judge the construction activity and time your entry... Subterminal cleans up your in-close RW act."

The 2nd place Seattle team was built of two 4-man RW teams, plus two. Besides big money, Montana provided big boogie and a world-record 11-man moon on the dance floor. . .great band, good activities.

TEXAS TRIP-OUT. The Sutton Memorial Ten-Man Meet-Party at Valley Mills in October was termed a blast by all who attended from as far away as California, Ohio, Illinois and Florida. "Those crazy Texans" put on a party and a meet that'll be talked about until next year's. Their format was a good one for a fun-type, yet serious, meet: five jumps, three of them plain ol' vanilla 10-mans, one a reverse order and one a "draw-your-position-from-a-hat."

When the dust cleared from the hot and heavy competition, V-Mills came up the winner, followed by the Greene County-Atlanta group and Kansas Home-grown, third. Texas walked off with the C.G.Godfrog Good-Times and Good-Vibes Award, too, which was originally presented at the Nationals to A-1 Unlimited.

STAR-CREST SCRAMBLES. Ted Webster's 1972 StarCrest Scrambles and Tracking Contest was the biggest FUN parachuting event I've ever been to. Twenty-nine teams. That's 232 skydivers doing it out of three Twin Beeches and a DC-3. Many of the World Meet contestants stayed in the USA for the Labor Day Event. The scheduled RW consisted of three jumps: an 8-man star; an 8-man snowflake;

1972 U.S. Nationals and XI World Parachuting Championships

"Another decision affecting the '72 Nationals was a far-reaching decision in my estimation, for both the sport and the USPA. The 1972 Nationals included yet a fourth event—10-Man Stars." —*Norman Heaton*, Meet Director and Executive Director, USPA

Norman Heaton

As reported in *Parachutist* Magazine, September 1972:
"In June of '66 we conducted our first Nationals in Tahlequah, Oklahoma. There were 97 contestants that summer. We've returned to Tahlequah for three other Nationals, and June 15–25 of 1972 witnessed the conduct of the largest single parachuting competition ever held, anywhere.

For starters, we had 204 entered in the individual events, then you add nine teams in the 4-Man RW event, and top it off with six teams in the 10-Man Star event, giving you a grand total of 304 registered contestants . . .

This year's Nationals were so tied in with the XI World Parachuting Championships it's difficult to relate the story of the Nationals without plugging in the story of the preparation of the World Championships.

The 10-Man Event

Thursday and Friday were designated for the 10-Man Star Event, and we got it underway the morning of the 15th. By late afternoon we had a lot of people newly initiated to big star relative work and 10-man teams became a new topic of conversation with the local townspeople.

By late that afternoon we knew something else—we had a world record time for building a 10-Man and a fine selection of teams: Jerry Bird's All Stars, 10-High Bunch, V-Mills Texans, Hickley All of the Above, The Flying Farkle Family, and A-1 Unlimited.

The sixth and final round of the 10-Man event was completed late Friday afternoon with Jerry Bird's All Stars being undisputed National Champions of 10-Man Stars." —*Norman Heaton*, Meet Director.[57]

---

57. Norman Heaton, Meet Director, "A Report on the 1972 National Parachuting Championships, the Largest Meet in Parachuting History." *Parachutist* Magazine, September 1972, 9–21.

In Bird's words

"During this time [1968-1972], Jerry Bird's All Stars had a core membership of four people—Sam Alexander, Dick Gernand, Bullet Bob Feuling and me—and over that five-year period there were 38 different people that jumped as Jerry Bird's All Stars, winning competitions which included the '69, '70, and '72 Rumbleseat Speed Star meets. The Webster Sweepstakes in 1970 that became the U.S. Exhibition Team in the World Championship Meet at Bled, the Ken Dobell Memorial Meet in San Diego, BJ Worth's Missoula Montana Money Meet, the State Championship in the Texas Speedway Meet, and the 10-way Speed Meet in Santa Nella, California.

U.S. National Speed Star Champions. Jerry Bird's All Stars pose for the camera prior to their last competition jump. Kneeling (L to R) Bill Stage, Sam Alexander, Lynn Fogelman, Rich Piccirilli, Bob Westover. Standing (L to R) Mike Centracco, Tom Phillips, Ron Haun, Jerry Bird and Charlie Wickliffe. *Parachutist* Magazine, September 1972.

This was, of course, with round parachutes—red, white, and blue Para-Commanders bought for us by a rival team. Their sponsor, Joe Garcia, made the A-1 jumpsuits. He said, Bird, if you beat the Downers (which was called the A-1 Team at the Nationals) I will buy your team new canopies. We won the National Championship, Joe lived up to his word and he bought us matching red, white and blue Para-Commanders which had All Stars put on the side flaps so we really looked like a professional team and it made great photography with Carl Boenish filming and Sam Alexander shooting point of view, along with Dick Gernand.

USPA had started 4-way competition and wanted to have the first 10-way so they picked the top teams from the competitions around the country and invited six teams to come to the Nationals. The winning team would go to the World Championship as the first National Champions and do demos. We won first place. We were the first team to break 20 seconds with a 19.5 second star out of a small-door Beechcraft.

Tahlequah, Oklahoma, our last hurrah. At the 1972 World Championships, after the Style and Accuracy World Meet was over, the organizers said since we have three Huey helicopters and the record is the 24-way you made in Perris Valley this year, we will give you one free jump to attempt to break the world record.

Jerry Bird's All Stars on the Huey for a demo jump at the 1972 World Meet.

I knew more people there than anyone else on my team because I had done some traveling, and I knew a lot of the Style and Accuracy jumpers who were also good at RW. So, out of the people that were there, I selected 26 and we went up on one jump and we made a 26-way round star to set the record. It was done on one try with a walk-up group of people.

The World Record 26-Way Star Jerry Bird organized at the close of the XIth World Parachuting Championships in Oklahoma. Carl Boenish, photographer. Cover of *Parachutist*, December 1972.

Southern California was the hub of RW, especially the 10-way speed star. But now there are 10-way teams all over the place. There is the Flying Farkle Family team, The Valley team, the Downers, the A-1 team. Later, there was Al Krueger's Captain Hook and the Sky Pirates. When the '72 Nationals came along, the local meets didn't continue as much. Teams trained and qualified locally to go to the Nationals. But we wanted to set records, we were always trying to make bigger formations." —*Jerry Bird*

15

Sequential RW

Jerry Bird's All Stars 4th maneuver in their signature sequential dive. Carl Boenish, photographer. *Parachutist* Magazine, March 1973.

One of the first exhibitions of Sequential Relative Work—forming a series of patterns in freefall—was performed by Jerry Bird's All Stars. They did not invent sequential flying but they were doing it. Having gotten so consistently fast at building a 10-way star, they had plenty of time left to make another pattern or two after the star was complete.

Small groups of skydivers, particularly in Southern California and the Seattle area had been experimenting with non-round, free form patterns, sky dancing, and other possibilities of body flight—experimentation that laid the foundation, not only for sequential relative work but for vertical and hybrid dives which would eventually follow. BJ Worth would organize sequential skydiving and introduce it to the world through the film he made with Carl Boenish, titled *Wings*.[58]

BJ Worth and Sequential RW

"I came up with my idea because Jerry Bird in 1972 did a sequential exhibition at the World Championships in Tahlequah, Oklahoma and they had their 10-way team build a speed star and then they'd break it into a line and break that into two 5-way stars and make a snowflake. It was so cool, and it was color-coordinated so you could follow what was going on." —*BJ Worth*[59]

BJ would begin to form the second USFET (U.S. Freefall Exhibition Team) in 1974, further experimenting with and showcasing the many possibilities of Sequential Relative Work; techniques such as compressed accordion bases, back-ins, side docks, donuts, flying pieces and no contact formations. Team members, alternates, and support included Jim Baker, Ruben Casarez, Jim Captain, Ed Dugan, Rich Fiegel, Matt Farmer, Skratch Garrison, Steve Gras, Steve Haas, Karen Thompson, Dianne Marsh, Robin Mills, Bob "Chirp" Navrotski, Charlie Greenfield, Max Kelly, Mike Larson, Ron Luginbill, Pat Melroy, Steven Maness, Bob Schaffer, Gary Sanders, Dave Singer, Bob Taylor, BJ Worth. Camera Team: Carl Boenish, Ray Cottingham, and Rande DeLuca.

---

58. BJ Worth (director) and Carl Boenish (producer), *Wings*, a film shot on 16mm.
59. BJ Worth, Ground Rush Productions interview in Elinore, November 20, 2021.

Jerry Bird's All Stars Scorecard

3rd Rumbleseat Meet Taft, November 1969: JB All Stars 1st place

Bob Hughes Meet Elsinore, May 1970: JB All Stars 1st place

Ted Webster Sweepstakes Elsinore, July 1970: JB All Stars 1st place

Ken Dobell Memorial Meet Otay, October 1970, Otay, CA: JB All Stars 1st place

4th Rumbleseat Meet Taft, November 8, 1970: JB All Stars 1st place

Santa Nella May 22, 1971: JB All Stars 1st place

Valley Mills Waco, October 1971: JB All Stars 1st place

5th Rumbleseat Meet Perris Valley, November 14, 1971: JB All Stars lost to the Downers and received 3rd place.

Back story on our loss to the Downers: After the 4th round, Jerry Bird's All Stars were ahead by over seven seconds. Jerry, never to miss an opportunity to impress, told the team that the meet was won—he wanted to use the last jump to set a new record for the fastest star. Charlie went low and didn't get in until after break time, so we finished with a 9-man. A bitter pill. Still, Charlie was one of the fastest and most dependable 10th guys out there. —*Sam Alexander*

U.S. National Parachuting Championships Tahlequah, June 16, 1972: JB All Stars 1st place (won by 18.9 seconds in four jumps). Bob Westover, Mike Centracco, Ron Haun, Chuck Wickliffe, Sam Alexander, Bill Stage, Lynn Fogleman, Rich Piccirilli, Jerry Bird, Tom Phillips.

BJ Worth $$ Money Meet Missoula Montana, October 22, 1972: JB All Stars 1st place

6th Rumbleseat Meet Elsinore, November 18, 1972: JB All Stars 1st place:

Bob Westover, Lynn Fogleman, Bill Stage, Bob Feuling, Sam Alexander, Tom Phillips, Ron Haun, Rich Piccirilli, Chuck Wickliffe, Jerry Bird.

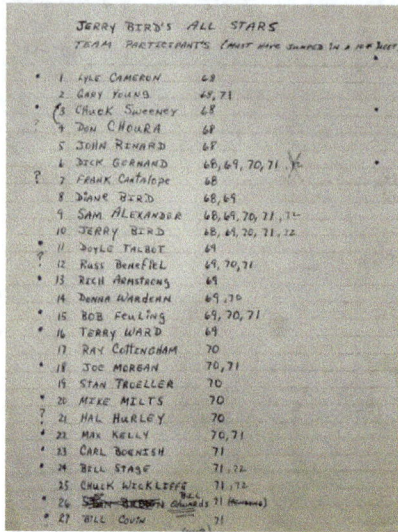

Jerry Bird's All Stars Roster

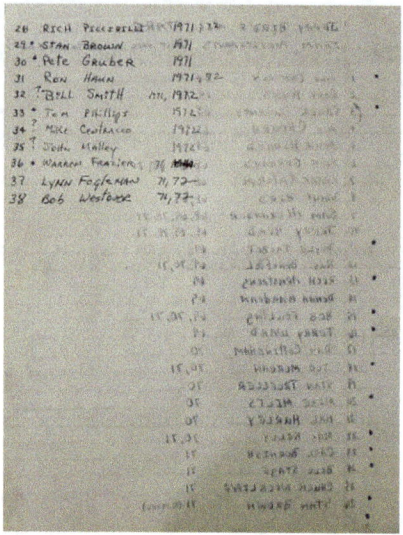

Jerry Bird's All Stars Roster pg. 2.

Jerry Bird's All Stars memorabilia. "The patch on the bottom left is my team patch. I was the ninth out on our first team. After that, I changed positions a few times so the number only meant I was the ninth member of the team. Bottom right is the first place medal for winning the 1972 National Championships. The coin above that is the Pioneers of Excellence award we received in 2024." —*Sam Alexander*.

16

Beyond California

In Bird's words

"And that was the end of Jerry Bird's All Stars. The remnants of that team kept the jumpsuits and the canopies and called themselves the Elsinore All Stars or the California All Stars, but Jerry Bird's All Stars were retired."

"About that time, I left California. I had my 1959 half-ton panel truck with Jerry Bird's All Stars on the side, painted by Smitty the Jumper.[60] On the back it said Matt's Plumbing Service.

In Tahlequah, where we set the record at the 1972 World Championships, one of the guys that was on the jump was Leon Riche. He had a drop zone outside of New Orleans and he invited me to their Mardi Gras Boogie. That's where I met the group from Columbine Parachute Center in Colorado which included a bunch of young ladies—Charmian Cliff, Patty Pitcher, Crissy Shinn, and others. I was highly encouraged to move to Colorado and jump with them.

---

60. Smitty the Jumper—Harold Truesdell Smith (1898–1995) was a pioneer parachutist during the American barnstorming era of the 1920s and '30s, making exhibition parachute jumps across North America. He continued jumping for decades, showing up at skydiving competitions and boogies well into the 1980s and published a booklet: *"Smitty"—His Exploits of Early Day Jumping*. Smitty was once a professional sign painter.

They were a bunch of fun people and they had a really tight membership. It seemed like there were more women than guys. They were all young, had a great attitude and had never competed. The company that owned the aircraft was Columbine Aviation, run by Mike Larson, Mike McCosh and Tom Fiore.

Bill Covin, Stan Brown, Jim Heydorn, Jake Lombard, and I lived in Southern California around Elsinore. In 1972 all five of us moved into the Columbine Clubhouse in Denver. Five different guys chased girls to Colorado. Charmian and I became girlfriend and boyfriend."

—*Jerry Bird*

17

1972–1976: It Happened at Casa Grande (the Gulch)

"Some of the best RW was going on there." —*Jerry Bird*

At the Columbine Airport, just south of Denver one November morning in 1972, Mike Larson was doing his pre-flight. He had been invited to fly his Beech to Elsinore for their 10-man star competition. Getting there is a story in itself, which Mike relates in his flying memoir, *Tales of the Cessna 195*.[61]

Spoiler alert: They made it to the drop zone in time for the meet and it was a profitable trip for him, in spite of the harrowing experience getting there. Over the weekend he met a couple of Arizona jumpers who wanted him to bring his Beech to their drop zone for a 20-man star attempt.

Mike Larson

"If you are reading this and you're not a skydiver you probably don't know how Casa Grande became a significant footnote in skydiving history. We made several flights back there and the jumpers kept begging us to return. The guys running the parachute center weren't as enthusiastic about sharing the weekend revenue. They finally advised us not to come back unless we were invited by them. Unfortunately for them, however,

---

61. Michael D. Larson, *Tales of the Cessna 195*, Erie, Colorado, 2014.

we had just bought the Casa Grande FBO. Columbine Airport had been sold by the sleazy owner and the airport would soon be sprouting houses. We were moving the whole operation to Arizona. The Arizona operators didn't like being second fiddle on the airport, so they packed up and moved their operation to Coolidge. Most of the experienced skydivers stayed with us at Casa Grande and by February we were busier in Arizona in winter than we were in Colorado in the summer."[62] —*Mike Larson*

Skratch Garrison

"Casa Grande is not a very big operation compared to, say, Elsinore," Skratch wrote in "Patterns in the Sky," published in *Parachutist, July 1975*. Their Lockheed Lodestar carries 24 people. Besides the Lodestar there is a Beech and a C-195. It is a perfect wintertime drop zone. Seattle—Snohomish—is the place to go in the summer.

 Seattle had called down Saturday night to tell us they had made a 21-man wedge—an extremely difficult maneuver because it floats so much. They had had a break in their winter rain and fog and had gotten together and done it. There is already some rivalry between Seattle and Casa Grande—as well as a healthy cross fertilization of people who follow the seasons and oscillate between the two. So, on the last jump Sunday BJ decided that there were enough people around to try a 24-man sunburst-flake. We made it smooth and high, with only a couple of small vertical warps about halfway through. And Rande got some nice shots of it.

 That was a good jump, and I enjoyed it. It makes a nice picture. And it is nice being in a first or in a record of some kind once in a while . . . Rande Deluca and Ray Cottingham at Casa Grande—there is always a cameraman involved when our knowledge of skydiving makes a quantum jump . . . Well, that's the kind of skydives you can expect to make on a typical weekend at Casa Grande.

 I'm just having fun making skydives with a very professional group of people—The [second] United States Freefall Exhibition Team. We were talking about it all one night after studying the films and BJ said,

---

62. Larson, *Tales of the Cessna 195*, 21.

'It's gonna spread like wildfire.' I think he is right. It sure gives me an airgasm." *Skratch Garrison*[63].

Matt Farmer

In his group skydiving memoir, *Above Us Only Sky*, Matt Farmer praises Mike Larson as "a brilliant drop zone operator who kept his fleet of large, antique airplanes flying and the freak show of 1970s relative workers they attracted from going completely off the reservation. At the same time, he offered the kind of open environment that fostered experimentation and excellence. If I had to pick the one person most responsible for the quantum leap the sport took from speed stars to formation skydiving in the early 1970s, I'd pick Mike Larson."[64]
—*Matt Farmer*

Jim Captain

"I think I spent five winters and one summer jumping at Casa Grande, or the Gulch, and for me it was really just about being at the most progressive jump center there was in the country. It really was a magnet."[65]
—*Jim Captain*

Jackie Smith

Parachute accuracy champion and member of Great Britain's Red Devils Freefall Display Team, Jackie relates her experience at The Gulch in her skydiving memoir *Marooned*:

"Casa Grande was THE place to be for progressive skydiving and each day we watched in awe as those sky-gods we'd watched in the movies were performing before our very eyes, the skies above were filled with 16-man formations. Throughout the following weeks, we skydived

---

63. Skratch Garrison, "Patterns in the Sky." *Parachutist* Magazine, July 1975, 16–25.
64. Matt Farmer, *Above Us Only Sky: Tales of the Kansas Homegrown*, 47.
65. Jim Captain, Ground Rush Productions interview, Erie, Colorado, September 12, 2021.

our butts off doing some amazing stuff and ultimately jumping with the USFET to achieve our 8 and then 16-man patches."[66] —*Jackie Smith*

Mia Elmsater

I met Jerry Bird in 1973 at Casa Grande, also known as "the Gulch." He had put together a group of the best skydivers and then there were the "Bird Chasers," of which I was one. We got a solid formation to swoop after—and we learned so much listening to Bird afterward. The thing about Bird that is amazing is he saw everything. After the jump he would go through the dive with everyone on it—the people on his team and the Bird Chasers. His feedback was always positive.

As a less experienced jumper, when we came to the drop zone we were often met by what we called "sky gods"—those who had a lot more experience and in some cases, really couldn't be bothered to even talk to us. They would walk around . . . just a little bit better. And it would never occur to them to jump with us.

Bird was never like that, although he had every right to be a sky god. He was there for the skydiving, and I think he wanted to see everyone have the opportunity to improve. Skydiving would not be what it is today had it not been for Jerry. —*Mia Elmsater*

First All-Girl 16-way

November 30, 1974: Sixteen women, organized by Patty Wickliffe, got together over the Arizona desert for a world record women's star on November 30, 1974. In the star were Rolayne Mattsson, Pat Davis, jeanni McCombs [she insisted on the lower case "j"], Nancy Gruttman, Linda Heath, Pat Pitcher, Mary Holdredge, Helen Fraser, Ruth Lanier, Donna Wardean, Patty Wickliffe, Karen Collett, Diane Marsh, Debra Zweifel,

---

66. Jackie Smith, *Marooned*, Kindle edition, 2017, Location 2896.

Charmian Cliff and Betty Hawkins. Ray Cottingham, photographer.[67] *Parachutist* Magazine. December 17, 2024.

THE CAMERA'S EYE — Sixteen women, organized by Patty Wickliffe, got together over the Arizona desert for a world record woman's star on November 30, 1974. In the star were: Rolayne Mattson, Pat Davis, jeanni McCombs, Nancy Grutman, Linda Heath, Pat Pitcher, Mary Holdredge, Helen Fraser, Ruth Lanier, Donna Wardean, Patty Wickliffe, Karen Collett, Diane Marsh, Debra Zweifel, Charmian Cliff, and Betty Hawkins. (Photo by Ray Cottingham)

BJ Worth

"By 1973 Jerry Bird had won the world championship, the World Cup, in 10-Way Speed Stars and he was hanging out in Casa Grande Arizona, so I packed up all my stuff and I went down to Casa Grande, Arizona. I have a journal, and I wrote, Today begins the first day of the rest of my life" —BJ Worth[68]

---

67. *Parachutist* Magazine, (online) December 17, 2024. http://www.parachutist.com At the end of the century, September 5, 1999, 118 women set a world record all-woman formation at Perris Valley, California in a breast cancer awareness-raising *Jump for the Cause* (a non-profit organization) Paige MacDonald. "Cause for Celebration." *Parachutist* Magazine, October 1999, 28–33.

68. BJ Worth, Ground Rush Productions recorded interview at Elsinore, November 20, 2021.

18

Columbine Turkey Farm

1973 U.S. Nationals

In Bird's words

"**Larson's whole operation** moved from Denver to Casa Grande, Arizona. We took over the airport and we would jump real early in the morning and in the evening. We jumped every day.

The California All Stars, with their blue and white striped jumpsuits and their All-Star canopies, came to Casa Grande to qualify for the National Championships. They won the Conference Meet to qualify, and I jumped with my new group, and we were barely able to qualify under the qualifying time.

Someone said, Bird, you really messed up by leaving California and jumping with these turkeys instead of us. So, we called our new team, The Turkey Farm—the Columbine Turkey Farm—because Columbine Aviation was sponsoring us and because the columbine is the State Flower of Colorado. We took our California guys with a mix of guys from Colorado and Arizona and made this new team.

The California All Stars team was averaging 25 seconds a jump and we were averaging 35 seconds. My new team—the Columbine Turkey Farm—we show up and they have the matching gear and arrogant attitude and that is where in the pictures you see us standing on one foot and gobbling at them. They didn't like that.

On our first jump of the 1973 Nationals a new world record was made, not by the California All Stars but by Jerry Bird's new team, the

Columbine Turkeys gobbling smack.

Columbine Turkey Farm:15.6 seconds. We went on to win the meet and we averaged 17.63 seconds for the six jumps in that competition."
—*Jerry Bird*

1973: Columbine Turkey Farm Wins First World Cup of Relative Work

"All men were brothers at the First World Cup of Relative Work, where representatives from seven countries came together to do that which they love best . . . to fly. For the first time in history a world parachuting meet happened without a single protest filed. We were pleased to see teams doing relative work on the ground as well as in the air," wrote Pat and Jan Works in an article for *Parachutist* in October of 1973.[69]

The international meet was held at Fort Bragg, North Carolina that year, and included 4-man and 10-man relative work events. This first

---

69. Pat Works and Jan Works, "How it was at the First World Cup of Relative Work," *Parachutist* Magazine, October 1973, 16–25.

World Cup of RW was the result of several years of planning by members of the Relative Work subcommittee formed in 1972, with Eilif Ness of Norway as Chairman.[70]

Andy Keech, author of Skies Call 1-3, captures the Columbine Turkey Farm as they exit the Chinook helicopter at the First World Cup of Relative Work. (Garry Carter confirms it was the Columbine Turkey Farm and not the All Stars as incorrectly identified by Eilif Ness, Chairman of the FAI RW Subcommittee, 1976.)

Garry Carter

"Once Jerry Bird is on the drop zone people from all over the world will show up to skydive with Jerry Bird." —*Garry Carter*

When I finished college, I went into the Air Force to be a pilot. I was stationed at Williams Air Force Base, south of Phoenix—outside Chandler, Arizona—not far from Casa Grande, where Jerry Bird would later put a new team together with his Columbine, Colorado followers.

His team later became known as the Columbine Turkey Farm—a combination of Columbine, where many of the team members were from, and 'turkey,' an expression I'd picked up from one of my skydiver friends at the University of Arkansas. Somewhere along the way, I referred to

---

70. Works, *Parachutist*, October 1973, 25.

Jerry's team as the Columbine Turkey Farm. It stuck and was used as the formal team name through Fort Bragg's RW Cup.

I had known Jerry from the Elsinore days and trained with the team on days I had off from pilot training. I became their designated alternate for the Nationals that year, and later a starter at the 1973 World Cup.

Me going to the World Cup is a story in itself—and a testament to Jerry's stature in the skydiving and military communities. After pilot training, I went to Luke AFB, west of Phoenix, for seven months of F-4 (RTU) training. When the team went to Raeford to train for the World Cup, I couldn't go. The Air Force does not permit anyone to take leave from the strict RTU training regimen.

Nevertheless, one afternoon an officer interrupted a flight debriefing and told me the Squadron Commander wanted to see me—NOW. The commander told me that the Pentagon had contacted the Air Force, and I was to be excused from training for the period of the RW World Cup at Ft. Bragg—and that I should catch the earliest flight to get there. The commander went on to comment, 'You must know someone at the highest level."

Yeah. Jerry Bird.

Apparently, one of the team members was not holding his own while practicing at Raeford, so Jerry started the quest to get me out there to join the team. Although he had been told it was impossible for anyone to take time off from F-4 training, Jerry—with his stature in early skydiving, RW, and military circles—gave it a try and pulled it off. How he did it is best told by Jerry, but I made it to Ft. Bragg and joined the team thanks to Jerry. The rest is history.

—*Garry Carter*

In Bird's words

"We went on to Fort Bragg, North Carolina, and won the World Cup Championships with our team, The Columbine Turkey Farm. That is how relative work spread. I took my show on the road." —*Jerry Bird*

JERRY BIRD

Aussies, Yanks, and Brits at the World Cup, August 4, 1973. Joe Gonzales, photographer. "The Gully Cats from Sydney were the Aussie 10-Man team representatives at the first FAI 10 and 4-Way World Cup in RW held at Fort Bragg, Norh Carolina. Australian team on the left: Bob Barry, Dave Hobbs, Geoff Bingham, John Parker, Andy Ski, Ken Hills, Peter Stevenson, Ed Smith, Russ Cocking, Ian Swinbourne." —*Annie Swinbourne* "Jerry Bird's U.S. team in the middle: Jerry Bird, Jim Heydorn, Tom Fiori, Stan Brown, Tony DeRosa, Garry Carter, Steve Haas, Jake Lombard, Nixon Lange, Bill Covin." —*Garry Carter*. "British team on the right: Alan Skennerton, Mike O'Brian, Dave Moody, Terry Fawdon, Dave Waterman, John Partingdon Smith, Jeff Lancaster, Mark Miller, Dave Fiddler, Tony Unwin." —*Dave Moody*.

Columbine Turkey Farm, the 1973 World Champion 10-Man Team. Standing, left to right: Jerry Bird, Captain, Casa Grande, Arizona; Jim Heydorn, Casa Grande, Arizona; Tom Fiore, Denver, Colorado; Stan Brown, Denver, Colorado; Tony DeRosa, Tucson, Arizona. Kneeling, left to right: Garry Carter, Fayetteville, Arkansas; Steve Haas, Phoenix, Arizona; Jake Lombard, Denver, Colorado; Nixon Lange, Tucson, Arizona; and Bill Covin, Los Angeles, California. Joe Gonzales, photographer.

Charmian Cliff: in Bird's words

"After the World Meet, everybody went home and my home was in Denver, Colorado with my British girlfriend whom I met at the Mardi Gras in New Orleans about two years before, Charmian Cliff, a young British jumper who was a member of the club in Denver. Char was on the first women's 16-way star, formed over Casa Grande. Not long after, a group of the Columbine gang—Pete Gruber, Steve Curry, Patty Pitcher and Charmian—drove to Arizona to a Meet. I couldn't go on this trip so away they go. The next thing I knew, I got a call from somebody who said they had been in a car wreck. I immediately got on a direct flight to Phoenix.

She was taken to Barrow Neurological Center, one of the highest rated brain trauma centers in the nation. The first time I saw Charmian, she was in the ICU ward where everybody in there had traumatic brain injuries. There were probably a dozen beds and they were all in one big, open ward. They could pull a curtain around the patient for privacy. There was a waiting room outside where the families could stay for 24 hours a day. The chairs reclined into almost a bed. The staff would bring pillows, sheets and blankets and there was a cafeteria where you could eat.

Unfortunately, many people there were waiting for their loved one to die. Charmian's initial prognosis wasn't good; she wasn't expected to survive. Her parents in England could not come right away. Because I was her boyfriend, I became her custodian. I made a promise that she was not going to die alone. I was going to be there, along with her other friends.

Charmian's body was cooled to decrease brain swelling. Because of the lowered body temperature, she felt like she was dead when I touched her. They weren't doing anything to repair the broken bones because if she didn't live, then there was no reason to, and she wasn't strong enough to go through surgery.

Every day was the same but one of my friends, Jim Heydorn, from our Columbine Turkey Farm Team, was living in Casa Grande, working as a crop duster pilot, and skydiving. He was part of the group that moved from Elsinore to Colorado to Casa Grande with me and he was one of my best and longest friends out of this group. It was about an hour's drive from Casa Grande to the hospital in Phoenix. He arrived with his shaving kit and said, I'm here with you for the duration, and he stayed with us for days. If I wasn't sitting by her bed, Jim would be there holding her hand and talking to her, or he would keep me company in the waiting room.

After a week, Jim told me he needed to go back to the Gulch to pick up some clothes and to do a crop spraying job. And he wanted to do some skydiving on the weekend.

I'll see you in a few days, Bird.

The next thing I know, some friends came to the hospital and told me that Jim had died in a skydiving accident. He had a streamer malfunction and was too low to cut away. In those days, with round parachutes and Capewells, you didn't cut away anyway. He deployed his reserve but one, he pulled too low, two, he had a terminal speed malfunction and three, he held on to his main ripcord and it burned into his reserve lines in the entanglement. This was a front-mount reserve and when he opened his reserve, somehow the handle and a cable got entangled and it wrapped with the main and Jim Heydorn died. He was 28 years old. He had served in the Army and was one of the best pilots I knew. He was a world champion on the 10-way speed star and was a great skydiver. He was from Elsinore, and a really nice man. Everybody loved Jim Heydorn.

I was at the hospital and I knew his girlfriend, Diane Farencie, was flying in to Phoenix so I went to pick her up. She knew about the car wreck and that Jim had been staying at the hospital with me. We get in the car and I'm crying, and she goes, Oh my God, Charmian died. I had to tell her, No, Charmian didn't die, Jim died.

After about 17 days, Charmian started to wake up from her coma. Eventually, they corrected all the problems they could and now it was time to start rehabilitation. Charmian was from Colorado, so she was transferred to a very good neuro rehab facility in Denver [Craig Rehabilitation Hospital].

At first, she could hardly talk or move anything. She couldn't remember words but as she worked through rehab, words started to come back to her. One day I was spoon feeding her mashed peas and she said, I don't like peas.

She didn't have any memory of who any of us were. I went every day to the rehab facility for about five months.

Another friend, Kung Fu Charlie, who was a graduate of the Al Dacascos Academy, was working as a rigger in Denver. He was one of the greatest Kung Fu fighters ever and every day after work he would come over to the rehab center. At the end of the week he would give me money from his paycheck so I could continue supporting and being with Charmian. A lot of the other Denver skydivers acted as a support team. One nurse said that the skydivers had been more responsive to one of their own than many families. Charmian had somebody visiting her every day, all day, and that is why she made so much improvement. We wouldn't let her quit and she didn't.

There came a time when Charmian could walk and talk, and it was time for me to move on. I had an invitation to go to Utah. The Columbine Aviation group, including Tom Fiore, Mike Larson, Denny Button and Bruce Reddish had moved back to Colorado from The Gulch. Unfortunately, one of our other buddies and one of the owners, Mike McCosh, had been killed in a hang glider accident.

I knew that Mike Larson had deep feelings for Charmian. I was managing her affairs and the only other person I completely trusted with handling her finances was Larson, so he took over as her caregiver.

They have been happily married for almost 50 years and have two children, four grandchildren, and one great-grandson. Mike had a successful career as an airline pilot and at one point was the Vice President of the International Cessna 195 Club. Charmian and Mike fly all over the country in their airplane. If you were to see Charmian walk by, or sit and talk with her, you probably couldn't tell that she had ever been in an accident. In those days you didn't usually come back from a traumatic brain injury like the one she had, but I think she did because of the stimulation and the extra work from skydivers and her own determination. Charmian exceeded the doctors' expectations for her recovery from a severe brain injury. She is a beautiful lady, and an accomplished skydiver. She and Mike seem like two of the happiest people in the world." —*Jerry Bird*

19

Bird and BJ

"I could never have accomplished what I've managed to do without Jerry Bird's leadership, inspiration, guidance and encouragement." —*BJ Worth*[71]

BJ Worth

Champion sequential formation skydiver, professional aerial stuntman, filmmaker, USPA leader, World Team organizer, and a great human being, BJ Worth is known and respected among skydivers worldwide. BJ was the driving force behind the champion 8-way team Mirror Image. While National Director of the USPA, BJ orchestrated the Olympic Rings freefall demonstration for the 1988 Olympics in Seoul. Following that, with his wife Bobbie, he established World Team, the pinnacle of big-way achievements. World Team has set multiple FAI World Records, culminating in the historic 400-way over Thailand on February 8, 2006.

Here's how BJ and Bird met:

In Bird's words

"I was jumping in Southern California in the '60s and first met BJ when he came to one of the competitions. He was going to school at the University of Montana in Missoula and in 1972, he and his skydiving club wanted to get to know Jerry Bird and the All Stars, but instead of their

---

71. Brian Giboney, "Profile; B.J. Worth D-3805" *Parachutist* Magazine, October 2018, 13.

club traveling to Southern California, they put on their own 10-way star meet and invited the All Stars.

One way to attract us was to make it a money meet, so they offered $1,000 to the winning team. Well, that was sort of unheard of in those days. Jerry Bird's All Stars had won a free trip around the world in 1970 at the Webster Sweepstakes but this was cash money. Instead of getting a trophy, each team member got a $100 bill. We went to Missoula, Montana and jumped in that meet and won. That was the second time that I met BJ.

I later moved to Casa Grande, and it became The Place to jump in the wintertime for people who wanted to jump big airplanes. Some of the best RW was going on there." —*Jerry Bird*

BJ Worth

Transcribed from a video recording of BJ with Ground Rush Productions at Elsinore in 2021:

"I met Jerry Bird in a very interesting way . . .

Spokane, Washington was the nearest other drop zone to our little drop zone in Missoula at the University of Montana. Tom Cannarozzo, from Spokane, and I came to Elsinore California in '72 where the best skydivers were and we asked some people, who can we jump with, we want to get our SCR and they said, oh those three guys over there will find some people for you. So, we got some jumpers that were really hot. Terry Ward was one of them. I'm not sure who the others were. Terry was having kind of a rough day. His two friends picked him up and put him inside the Beech because he had a hard time walking. For the young kid from Montana this was, um, pretty unexpected. We didn't know what to do and so we went out first, we built a 4-way and we said where are those Californians, they're supposed to be good and all of a sudden, boom-boom-boom, the other three came in and we built a 7-way. One of our guys was low and it was my first experience with Southern California skydiving and that started me thinking beyond Montana.

Later that year Tom Cannarozzo and I conducted the first money meet for 10-way speed stars. We put the red stamp on the hundred-dollar bills and then we advertised that we're going to have a money meet and the top team took the thousand bucks away. Jerry Bird brought his team up. Sam Alexander was on that team and Rich Piccirilli, and everybody from Southern California. Jerry Bird's All Stars came up and we had a big party and they won the competition, they got their hundred dollars each and they actually started dating our girlfriends and stuff, but we had a great time and from that point on I had a connection—we had a connection—with people outside of Montana. We were thinking that we could possibly do what these guys were doing, we were seeing what we might be able to learn, what we might be able to do in Montana, so that's kind of how it started.

I somehow managed to stay and graduate in four years with my degree in zoology, and that didn't come into play again for another thirty years, but I actually graduated, I jumped into my graduation with cap and gown in 1973, and then after that I went to find out where Jerry Bird was.

By 1973 Jerry Bird had won the world championship, the World Cup in 10-Way Speed Star, and he was hanging out in Casa Grande Arizona, so I packed up all my stuff and I went down to Casa Grande. It was 12 degrees when I left, frozen in my little Volkswagen, and managed to get all the way down there and started skydiving. When I ended up in Arizona there were several other groups that were showing up there because it was the mecca of skydiving because that's where Jerry Bird was. And there were other people from Texas, some people from Kansas, and people from Seattle and we wanted to push the envelope. Not only did we want to push the envelope with 10-way, we tried making some different sequential formations of different geometric shapes. We did not invent it; people were doing this. Skratch Garrison was one and Rich Piccirilli. We saw what people had done and we tried to take it to the next level. We were willing to try things and have them fail just so we could learn to see what we could do, what the possibilities were. That winter of '73 in Casa Grande was an awakening for all of us. And then we went back to our home drop zones, a lot of us, to show our local friends what we were doing. And we all planned to come back again the next year and do it again.

When I first went to Casa Grande all I knew was that it was a drop zone and Jerry Bird was there and so I wanted to go; I wanted to learn from this guy and hopefully if I was there long enough, he would actually talk to me. But of course, Jerry Bird is really cool; he'll talk to everybody.

Casa Grande was real bare bones. There were really cool aircraft and there were great skydivers but it was just dust and gravel and not much more, but the people came there, they felt like—not quite bandits but we were out on the fringe. We could kind of do what we wanted. Casa Grande got a reputation for being lawless. We as a group came up with the idea and actually Bullet Bob came up with the expression Sport Death. Sport Death wasn't that we were trying to cheat death; Sport Death, we all knew it meant pay attention. Because if you don't pay attention it's gonna bite you, the sport is. But everybody else saw Sport Death, the expression, as our flaunting and not worrying about the safety.

After that wonderful year at Casa Grande I asked Jerry Bird, could I come skydive with you, could I be on your team, and he said, Well, if you're not in Orange Massachusetts you can't be on the team. He didn't say yes but he didn't say no and of course I had to skydive to be able to hold my slot. Jerry was the greatest skydiving organizer at the time and I wanted to learn what he was doing.

So, I went back and did a whole season with Jerry Bird. We came to the Nationals, we made a mistake during the competition, and we came in second place, but we had the best team, and we ended up taking that team and going to South Africa to compete in the World Cup because the team that won couldn't go on their own to South Africa. So, we went and we won the World Cup in '74, came back to France and went to a 10-way meet. We won that meet, made the first 20-way, I think, in France with our French friends.

While I was in France, I came up with this crazy idea of making a movie and teaching people how to do sequential relative work. I came up with this idea and put all the pieces together and figured I'd go to Hollywood, find a studio that would make a 35-millimeter, 90-minute movie and then we would teach the whole world how to skydive from this movie. Well, I didn't know really where to start so I came back and I contacted the best skydiving photographer and filmmaker I knew, which was Carl Boenish. He laughed and he said, That's interesting but the studios won't let you in the front door, that's not how it works, but I love what you're doing. I've seen the stuff that Rande Deluca had shot with stills, and Ray Cottingham had shots of our team, and he said, tell you what: I'll sponsor, or I'll produce the show, I'll put the money up to do it. You direct it and I'll get Ray Cottingham to come over and film it and he'll teach Rande Deluca how to film so we can make a film together. And I said OK. It's not a 90-minute feature film but it's a film. And we're going to use this film to teach people how to do sequential.

I came up with my idea because Jerry Bird in 1972 did a sequential exhibition at the World Championships in Tahlequah, Oklahoma and they had their 10-way team build a speed star and then they'd break it into a line and break that into two 5-way stars and make a snowflake. It was so cool, and it was color-coordinated so you could follow what was going on. But convincing a bunch of very broke skydivers to go buy jumpsuits and do something that's kind of highbrow; I got some pushback from several people. They didn't really want to do that, but they eventually agreed, everybody agreed to do it. We didn't have 20 people, we wanted 20. We ended up having 15 people and we needed one more person.

I met up with Skratch Garrison and I told him what we were doing, thinking he would just think, well that's cool. And then Skratch calls me and says, I want to come play. What do I have to do?

Well, Skratch was maybe 20 or 25 pounds overweight and enjoying life a little bit and he was really old by then, I think he was probably 30, maybe 35, but he wanted to come play. And I said, we'd love to have you here. And Skratch was out running—I don't know if he'd ever run before, but he was running, he lost some weight, and he became one of the key members of our team which ended up being called the U.S. Freefall Exhibition Team and with that team we did the skydives for the movie *Wings*. *Wings* was designed to show the skydivers of the world—not just the United States but the world—what was possible. Not how cool we were but how much fun they could have.

It took a while to get the film finished and we wanted to go to a world meet. We finally got the invitation to go to Germany for the first world championship of 10-way speed stars. So, we took a team over there with 16 of us and with our color coordinated jumpsuits at the opening ceremonies we made a 16-way diamond then broke four color-coordinated diamonds away and tracked them off with smoke, so it was a big success and the skydivers there at the meet, they knew what we were doing but I didn't realize the world was kind of following what we were doing. So, we agreed we were going to show the movie *Wings* before it was finished. We had all the footage, but we didn't have it really polished, but we had a soundtrack on the side and a 16-millimeter projector so some people said, well look, can we just get a sneak preview? I said where can we go and they said there's a bar down here, why don't we just set it up and we'll do it there.

We didn't know it, but the word spread like wildfire that we were going to show the movie, and we got to the bar and there was standing room only—300 skydivers to pack into this bar. We got a bed sheet or something and put it up and synced up the music with the 16- millimeter and we showed it. When it was over first you could hear a pin drop and then the cheering of the skydivers and it was probably the most momentous moment, or one of them, in my skydiving career because the skydivers just couldn't believe what they saw—but they believed that they could do this.

The competition started the next day and when teams made their 10-ways they would separate after completing their 10-way and then they would start doing sequential. By the end of the meet everybody was doing sequential. Except I'm not sure Captain Hook Sky Pirates were, they were competing at the world meet and they were really serious. I don't think they did sequential. And the French, who came in second didn't do sequential, but everybody else from bronze medal on down, they all did sequential and the whole world of skydiving pretty much was transformed overnight.

January, maybe April of 1975 was one of the coolest expansions of our sport, I think. The Kansas Homegrown people, Matt Farmer, Jim Baker, Jim Captain were in Casa Grande for the whole time and Ron Luginbill came up from Texas. We had people come even from Australia. I convinced Hod Sanders to come down from Montana where he was still in school, and Skratch Garrison came over from California and we coalesced into a really fun team trying new things. We would try some

16-ways because we had 16 of us but we did a lot of smaller things like 10-ways and 9-ways. The Kansas Homegrown did a 4-way sequence that had about six or seven different formations in it. We tried to get a variety of sequences every week, some large, some small, and after we had filmed for two days, I would grab the film, drive back to L.A., go down to the studio or to the processing store and we would put in the film. I'd hang out with Carl for a day. The next day we'd get the work, Carl and I would look at it together and make comments and then I'd drive back to Arizona and then I would design formations for three days and some of the other guys would as well because it was a joint project, a team project. As we went one week to the next, we would take what we learned and apply it to the next week. We had a few formations that we tried several times that we just couldn't quite do, but people were willing to persevere and finally we would do these formations. Today it would still be considered a pretty hot skydive, so it was a magic moment for those 12 weeks we all worked together.

One of the fun things we would do is on Saturday night we would show movies, the 16-millimeter movies. I got out my projector and everybody would sit around, and we would watch ourselves. Two or three weeks into it we knew we were doing something special. We knew we were learning as a team. We were able to build on what we were doing and every now and then somebody would come in from some other place and they would join us. That was the idea. And they would go, and they would talk about it. Rande Deluca did a super job with the camera. Ray Cottingham did a super job, and they captured what we were doing all weekend long.

I did go down the competition road. We managed to win the Nationals, we managed to win the World Championship, and we didn't know where we were going to go next. We were kind of resting on those laurels but by this time I'm really broke. I didn't have any money to begin with and now I spent every penny I had. There were no sponsors, there was no anything. We bought our own gear, bought our own jumps and I was completely broke, didn't know what I was going to do. And then out of the blue I got a call from Michael Wilson, he's the executive producer of the James Bond films. And he said, I've got this idea about doing a skydive for a Bond film and I thought you might be interested." —BJ Worth[72]

"Jerry Bird, as a leader in our sport as well as being a principled human being who has a heart of gold, has been a skydiving mentor," BJ said in a 2018 interview with *Parachutist*.[73] Although Jerry Bird and I have different organizing styles, I never could have accomplished what I've managed to do without his leadership, inspiration, guidance and encouragement." —BJ Worth

---

72. BJ Worth, Ground Rush interview, Elsinore, November 20, 2021.

73. Brian Giboney, "Profile; Interview with B.J. Worth D-3805," *Parachutist* Magazine, October 2018, 13.

20

1974: Wings of Orange

I have vivid memories of the Wings of Orange. I was an impressionable 17-year-old, making static line jumps, working on the ground crew shagging students, field packing rigs, helping fuel planes, etc. at Orange Sport Parachuting Center where the team trained in the summer of '74. The team made multiple training jumps each day and we would drive an old Ford van out to retrieve them so they could quickly repack. One perk was the discovery of Coors beer, which at the time wasn't sold on the East coast. The team members were hauling it to Orange with them. Mike Wheeler and Tim Pond of this group were also on the ground crew with me. —*Jim Holston*

In Bird's words

"In 1974, we went to Orange, Massachusetts and BJ joined as a new person on our team. We became the Wings of Orange.

Jacques Istel[74] owned Parachutes Incorporated, the company that made the Para-Commander, and he says, We want to sponsor your team. So, I essentially took the wings of the Columbine Turkey Farm and said, we are moving to Orange, Massachusetts from Casa Grande and we're going to develop gear. We have a new sponsor, free jumps, free housing money and our whole team used their input to develop what we call the Jerry Bird rig. In '74 we went to the Nationals as the Wings of Orange and wearing the Bird gear—round reserve, round main, the lightest rig ever made. In South Africa, wearing the Bird gear, we set the new world record." —*Jerry Bird*

The Bird Rig

In Bird's words

"We were wearing all kinds of mismatched World War 2 equipment and we were national champions.

People at that time were just starting to make bad versions of piggybacks that didn't work. The packs didn't open, the handles broke off, or whatever, and I said I need to make some streamlined gear. So, me and a friend of mine, Charlie Shields, who was a rigger, we sat down with my drawings to make and patent what was called the Bird rig.

What was different about the Bird rig was the front mounted reserve pack was designed like an envelope, with a triangular flap. The pack was wedge shaped, no metal in it, all cloth. It had a front flap that was Velcro closed. To open that rig you reached down and pulled and grabbed the

---

74. The French-born American, Jacques-André Istel, did much in the late 1950s and early '60s to promote parachuting as a sport in the United States, including establishing the first commercial parachute company and dedicated commercial drop zone at Orange, Massachusetts. Istel served in the U.S. Marine Corps in the Korean War, led the U.S. Parachute Team he organized in 1956, and hosted the Sixth World Parachuting Championships at Orange, Massachusetts in 1962—the first time the United States had held the event. Istel did much to legitimize skydiving as a civilian sport in the United States, and he was a credited technical advisor of the first skydiving documentary film "A Sport is Born" (1960) about his parachute operation. Later in life, he sold his parachute business and founded a unique outdoor museum in Felicity, an unincorporated community in California near the Arizona border.

canopy, threw it in the air if you had to use it. (People with Capewells back then couldn't do a cutaway quick enough on a terminal speed malfunction; sometimes they hit the ground trying.) On the back we made our backpack a tear drop shape. The pins, like on your rig today, were down low on your back so you couldn't bend your pins. Our rig was aerodynamic. When you put it on there was a strap that went from the reserve back to the backpack in a triangular shape. We had this thing about calling "hug me" and the guy in the lineup would grab those two straps and like a woman in a corset, would pull it tight around you. If we're lined up right, we fit together like a jigsaw puzzle. With the rig on it looked like you had a fat belly. You didn't have to arch so much, you had ten pounds of weight right here in front of you, it was automatically your center of gravity. We were so stable you could hit our stars really hard, and you didn't knock them out of the air."

Wings of Orange over Orange, Massachusetts.

I only had a one year sponsorship in Orange, where we developed the gear. We did that and promoted it, and after that our job was done. None of us lived in Orange and we didn't have a free place to stay anymore, so everybody went home.

BJ was jumping at Casa Grande. He did sequential relative work and he and Carl Boenish made a movie called *Wings*. BJ filmed some of the first color-coded Sequential RW.

About this time, the switch from 10-way to 8-way was happening and

1974: WINGS OF ORANGE

Wings of Orange team photo, displaying their Bird Rigs.

BJ was one of the first ones to get on that bandwagon and said 8-way was going to be the wave of the future. He started jumping with a team from Seattle, Craig Fronk, The Clear Eye Express and the Casa Grande group. BJ formed a team, Mirror Image, in '77 to compete in the first World Championships for the new 8-way formation flying. His team won the National and the World Championships, becoming the dominant competitors in 8-way sequential.

I moved back to Colorado." —*Jerry Bird*

21

First Door to Your Right, Then First Star to Your Left

In Bird's words

"It was in Pretoria that Wings of Orange won the 10-way Speed Star competition and set a new world record at 12.76 seconds. All these teams were specifically designed to compete in 10-way speed star national and world championships. International skydiving competition hadn't yet changed its format, but Speed Star was soon going to be on its way out and Sequential RW or Formation Skydiving was on its way in.

What we had learned by going to the desert with the Columbine Turkey Farm where we became a professional team and jumped every day was that just like any other endeavor, if you practice something every day for two years you'll get better at it. So, from now on, my goal was let's out-practice everybody else. We said, let's outthink everybody. How can we do what we're doing better? Let's do it like a football team does. So, we sat in the classroom and drew pictures and explained to the jumpers how and why we are doing it this way. Now, we've added the mental aspect to it.

The most important thing in those days was how do you get ten humans wearing bulky objects to go through this three-foot-wide rat hole as quick as you can. Then you could skydive when you were outside that rat hole. Speed Star now became a contest of how quickly you can get through the door. If you took seven seconds to get out of the airplane you weren't going break 40 seconds on making a star! So, now we're thinking in terms of using smaller and more athletic people who were willing to get in an airplane and practice and run and dive out onto a blanket so they could learn to move as a group through a tunnel, so to speak, and then dive out the hole. Now that you are outside, you can skydive! Before that, you were land mammals in a box with a hole in the side of it. The size of the aircraft and the size of the hole in its side were dictating how fast you could make a star, so we designed and made smaller, more streamlined equipment.

Small door Beech at Hartwood, Virginia. Dave Tylcoat, photographer.

My belly mount went under his main pack so our exit line was probably four feet shorter than everybody else's. And because we had nothing on our shoulders, we were built specifically for a small door aircraft. Now, your pack wouldn't hit the door because there was nothing on your shoulders. Now, you get out in the air and you can do RW.

We'd always say Chuck Wickliffe was our fastest skydiver; later it's Tony DeRosa. So, our technique in '74: we went out and when we'd built a 2-way we asked our tenth man, what's your line? What do you like? A little bit to the right, a little bit to the left, come straight down the middle? We would build the 2-way and aim that slot at number ten and nobody was allowed in his quadrant. Now our 10th man can go as fast as he can, and the other seven people, because there's already a 2-way there, have to get in or at least tie him, so we went to the sides and to the back, and over the top, and everywhere else. But this first slot we made was for the 10th guy, and don't anybody get in his way because the clock stops on him!

"We trained at Pelicanland from a Twin Beech. At the time the rule was no show, no holds. Just look at the gear we were jumping and imagine just how long it took to exit the Beech with those large front reserves!" —*Dave Waterman*. The Bird rig allowed exits to be faster.

By '73 and '74 the sport was changing. The aircraft were beginning to change. Twin engine Beechcraft, tail draggers, were aging and becoming less popular and even more dangerous because there weren't enough pilots qualified to fly those World War II aircraft. Jumpers started experimenting by getting DC-3s, like Zephyrhills, Utah and Southern California. Now, because of the bigger door you're no longer on your knees trying to crawl out—jumpers were standing up and running out the bigger door—thus the emphasis is no longer on the exit. For instance, today in a Sky Van where there's just a tailgate, you all walk off the ramp at the same time and you only have to practice exits for a few minutes. In the Beech age we'd practice the exit for hours. Everything changed. No more awkward equipment or ducking down in a weird position and running to dive out that hole." —*Jerry Bird*

Twin Beech exit. Dave Duncan, photographer. #54 in Andy Keech's Skies Call 3.

22

The Thrill of Victory

In Bird's words

"**Jim Hooper,** who I went through Russian language school with at the Defense Language Institute in Monterey, California, was the owner-operator of the Zephyrhills drop zone and he had 60 or so Arabs who needed to be trained from military static line to freefall and transition to squares. He hired some people from around the country—Garry Carter, Jack Gregory, and me—then had us come to Z-hills to take on this program. This was before the AFF method [Accelerated Freefall] was official. That got me to move from Utah to Zephyrhills.

Then, lo and behold, because the World Meet was going to be here in '81, Mirror Image decided to move from training in California to Florida to jump out of the DC-3's." —*Jerry Bird*

Mirror Image, 1979

Jim Captain, Mirror Image team member: 1977, 1979 and 1981

Jerry showed up to the 1979 Mirror Image training camp at Pope Valley. He joined the team as one of our alternates, in addition to Steve Mayes. After watching a few dives, he began telling us what we were doing wrong and what we needed to do. He didn't hold back and told it like it was. A bit harsh at times, but always right on point. When Jerry was in the air with us, he was able to debrief the dive down to the split second what everyone had done, mostly what we could do better. His "air clock" was incredibly accurate. He would say something like: 'Captain! At 46 seconds you should have keyed that donut faster.'

We won Nationals that year by a large margin, set two or three world records, including one on our last practice jump and one during the meet. Fast forward to the World Championships held in Chateauroux France. The aircraft was a Nord Noratlas with a ramp or tail gate exit. Near the end of the last day of official training jumps, Jerry pulled the team together and said, "Let's set a world record", of course what a good idea and confidence builder. Then he said, "A speed star record!" Wait, what? This is an 8-way competition. Because he was a big reason why we got there, so what the heck, let's go for it! We notified the judges of our attempt and up we went. It was getting close to sunset which was going to make it tough for the judges to see (telemeters were still being used). We had a perfect exit and completed the star almost instantly. I remember packing after that jump and heard over the PA system, in French, *"Etats Unis . . . record du monde . . ."*

Yahoo!! The meet was definitely going our way, so BJ decided to sit out the last round or two and had Jerry fill in on one jump and Steve Mayes on another. I believe our winning margin was 17 points. A great way to end the 79 season. Both Jerry and Steve moved onto the starting line-up for the 1981 team, which would be a thrilling season with two come-from-behind victories.

—*Jim Captain*

U.S. Nationals 1981

Paragraph:

"Shortly before the [1981] Nationals, Mirror Image turned a staggering 14 maneuvers in 48.3 seconds. The jump was witnessed by appropriate judges and has been recognized as an official World Record by the FAI. Participating in the record breaker were BJ Worth, Jim Captain, Mike

Eakins, Steve Mayes, Gary (Hod) Sanders, Mike (Michigan) Sandberg, Jeff Barbani and Jerry Bird."[75]

Jim Captain

As we did in the past, the 1981 team carried over six members from the 1979 team: BJ Worth, Michael Eakins, Gary "Hod" Sanders and Jim Captain returned for their third season, while Jerry Bird and Steve Mayes, 1979 alternates, moved into the lineup. Mike "Michigan" Sandberg and Jeff Barbani joined the team as new members. Roger Ponce was added as an alternate and Jim Baker, to replace Rande Deluca as photographer.

The team moved to Zephyrhills as a new training site. Like in the past, we trained during the week and took the weekends off. For the first time since the team formed, we finally came up with a decent exit piece we called the tarantula.

Mirror Image's tarantula exit. Jim Baker, photographer.

---

75. Paragram "Broken Records," *Parachutist* Magazine, September 1981, 12.

Moving from the west coast to the east coast, we gained a three-hour advantage over our main rival, Visions. When learning of a world record attempt by Visions, we brought in a judge and broke the current record before the sun came up on the west coast.

That year, our teams were evenly matched. At the 81 Nationals we had an epic battle as the lead changed hands until, going into the 10th round, we found ourselves one point behind.

Team dirt dive. Jim Baker, photographer.

An Oklahoma TV station sent a film crew from the show PM Magazine who followed us at the meet. We learned from the cameraman that there was a curse; other teams they covered always lost. Nice. While dirt diving for the 10th round, the reporter was having a difficult time getting through her take, causing us to start and stop our dirt dive a couple of times. We managed to get through our practice and circled up for a final team cheer, then headed out to the DC-3.

The dive started with a Hope Diamond, which, back then, was still a difficult maneuver. Visions was set to go first, with their one-point lead, Synergy went second, and Mirror Image were out third. The ground supporters for all three teams filled the video tent, as the judging was still being done using ground-to-air video. The tension was building as each team exited and the DC-3 went around for the second, then our turn on the third pass.

Our dive started off clean and even though it went smoothly, it felt frantic. We went through the sequence the first time then through it again. I don't really remember the dive as clearly as I remember hanging under canopy looking down to see which way the crowd was running. We did not know yet that Visions only scored 7 points.

The crowd was running towards the landing area. WE DID IT! We scored 9 points—we had just won our third national title and were now set to defend our two previous World Championships.

For me, being a competitive person, that jump would go down as one of the best of my skydiving career—even more meaningful than our jump into the Seoul Olympics Opening Ceremonies.

The U.S. Army Golden Knights won the 4-Way event, giving the 1981 U.S. Team the best chance to sweep both 4 and 8-Way on our home turf at the World Championships in Zephyrhills Florida. —*Jim Captain*

World Meet 1981

Jim Captain

After a few months off, the team reassembled in Florida and began a short training camp before the World Meet.

Between the Nationals and our return to Florida, the DZ had moved to a new location on the airport. Everyone pitched in to lay down new grass on the landing and packing area and a new chant was born: "Blue Skies . . . Black FEET."

Our training was going so well that on almost every dive we were scoring more points. This was at a time when "set sequences" were being used, so that half of the rounds in the meet were dives that could be practiced over and over and we were consistently scoring 10-12 points per jump. I believe we actually peaked a day or two before the start of the meet. On one of our last training jumps we set a new world record of 16 points.

After the first five rounds at the World Meet, we found ourselves behind by 7 points. For the first time in three seasons, through six competitions, Mirror Image had two scoring busts and, on one jump, lost a floater on exit. We had never before lost a floater on exit. For an undefeated team, this was a nightmare. We made an official protest (not my idea) claiming the DC-3 was flying too fast but the protest was denied.

That night, BJ invited Michael Collins, Apollo 11 Astronaut, to hang out with the team in our Plant City hotel room. Hod Sanders broke out his bottle of champagne from the '79 World Meet in France.

I don't remember exactly what was said, but it was definitely an energizing experience. After drinking the champagne and after astronaut Collins left, we went out to the parking lot and dirt-dived the next five rounds of the meet.

The first jump the next morning started with the long diamond, another difficult maneuver for us back then. I remember sitting with a few of the British team at breakfast that morning and they kind of chuckled when I told them we were going to score a 10 on the next round.

Round Six, 10 POINTS!

Rounds 7-10 we were able to make another comeback, although our final score was 6 points less than we did at the Nationals, we managed to win by one point over Canada and 2 points ahead of Australia.

WHAT A SEASON!

This would be my third and final season with the team. Mirror Image would reform and compete at the 1983 and 1985 Nationals with a mix of team members from Synergy, the Army, Navy, and a few from the former Mirror Image teams. —*Jim Captain*

In Bird's words

"It was BJ Worth's team. He was the one that got us our sponsorship. He was the one who came through when you didn't have any money. BJ was the motor behind Mirror Image and was a three-time World Champion. He was part of the Olympic Rings demonstration jump in 1988 and organized the World Team 400-way. He deserves to be in the Hall of Fame.

The '81 Mirror Image Team produced some excellent skydivers. Jake Brake was one of our alternates and helped us a whole lot with our sponsorship and rigging and support. He was ready at any time to step into the lineup. He was a former National Champion and the Golden Knight of the year. Roger Ponce was our other alternate and was later inducted into the Hall of Fame.

Of all the competitions, those two jumps were probably the most exciting I ever made."

By 1981, Mirror Image had been together for about six years. The constant training was hard on our families and made it difficult to keep a permanent job. So, after the World Meet, most of our team went their own way." —*Jerry Bird*

23

Utah Daze

In Bird's words

"In '74, after winning the World Cup in South Africa, there was sort of a split up and people were going their own way.

I moved to Utah and hooked up with Mike Hurren, Jim Fonnesbeck and Jody Pond. That was the beginning of the Seagull Aviation, Pacific Utah Air, the C-47, and the Utah Daze

First, we had a company called Seagull Aviation, which was the drop zone business, and later we had a company called Pacific Utah Air, which was the aircraft business. Mike Hurren, Jim Fonnesbeck and I were the owners; Jody Pond was our chief pilot.

When we first moved there, we had a Twin Beech to jump—small door Beeches we used to call them. At first, they had a drop zone along the Wasatch Range in Northern Utah. Just south of Brigham City there's a place called Fruit Way where the settlers grew peaches, cherries, apples, fresh fruits and vegetables. That's where I ended up living, in a little town called Perry which is real close to Brigham City. There's a big sign as you drive into the city that says, *The World's Largest Migratory Bird Refuge*.

At that time probably over 90 percent of the people around me were Latter Day Saints. They were nice people, always polite to us. It was beautiful, we loved it there. Brigham City had a small airport. Across the mountain, not far to the Northeast of Brigham City is Cache Valley where our guy, Mike Hurren, grew up. Cache Valley is a farming valley.

While I was in Utah, my partners showed me the good life. Mike Hurren taught me to play golf. After a while all four of the owners were driving Porsches. I had a 914, which is a cheap Porsche, but it was a little orange one and a great car.

The first year we flew a Beechcraft and we charged people X dollars to be on Jerry Bird's team. So, we have, let's say ten people who each throw in $1,000 to cover their jumps that year. and we would guarantee 300 jumps. We took the money we collected to Jimi Hendrix's brother—that's what we used to call him—but his name was really Ray Hendricks. He was a great pilot. We said, Ray, you told us that you could go to Arizona and get a Beechcraft. So, he took the money and a week later came back to Utah in a Twin Beech from a government auction. He was a mechanic and could do everything. The Beechcraft probably only cost about $6,000, so all he had to do was make it run and fly us. At the end of our training camp, he owned the airplane. With the extra money, we bought gas, but everybody's jumps were paid for.

We went to the Nationals, and I think we were the best team there, but now exits had become a big thing. You were not allowed to hold on, but people realized that they're shooting this from the ground, and they can't see you cheating, going through the door. The times would be really close, but we didn't win another 10-Way at Nationals.

You could jump on Bird's team if you went to Logan, Utah. It was off the beaten path, but a lot of the world's great skydivers showed up there. During that time, we had Bent Laurssen who showed up from Norway and couldn't speak English, learning with us. Usually, you just get on the airplane and you follow Bird's team and they would do star, back loop, star or something and then you were allowed to dock and we had already made the star, back loop, star before they could get there, so we would let people jump. We didn't have a ticket office; you just got on the airplane and jumped for free. Your money for nothin' and your skydives for free.[76]

I think one of the greatest photographers we jumped with was a guy by the name of Peter Boettgenbach. Peter B wanted to film all aspects of us so he built a step to put behind the door. At the time it was a no-show

---

76. "Money for Nothing" a song by Dire Straits, the second track on their studio album *Brothers in Arms* (1985) a satirical song about the public's perception of the enviable life of musicians during the MTV era. "That ain't workin', that's the way you do it, Get your money for nothin' and your chicks for free . . ."

exit, so he would climb out first as a floater and he had built a little step and a gripper. A lot of planes have them on now. Our cameraman would be first one out and would leave with the guys. He was wearing a 16-millimeter movie camera and maybe a Hasselblad and he would float right beside the floaters like free flyers do today. He could stay right with them and float and film them. These are the greatest floaters in the world doing this technique, and Peter B was always right there with them. When he put the camera down, he could step up and jump on our team as a team member. That was how skilled he was.

Jody Pond, the fourth member of the group, was a bush pilot. He flew a 180 with floats back and forth to Alaska, usually from Seattle or somewhere in the state of Washington. During his travels he met Don Gilbertson who was the owner of Pacific Alaska Air.

One day Jody Pond showed up with the Pacific Alaska C-47, which we later named Pacific Galactic, and we became Pacific Utah Air. I was the President of that corporation. Mostly we just flew in Utah, but we flew to the Nationals and carried skydivers—that was in 1977.

One year we went to the Z-hills Turkey Meet from Logan, Utah. We made some late-night pit stops, some people never got out of the airplane. We took on fuel. Early the next day, somebody yells, twenty minutes to jump, run, and the people that were on the team got their gear out of their kit bags and suited up for a gear check. We popped the door over Zephyrhills and before landing we jumped and made a 20-way for our arrival at Zephyrhills. The people that didn't jump and the dogs and the motorcycles were in the airplane. We brought our whole entourage. Somebody said, Yeah Bird, that was the longest jump run ever.

About the time I went to Utah in '75 was when they were starting to switch over to 8-way sequential. That's when the transition was happening. Ten-way was only a secondary event anymore. Eight-way formation flying—8-way sequential—was now the number one event. Because 10-way was no longer king, there weren't as many people interested in dedicating themselves to 10-way, so we were more like, hey, we still want to go to Nationals but we'll make up a walk-up team when we get there. At the same time we entered some other events.

One time on a 10-way event they had 10-way back loop to snowflake. They were going to see about putting back loops or other things into events so there was one time on your last jump or maybe it was an extra jump that you were to make a 10-way star but that wasn't timed. When you broke grips, they timed how long it took you to build a snowflake 5-way star with five people on the legs and our Utah team took first place in that. We could do star, back loop, snowflake in under five seconds with a 10-way team. That was pretty good.

The Migratory Bird Refuge doing star, backloop, snowflake out of the Galactic DC-3 over Cache Valley, Utah, 1976. Larry Bagley, photographer.

I went to the Nationals and then I jumped into an event that was a 4-way event with accuracy. This was the end of an era for Jerry Bird because we had jumped by the name of VegetaBill and the Snowflakes, and the captain of our team, Bill Sweeney, didn't show up. He left Utah to go to the Nationals on his motorcycle and somehow went somewhere else. We named our team in his honor. But we had Mike Hurren, and we had a young jumper who had won the National Championships while he was on the Golden Knights.

Jake [Jack] Brake jumped with us. He was the national accuracy champion. Three of the four members were jumping the new square parachutes, and I was still jumping a round parachute, a Para-Commander. There was relative work and accuracy combined, and the judges were spotting us from the ground to do the relative work part of this thing. We did real good on the relative work part but we didn't have a good spot and I couldn't make it back, and so three guys get measured for accuracy and I don't. We're still in the top three or so, and on the spot, one of the ram air parachute manufacturers comes over to me and says, Bird, do you want to try one of these Units? I said, Sure, and I start jumping the square parachute. The rest of the jumps, I was in the pea gravel. They only held that event, I believe, one time and it was only because we were at the Nationals anyway.

I saw doom coming. Mike Hurren was one of my best friends in the world and I tried to warn him. When they got in trouble, Mike spent seven and a half years in Federal Prison, his wife spent six and a half years in Federal Prison and the pilot spent four years in Federal Prison.

Jim "The "Beak" Fonnesbeck was Mormon, and his Dad was big in the Mormon Church. They would rather refer you back to the Church than send you to reform school. In his case, they gave Jim a choice: He could move back to Idaho where his dad was and go to the University of Idaho for four years or he could go to prison for four years. What's your choice? Jim got a degree in Engineering and moved to Las Vegas and was the Engineer for the City of Las Vegas for the next 25 years. Jim always taught students at drop zones. He was a tandem master and he had a traveling demo group called, The Skydiving Elvises.

Jim Fonnesbeck always loved me and he said, Bird, come do one of these jumps. Well, he always had a con. I think he got these contracts to do a one jump demo for about $25,000. He had some others go on the jump but he was the leader. Having been one of the Flying Elvises in the film *Honeymoon in Vegas*, he had the flashiest outfit. And he could play the guitar and sing. He didn't have to pay for airfare for all these guys to come there. The people he always chose were airline pilots; Val Thal flew for Fed Ex and her husband Slocum, also flew for FedEx. Val had to have a sock in her pants to be an Elvis. Beak paid the people $1,000 for the jump.

He didn't have an airplane, but he would find the closest drop zone that had a Twin Beech and pay them good dollars to rent their airplane. So, he leases somebody's airplane, and we jump into a Jimmy Buffet concert called Margaritaville. They built this great big stage and had a roped-off area, and they are selling Margaritas. They've been doing it all day, so by the time we jump in as The Skydiving Elvises, the crowd is whooped up.

They tell us after we land right by the stage to go out in the audience and sign autographs and I'm still in costume as Elvis #7. The crowd is so happy to see us. All the women want to kiss you. Bikers want you to sign their wife's boob and take a picture with us. And Val is in a skin-tight Elvis costume, like we all are. It seemed like 30 minutes doing this and we make it back to the stage to get ready for Jimmy Buffet to make his entrance.

We go, hey, that was kind of fun. You got groped, you got to sign women's tits. This is kind of cool being Elvis. And Val said, I had to tell three different women, this is a sock; I am a woman.

Now Jimmy Buffet walks out on stage with a rig on, like he has just landed. Our guy Jim, The Beak, starts singing don't be cruel and Jimmy says, Hey Elvis, this is my show. Thanks for the jump now get out of here. And the concert would start.

About the Syndicate: After they got out of prison, Jody Pond went back to Alaska and became a bush pilot again. He'd done his time, and he got into the DC-3 business, and he actually had a DC-3 as his bush plane operating in Alaska. It was probably around 1980 when those guys got in trouble. By the late 80's, Mike was back in the skydiving business working for Larry Bagley, because they loved him. He was such a nice guy. Jody went back to flying. Fonnesbeck moved to Las Vegas and was an engineer for the city.

That was 1979, I was with Mirror Image, training in Pope Valley. We went across the country and stopped at my house that I had in Utah and visited for a day and took a break and then went on to go to the Nationals in Richmond, Indiana. We won the Nationals, then we won the World

Championships in Chateauroux, France. The Mirror Image team were world champions again. That was the team that set the 10-way speed star record on our practice jump that still stands at 5.1 seconds.

I still had a house in Perry Utah that my girlfriend, Linda Waterman and I owned. I had a full house and a collection of Studebakers, but I hadn't lived there in a couple of years. I got the offer to go to Florida to teach some skydivers from Saudi Arabia. They were going to pay us good money for skydiving seven days a week and I had a free place to stay. Linda is a nice person and a great skydiver, but I was traveling and she had a job and she couldn't be involved with me or my friends anymore. I left in the '80's and came back around the year 2000 to sell it. I was going to go to Idaho and do a boogie so Linda flew me up there in her airplane. When we came back, she gave me one of her Cadillacs to drive and then she bought the house from me that we used to own together. We were good buddies and I love her dearly.

Mike Hurren had reopened the drop zone. He had done his penance

Studebaker Acres in Perry, Utah, 1978.

for his evil ways. He didn't try to hide that from anybody, and he broke his habit. King Airs were popular at that time and he rented one as an emergency King Air to rescue or transfer out ambulatory people. The government signed a contract where he made more in a year renting it than the airplane costs. He had a six-year deal. They rented his airplane and then gave him his airplane back in perfect shape. He ended up owning three airplanes, he had an airport business. He owned a house, ran the drop zone and he still skydived.

Mike was one of the smooth skydivers. He was on Wings of Orange with us when we set that world record. Everybody liked Mike because he was the best jumper and a nice man. So, Mike was going to also be my backer for the airport I had down here at Birdland. I bought a private airport with 55 acres. Mike owned Skydive Salt Lake and he and his group took his King Air south to get out of the snow country. They went to a boogie and spent Friday night and Saturday night. On Sunday night they're going to fly back. There were people waiting for him at Salt Lake International Airport, but they landed at a little airport, across the lake. Their pilot was an airline pilot so they always said they had a really good pilot.

When they didn't show up on time, his people figured they had turned around; they had enough gas to fly back to Arizona or California if they wanted to go to an alternate airport. Don't fly to Salt Lake City in a snowstorm in a plane that had been stripped down for skydiving, meaning not having all the right instruments for IFR and it didn't have working de-icing boots. Because the Great Salt Lake has extra salt, it never freezes and lots of times there was warmer air over the lake creating a hole in the clouds for visibility. So, the pilot does a 180 and now he's under the clouds and he is going to land at this little airport Tooele.

Nobody knows what happened, but when air traffic control took another look at the blips on the screen, they saw a blip do a nosedive. When the pilot turned, the airplane stalled, probably because it was iced up. The gear in back might have shifted around. But it stalled and turned over, and the pilot was just pulling out when he hit the Great Salt Lake.

Mike's wife was on that plane too, and a lot of his staff—young people who just got married, just graduated from the college, from Brigham Young or the University of Utah. That just devastated a lot of people there in Salt Lake City. In my opinion the pilot, who was an airline pilot, should never have put them in that situation. Mike was a passenger in the back at night in an airplane he owned.

At that time Jim Fonnesbeck was still alive so we go to the funeral. It was always Jerry Bird and Mike and Jim and Jody. At the funeral Mike's mother says to me, You're here, Jim's here, Mike is in the box. Where's Jody? Nobody knew where Jody was.

We're not sure, but that week Jody went missing in Alaska in a snowstorm. The reason he wasn't there was that Jody and his wife had crashed into the mountain, and he might've died the same day or within a day that Mike Hurren did. So, my three partners from Pacific Utah Air, Jim Fonnesbeck bounced and the other two died in airplane crashes. Jody was the pilot in command, and I would have never expected that to happen with Jody Pond, but this is in Alaska, bush flying. Consequently, we lost the airport. But he was my backer on a lot of the business I did. Mike was one of the great people.

Jim The Beak Fonnesbeck was a legend. He jumped "Bird Gear" longer than anybody. Jim was one of the great floaters and instructors and could do anything. He retired from the City and became a full-time skydiver, mostly a tandem instructor. One day in 2011 he was taking a 75-year-old grandmother on her birthday tandem jump and they had a malfunction. When he cut away only one side released and he ended up with a main and reserve entanglement, so they had a mass of fabric out when they hit the runway. Perfect spot, being The Beak. The passenger lived for a while but then she died. They both died. The Beak had more than 11,000 jumps and something like 8,000 tandem jumps. And bad luck.

That was the end of my Utah "Daze", but we left a trail through Utah with some great sky diving. Mike Hurren, Jim Fonnesbeck, Jody Pond, I loved every one of them. They were wild people—play hard, live young, die young.

So, now BJ, who is the reigning world champion, invites me to come back and join Mirror Image and train with the 8-way team in Pope Valley, California." —*Jerry Bird*

24

Bird Seminars, Bird Camps, and Coaching Military Teams

Jerry Bird was a rated military freefall Instructor as well as a champion sport skydiver. Many competitive military and civilian teams around the world benefitted from his coaching, as did weekend skydivers wanting to up their game and take part in bigger stars.

Beautifully round 21-way star over Z-hills, 1977.
Carl Boenish, photographer. Cover photo.

BIRD SEMINARS, BIRD CAMPS, AND COACHING MILITARY TEAMS

In Bird's words

"My buddy Mike Schultz was the team leader of the U.S. Parachute Team when we were in Bled. He says, Bird, you have some skills that nobody else has. He says, Let me show you how to make money. And that was by doing my seminars.

The very first one I did was Fort Bragg. Mike says, How about two weeks prior; I have a camp at Pelicanland and I'll sign up people? Well, the British 10-way team showed up to train with us. Schultz charged everybody $25 to enter the camp.

In 1973 I went to Canada, did a seminar there, and then in '75 I took the Canadian team to the World Meet. I trained them in Canada and then went to Germany in '77. Their organization asked me to stay and be a coach and team leader of the Canadian team. I went to Germany as their coach. We were trying to beat the American team Captain Hook and the Sky Pirates. Halfway through the meet the Canadians were in the lead, but they didn't win.

I coached armed forces teams from Canada, Venezuela, Peru, Mexico, Costa Rica, Iceland, Norway, Denmark, Sweden, Germany, France, Austria, Australia, Czech Republic, Poland, Bali, Thailand and the United States of America.

I trained the U.S. Air Force Academy Parachute Team, the PTWOB—Parachute Team Wings of Blue—out of Colorado Springs. I believe I've trained them three different times. I went there in the early '70s and did lectures at the Academy. One of the guys that I met when he was in the Air Force Academy as a student, and later as a fighter pilot and the captain in charge of the Academy team was Captain Eli Colotta. He showed up at Zephyrhills in an Air Force plane, a twin Otter. Says he has an inexperienced 4-way team going to the Collegiate Nationals in Deland and asks me to help them out.

Mike Schultz taught the Naval Academy cadets' parachute team. He was my partner and so I gave some lectures to some of the naval cadets, both in Maryland and Zephyrhills.

Back in 1972, when Jerry Bird's All Stars were the National Champion 10-Way Speed Star team, we were invited to the World Championships to demonstrate relative work. We put on some spectacular jumps in front of the World Style and Accuracy Meet and during this time we invited several people to come and jump with us. One was a Russian lady who was the champion. We took her up and put her in an 11-way star.

One of the other people we took was the young captain from West Point by the name of Chris Needels. Because he was the U.S. Army's Team Captain, we let him go out last.

The Army Golden Knights did not have a relative work team at that time. They had demonstration teams and style and accuracy teams. Needless to say, it took the captain longer than expected to get in—but being the showmen that we were we waited on him until he finally docked and then we dumped in a clump because we were pretty low. We couldn't embarrass the commander of the Golden Knights.

Later, between Captain Needels and Top Sergeant Bob McDermott, I was invited to Fort Bragg, North Carolina, to teach the Golden Knights how to do 10-way and RW. The Army had a parachute team but they were all style and accuracy jumpers. Somebody gave an order and said, You are now the 10-way RW team. They had famous people on there like Jake Brake, Chuck Collingwood and Halsey Richardson and a whole list of Who's Who in the Army that were champions of style and accuracy.

They showed up at the annual Turkey Meet at Zephyrhills later that year and their team was called Needels and Pins. And that was the beginning of the big RW Formation program for the Army Golden Knights.

When I coached them in the 1980s, I wasn't allowed to jump with them because Army regulations forbid civilians. I was giving them psychological help. On a day off though, Major Roger Pickett said, Captain Bird, would you like to jump with the Military Freefall today? We'll go over to our place but we are like a Black Delta Project, so if anyone asks your name, don't talk to them. It's need-to-know and you don't need to know.

In 1990, the new Zephyrhills drop zone, Skydive City had opened but the Golden Knights were training at the old drop zone. They weren't allowed to go to the new "outlaw" drop zone where I was, but Paul Rafferty and one other guy snuck over there one night and gave me an official United States Army Parachute Team shirt. On the back it says, "Coach Bird." Somebody disputed that, saying they never had a coach and

Rafferty said, Bird has coached us three different times. He's the only coach we've ever had. And so I have a Coach Bird United States Parachute Army shirt from Paul Rafferty, one of the good guys." —*Jerry Bird*

Coach Bird with the U.S. Army Golden Knights 8-Way Team. Zhills, 1989.

Bob Sturtivant

I was blessed to be a member of the Royal Marines Freefall Display Team who did their six week annual training at Z-hills in '82 and '83, February to March. The Birdman was a key part of our experiences and coached us on many occasions. We are still in awe of his amazing capacity to organize, motivate and participate and then recall, like a human video, everything that occurred on a dive. We hugely benefitted as a team and as individuals from his mentoring. Thank you Jerry, on behalf of all those Royal Marines that went before and after my time on the team.

You are indelibly etched into our hearts and memories. —*Bob Sturtivant*, former Royal Marine Corporal, British Parachute Association Approved Instructor, AFF Instructor, Rigger.

Rüdiger Wenzel

René Richter contributed this article, written by Rüdiger Wenzel and published in *Sportspringer*, February 1975. (Google translation)

"Jerry Bird has been a household name for all relative jumpers for years. The successes of the teams he has formed and led—Jerry Bird All Stars, Columbine Turkey Farm, Wings of Orange—have already gone down in the books of relative history. His leadership qualities, his ability to inspire, his motivation and enthusiasm, and his training principles and methods distinguish him as an exceptional team leader.

What is less well known is that Jerry Bird is connected to Germany in many ways. Years ago, for example, during his military service he was stationed with the Special Forces in Bad Tölz, albeit with short hair.

Jerry Bird, Torsten Werner and friends at Cottbus/Neuhausen Airfield after the Berlin Wall fell. Courtesy of Torsten Werner.

Victor "Lince" Nickolich

Victor Nickolich grew up in Castro's Cuba in the 1960s where he became a skydiver for the Cuban team and earned the title "Master of Sport for Cuba for his parachuting skills." His code name was Lince, which is Spanish for lynx.

Nickolich had long planned to escape the island and he took his chance in November 1977. Cuba has assembled a skydiving team to compete at the Pan American Parachute Games in Mexico. Their coach was Anatoli "Tolia" Yurenkov, a former U.S.S.R. champion and a member of a Spetsnaz airborne unit in the Soviet Republic of Ukraine. The team to beat would be the U.S. Army Golden Knights, the undefeated Pan American Champions.

Days before the team's departure, the Cuban intelligence services discover that one of the competitors intends to defect while in Mexico and that skydiver's call sign is Lince. To the Cuban regime, a victory against the U.S. Golden Knights is a most tantalizing prospective—but will that justify taking the risk that one of the skydivers might escape at the competition in Mexico? Unwilling to give up, Castro orders his top intelligence operatives into action.

This is the premise of Victor Lince Nickolich's memoir about his defection, titled *The Lynx* (2016). Written from the third person point of view, he talks about the influence Jerry Bird had on his skydiving, and on his plan to seek asylum in the United States.

From *The Lynx*:

"The Second World Cup of Formation Relative Work had just ended in South Africa. The Wings of Orange had set a new record of 12.7 seconds from a DC-3. On their way back to the United States, the champion USA relative work team made a surprise stop in Szolnok and performed an amazing demo jump. On that day, the incredible freefall skills demonstrated by the Americans virtually turned the style and accuracy world upside down."

After the American team landed, the author asked permission to speak to the captain and find out more about this novel skydiving discipline. He wanted to learn all about body flight, exit techniques and other details so he could put together a Cuban relative work team.

The captain of the USA team was a friendly guy eager to demonstrate on the ground everything that *Lince* asked him for. The team captain's name was Jerry Bird, a pioneer in the art of freefall relative work and a living legend in the United States"

In 1995, his skydiving life would come full circle in the skies high above Lake Wales, Florida. On that day, Lince and Jerry Bird flew next to each other on a 213-way freefall formation attempt to break the world skydiving record. Twenty-one years earlier, it was Jerry who gave Lince his first relative work lesson at the World Parachuting Championships in Szolnok, Hungary."[77] —*Victor Nickolich*

Endnote: Nick wasn't the first skydiving competitor from a communist country to defect while at an international parachute meet. At the 6th World Meet, held in Orange Massachusetts in 1962—the first one to be held in the United States, Milan Knor, a Yugoslavian skydiver escaped into the crowd. He later married Kim Emmons, a world champion parachutist on the U.S. Women's gold medal winning team that year. Kim Emmons Knor was inducted into the International Skydiving Museum Hall of Fame in 2013.

---

77. Victor "Lince" Nickolich, *The Lynx*, Shreiber Press, 2016, pp. 116, 117, 301. Jerry recommended this book.

25

1977: Smithsonian Air & Space Museum Display

In Bird's words

"**On the Bicentennial,** 1976, The Smithsonian Institution opened the new National Air and Space Museum. I and three other jumpers were asked by former astronaut Michael Collins [Apollo-11], the first director, to donate our skydiving equipment to go to the museum. I donated my equipment from the Wings of Orange 1974 World Record and World Champion team.

Bill Ottley had a tremendous pull in Washington, D.C. At one time he was the head of the NAA and the USPA. He was one of the first ones inducted into the Skydiving Hall of Fame. Hanging there beside me was Bill Ottley and Dick Fortenberry, World Champion Style and Accuracy jumper and Golden Knight. They needed one more person to finish it. It happened to be a young jumper who worked for the USPA, and he willingly donated his gear. That was Mike Johnston, the current manager of Deland. Mike is a fine guy and a good jumper. So, there were four of us that hung there, but it was mainly Bill Ottley's power in Washington, DC that got the skydivers in the Smithsonian Institute. He made sure that he was part of it. I donated my equipment from the Wings of Orange 1974 World Record and World Champion team."

—*Jerry Bird*

Bill Ottley was an advisory to the National Air and Space Museum since 1973. In 1977 Museum director and former astronaut Michael Collins asked Bill to put together a skydiving exhibit. In addition to photographs by skydiving photographers Tom Dunn, Ray Cottingham, Jerry Irwin, Carl Boenish, and Andy Keech, Ottley conceived of what he conceived as the world's greatest 4-way suspended over the heads of spectators and visible from the sidewalk below. These weren't just any plastic department store dummy, but bespoke mannequins designed to resemble the four specific skydivers chosen by Ottley. As Jerry said, the skydivers were U.S. Accuracy champion, Dick Fortenberry, instructor/examiner/rigger Mike Johnston, the inimitable Jerry Bird, and Bill Ottley himself, who was never a champion skydiver, but he was the skydiver's man in Washington D.C.

Bird's stand-in had longish blonde hair but was too big to fit into Jerry's jumpsuit, so the mannequin artists amputated its legs and performed a midline autopsy cut to slenderize the plastic form. Ottley's own mannequin was designed with his signature balding pate and glasses.[78]

Besides an homage to parachute technology—which NASA engineers use to decelerate manned space capsules before landing safely in the ocean—the exhibit was a testament to sport skydiving and freefall relative work, as well as to Bill Ottley's influence in Washington. Serving as the United States Parachute Association's Executive Director for more than a decade, Ottley did much to establish USPA as a lobbying organization to protect civilian skydiving.

(Twenty-first Century Post Script: The artifacts of the special 1977 skydiving exhibit are no longer catalogued at the Washington DC museum but were purportedly sent to the affiliated San Diego Air and Space Museum, according to a curator I queried. The San Diego Museum burned down in 1978 and although it was rebuilt, thousands of artifacts were destroyed. Was Bill Ottley's dream team among the casualties? California skydiver Jerry Swovelin says the skydiving mannequins went into storage at the San Diego's Gillespie Field annex but this cannot be verified. *Editor*)

---

78. Staff Report, "The Biggest Show in Town." *Parachutist* Magazine, July 1977, 30–35.

Jerry's mannequin suspended in the Smithsonian National Air and Space Museum, 1977.

Ottley's Dream Team in the Smithsonian's Special Exhibit.
"Staff Report" *Parachutist*, July 1977.

26

The 1980s

Boogies, the Bird Machine, and Beth

By 1980, rectangular shaped air foil parachutes—*squares*—were everywhere. Students still learned on round military surplus canopies, and some experienced jumpers still had their Para-Commanders, but the state of the art was "square."

By 1980, freefall relative work was the most popular activity at most commercial parachute centers, overshadowing parachute landing accuracy. And, by 1980, boogies—skydiving gatherings for fun instead of competition—really took off, drawing sport skydivers from all over the world. Big jump planes, big loads, and big parties after dark were the draw.

Nancy Dwyer aptly described a boogie as "a party in the sky." Her article "Boogies for Beginners" illustrates the rise of the boogie as a destination event for weekend sport jumpers looking for a new experience. "Some boogies offer special events such as RW seminars, movies, large formation attempts, canopy relative work or freefall photography seminars."[79]

The United States Parachute Association got in on the fun too, sponsoring boogies following the yearly National meet. USPA Executive Director Bill Ottley wrote an article summarizing the 1981 USPA boogie.

---

79. Nancy Dwyer, "Boogies for Beginners," *Parachutist* Magazine, July 1985, 21–23.

Bill Ottley

"It was a time for superlatives. Perhaps the best facilities ever organized for a Boogie event awaited more than 700—count 'em—skydivers and at least 700 more friends, who descended on Muskogee, OK, for an extra-long Independence Day party; July 1-5.

The parking and traffic control chores were handled on a volunteer basis by the Indian Territory Marshals, who arrived complete with horses (real), side-arms (real and loaded), and a portable jail cell (real and sometimes occupied.)

But mostly it was fun and fun jumping for all. Some 4000 jumps were made, almost all from 12,500 feet.

Jerry Bird and B.J Worth led a discussion of relative work techniques which played to an overflow crowd packing the conference room. Films, walk-throughs, questions and answers helped many less experienced Boogiers learn how national champions make it look so easy. On hand to help Jerry and BJ were members of the Mirror Image team, plus the U.S, Army Golden Knights. The United States Parachute Association—and also those who attended these seminars—appreciated the effort and cooperation of the experts who participated. The boogie and the boogiers benefited.

Now the aircraft were shut down for the last time and USPA threw open the bar for a no-pay Auld Lang Syne Beer Bust hosted by the Boogie staff and enjoyed by all . . . The lights finally flickered out in the wee hours of Monday morning. It was a hell of a party, for sure."[80]
—Bill Ottley

In Bird's words

"In 1980 I got hired by a former Army mate, Jim Hooper, to move to Florida and get paid. I had a place to stay and I think I made $100 a day, which as a jumper, was high heaven. He knew me from the past and he wanted me to oversee the training program and to help run the drop

---

80. Bill Ottley, "The 1981 USPA Boogie," *Parachutist* Magazine, September 1981, 31–35.

zone. I knew that in the very near future the Mirror Image team was also going to move to Florida to train, so I was in a good place.

When the team arrived, I dropped my other duties and became a full-time team member for the Mirror Image 8-way, training for the '81 World Championships. Consequently, we went back to Muskogee, Oklahoma and we won the National Championships, then we went back to Florida and won the World Championships for the third straight time.

We now held the world record for the most points. So, we were world champions, world record holders. After the meet finished, my teammates who were from out west in Montana, California and other places, most of them went back to wherever they came from and that team of Mirror Image, retired. Guys needed to go make a living. Some of them were finished with competitive jumping, or they wanted to join another team or whatever. I stayed in Florida as the chief instructor of the drop zone.

In December of 1980 I met Beth Baker. There was a drop zone in Muskogee where Beth learned to jump, and she was already past being a student jumper. She came to Z-hills with another girl, Bonnie Frazier, who had dated one of the other jumpers. They came to Florida for either a Turkey Boogie or the Christmas Boogie. I was introduced to Beth and we started dating. When her friend went back to Oklahoma, Beth stayed with me."

In '83 I was at the Nationals but I wasn't competing, maybe I was an alternate for a team. So I'm just hanging out. And that's also where my wife was from, Muskogee, Oklahoma. My friend Mike Scholtz and my friend Richard Pitt said that DC-3's were taking over skydiving. Twin Beeches were gone. They're flying DC-3's at all the boogies, so why don't we get a DC-3?

While we're there at that Nationals there comes in a different DC-3. It taxis up, parks, people get out and the pilot walks over and goes, Hey

Bird, here's your DC-3. That was the Bird Machine. The airplane was 66 Whiskey. They called it 66 Women with Diamonds and Cocaine and lots of money.

Now, we had a DC-3 and that was the start of The Bird Machine era. Mike Scholtz was our chief pilot. At times, Bill Morrissey was our copilot. So, Jerry Bird went to do his boogies and things around the country. I brought my own airplane, like I get to bring my own bulldozer to do all this work so when we leave, we leave with most of the money. We're not filling everyone else's airplane and letting them make money. Our plane was one of the first. Some people will go, DC-3's are kind of slow, but the thing about a DC-3 was you had seats to sit in. They are facing seats, but you could see everybody in the airplane or you could go to the bathroom in the back or to exit, you stood up and ran out the door, not crawl around on your hands and knees.

"The Bird Machine at the Genesee County Airport, in Batavia, New York. An annual boogie occurred there from the mid-'80s until 2008. Bird visited with the plane and helped to boost registrations nicely. Lots of guests from Canada and the entire Northeast." —*Jim Tavino*

And so at the end of the day after being on a DC-3, you've seen and met everybody at the airport. It was a different era. To entertain people in The Bird Machine, we put in speakers and a stereo system so you could play rock-and-roll or do anything on it. In the back, there was a full screen TV and in the front there was a full screen TV. If you wanted to watch the football game, because it's Sunday, we could turn on regular television and watch a football game.

Nowadays, when you land, you see them all run over and put their video in the machine to do their debrief. Back then, people would get back on the Bird Machine, put their cassette in the cassette player and watch the cameraman's view of their jump while they're climbing to altitude. They'd do their debrief, stand up and do their dirt dive in the back of the airplane and were ready to go again by the time it was jump run.

We became quite popular and we had a lot of fun doing that for about five years." —*Jerry Bird*

1984: Jerry Bird Awarded the da Vinci Diploma

Bill Ottley

Published in *Parachutist*, April 1984

"During the closing hours of the plenary meeting of the International Parachuting Committee, America's Jerry Bird was awarded the Leonardo da Vinci Diploma by a near unanimous vote of the delegates, defeating candidates proposed by Italy and the People's Republic of China. The da Vinci Diploma is one of the highest honors that the FAI can bestow on high achievers in sport parachuting.

The vote to honor Bird followed a very positive presentation by BJ Worth of Jerry's qualifications ... Jerry Bird was captain of the 1972 U.S. National 10-way Speed Star Champion Team; he was captain of the 1973 U.S. National Speed Star Team; he was a member of the 1979 and 1981 8-way Sequential National Champion Parachute Teams. In addition, he was captain of the World Champion Team at the Speed Star World Cup conducted in Fort Bragg, North Carolina in 1973 and again was captain of the World Champion Team at the Speed Star World Cup conducted in Pretoria, South Africa in 1974. He was a member of the 8-way Sequential World Champion Team at the Championships in Chateauroux, France in 1979 and was again a member of the 8-way World Champion Team at the Championships in Zephyrhills, Florida in 1981.

Therefore, Jerry Bird has been a member or captain of four U.S. National Champion teams and also has been a member or captain of four World Champion or World Cup Champion teams."

Bird's nomination was originally suggested by USPA Awards Committee Chairman Pat Works, approved by his committee members, and then endorsed by the USPA Board at their September 1983 meeting. All the world competes for this award, and only one American had previously been honored: triple world parachuting accuracy champion Dick Fortenberry, then a U.S. Army sergeant, received the diploma in 1974."[81]

---

81. Bill Ottley, *Parachutist* Magazine, April 1984, 27.

27

Friends to the Left of Me, Friends to the Right

"At one time I probably knew 10,000 skydivers." —*Jerry Bird*

Dieter Kirsch

Dieter Kirsch

Dieter Kirsch is one of the most successful big way and total break sequential designers organizing dives today. Kirsch credits the flying skills learned in 4-way and 8-way, of which he is a German champion, as the backbone for being on successful big-ways. In over four decades of skydiving he has scored nine FAI World Records, many of which he designed and organized, and a score of German records. Dieter organizes the Power Games—formation skydiving events that take place at various drop zones including Klatovy, Czech Republic, Eloy, Arizona, Perris Valley, California, and Z-hills, Florida.

Dieter Kirsch

Of course, Power Games is all about beautiful big formation jumps. But there is another important side: friendship and camaraderie. Enjoying the jumps with friends, reviewing the experience over a delicious meal, ending the day of jumping together with people from all over the world and from all walks of life.

Being at the right time at the right place is one key to success. Running into Jerry Bird in 1986 was such a lucky moment and had a major impact on my success in the skydive world. He never asked me about my number of jumps (300 at that time) or anything else. He jumped with me and I found myself on the Jerry Bird 40-way that year and I was the happiest guy.

At that time and throughout the following years, I learned from Jerry, especially about Big Formations and how to lead a team. He was outstanding.

I used a lot of this knowledge on all the World and German records I have organized. What I never reached, was the lightness, humor, and fun that he was able to give to a team and still get the biggest achievement out of it.

The most fascinating thing about Jerry, is his hard disk (brain) seems to have endless capacity. He is able to tell 40-year-old stories so detailed, like it was yesterday—a seemingly never-ending cornucopia of stories. Thank you Jerry! —*Dieter Kirsch*

Mike "Michigan" Sandberg

Mike Sandberg—AFF skydiving instructor, champion formation skydiver, pioneer freestyle flyer and choreographer, skydiving stunt person and jumpsuit designer—is known to the worldwide skydiving community as Mike Michigan. Mike recalls formative events from his skydiving career:

Before I can tell you when I first met Bird. Some of my personal history needs to be explained. I started hanging around a drop zone in Michigan at Austin Lake in 1972. My dad moved us there when I was 15, and the very first day we arrived, I was hanging out there. I started packing student rigs as soon as I could get them to let me. I got to know all the regulars and pretty soon they let me pack their rigs as well.

This was the home of the Rainbow flyers, who became multi-year national champions in 4-Man, and the Beechnut 10-Man team.

I was a sophomore at a country high school in Vicksburg. My English teacher's name was Suzi Coleman. During study period, I used to go to her class to help out with stuff she needed done. One day she asked me why I was always looking out the window daydreaming during class, and I said something about hanging out at the DZ. She said, "Oh, so you're the one." It turned out that she was the wife of Ken Coleman, who you might know as the guy who created the modern-day version of AFF. Ken took me under his wing and taught me how to sew and modify military round parachutes into student canopies. When I was over at their apartment, I'd go through all his *Parachutists* and *Skydiver* magazines. At that time, Bird was the man in the middle of all the big changes in the sport. Plus, back then, there were very few cameramen and the ones around were taking pictures of what Bird was involved in at the time. I read everything about him and actually wrote a report for my English class about him. I couldn't have written about him if Suzi wasn't my English teacher, and in the end, I think I got a C.

When Ken opened a new drop zone in Athens, Michigan, I went along as his packer. When I turned 16, I made my first jump. Because I worked there, as long as I was the fourth person on the load in the 182, I got my jumps for free. With just under 100 jumps, I became the alternate for the Beechnut 10-man team. It was perfect for me because someone wouldn't be available for practice for one of the days every weekend, so I got to fill in on every position but the base. At that time, I was 5' 2" and weighed in at 110 lbs. The four-man base weighed in at 1000 lbs. dripping wet, so I learned how to fall real fast for my size. That's who I was when I was about to meet Bird for the first time.

We went to Tahlequah, Oklahoma for the Nationals in '73. It was a huge experience for me. I got to watch all the big guns in person. I think we came in 5th or so.

I never was needed as an alternate but was standing by. All the teams stayed in the local college dorms. Each floor housed two teams. Our floor was with Captain Hook and the Sky Pirates. At the end of the day, from the room at the end of the hall, the music "Smoke on the Water"[82] would blast through the open door. It was the party signal, and everybody would fall out into the hall and make their way along with whoever else heard the calling. We would end up sitting on the beds across from each other to smoke pot out of a long plastic pipe that they had taken from a porta-potty. They had rigged a fish pump so the smoke from a big bowl would fill the middle of this 10ft long pipe. Then one guy would get on one end and another on the other. One guy would blow into it and the other would suck. I never partook in the ritual, but it was fun to watch, and we had many big names end up there at one time or another.

The very last day, we were getting ready to leave. Ken and I were passing the cafeteria on our way out. There were only two people there. Sitting at the end of one of the long tables was a very pretty girl and across from her was Bird. He was hitting on her seriously. Ken noticed me looking at them and said, Hey boy, you want to meet him? I stammered something like, No, that's alright, or something like that, not wanting to interrupt his moves. Actually, I was too nervous. Ken drug me over there anyway,

Bird, who never forgets anybody, looked up and said, Hey Ken, how you doing?

---

82. "Smoke on the Water" (1972) a song by Deep Purple, written after the 1971 Montreux, Switzerland casino fire during a Frank Zappa concert.

Ken said, Hey Jerry doing good. I just wanted to introduce our alternate, Mike.

I'm sure I was beet red and said hi. After that, I don't have a clue what was said. I pretty much floated out of the cafeteria, having met the biggest name in skydiving at that time.

A year later, we were back to Tahlequah as the Beechnuts. This time we were color-coordinated in red and white everything. Jumpsuits, introducing the SST piggyback rigs and five cell Strato-Star ram-air parachutes. At this time in the sport, having ten people jumping squares at the same time was unheard of. Seventy-four was the year of the gear war.

Captain Hook came with Paradactyls in small piggybacks, Bird came with a completely new system with front-mounted rip off-reserve and Tri-conical mains.

That year the Oklahoma winds were fierce, and for the week before the meet, we were the only team that could practice. We were at a grass strip down the road in Wagner, OK with another team called the God Frogs. One evening when the winds had died down, out of nowhere this white Twin Beech came flying over at about three grand, threw out some wind drift indicators, and proceeded to climb up. We had been practicing from 10,500 ft. these guys only went to 7,500 ft. It was a no-show exit but because of the low altitude, you didn't need any binoculars to see these 10 white suits pile out the door and throw together a blazing fast star. As if that wasn't cool enough, when they broke off, they didn't all turn 180 to track. The five on the DZ side of the star turned 180 and fanned out as they tracked but the other five tracked straight forward and filled in between the gaps of the other five. It was spectacular. Then they all pulled, and these little round canopies opened, landing right there in front of us. Wings of Orange had arrived. They hung out with us that night, and we got to party together.

The next day after a practice jump on which I was filling in for someone, I was over by a trailer trying to figure out how to pack one of these new square things; I always needed help. When I stood up and looked around, I didn't see anybody anywhere. I went to look around and saw a big circle of people. There were all the guys from the God Frogs, my team, and Birds team in a circle. I couldn't see in the middle, but I could hear Bird and John Sherman arguing the benefits of front-mounted reserve rigs versus piggyback rigs in the line up in a small door twin beech. Because I was only 5'2," I couldn't see over everybody, so I pushed between folks to get a better look. Well, I pushed a little too far and stumbled into the center with the two of them. Bird noticed me trying to back out and pointed right at me and said, in front of everybody,

"Hey, are you still alternate or did you kick Sherman's ass and get a slot?"

HE REMEMBERED ME!

Everybody was looking at me, I mumbled something as I shook my head, backing away, trying to disappear into the crowd. My team gave me so much shit for being so star-struck. They would say crap like, he puts his pants on one leg at a time just like you, and stuff like that.

And I would think to myself, Yeah, but he's standing on the podium, and we aren't.

So, that was just the first two times I met him—but we have a lot more history. Like the time we almost came to blows at the World Meet in '81, he and I. But that's another story . . .

"I was blessed with great mentors in my skydiving career. I started packing student rigs for Ken Coleman when I was 15. I had the National champion Rainbow Flyers as my jumpmasters in the very beginning when I finally turned 16. I worked at Strong Enterprises and lived with Ted Strong for a few years and learned the lesson of being true to myself in business.

But I think I learned the most about organizing and competing from Jerry Bird. I participated in many big-way formations in Z-hills Bird organized and I got to observe how he managed large groups. I also participated in other big formations organized by other organizers who used fear to get people to do the dives they had designed.

This approach, more times than not, was less than constructive and I witnessed very good skydivers perform worse than they ever had from the fear of being publicly ridiculed.

That was in stark contrast to the way Bird organized. He was always positive and never called out a person's less-than-stellar performance in front of everybody. He would take them aside, give some constructive advice, or move them to a place on the dive that was more suited for their skill level, but always building them up. I remember one year while competing on a 40-way team he captained, during the debrief Jerry was preaching to the choir and the guy next to me leaned over and said, "I think Bird is going to talk us into winning this thing."

And he did.

He could get people to perform better than they ever had. I worked that lesson into my own teaching style. Always highlighting the positive and never calling anyone out in front of the group. When there was a problem in a section of the dive Bird organized, he would ask the people involved if they had it worked out between themselves and if they had it handled he moved on. He always made you feel like you were being respected for your skills. One skill he had that always amazed me was his ability to remember people's names even years later.

That's what made it so special to get to be on a load he organized. Folks from all over the world came to Z-hills and left with memories of the jumps they got to do with him, never feeling anonymous. He met so many people over the years, but he could still remember where and when no matter how much time had passed.

When competing on Mirror Image with him he was at one end of the age and experience scale, I was at the other, but I never felt less than. We were the floaters and shared the secret floaters handshake that he came up with. We still use it to this day. He also taught me about respecting my sponsors and promoting their gear: *They believe in you, so you need to be responsible for their image.*

Bird also taught me that you have a responsibility toward people who look up to you. Even if I could handle a situation like high winds it was better to give the example of standing down for better winds than take someone up who could get hurt in a situation that was over their heads. It was a kind of Sky-God Karma thing.

I think the biggest lesson I learned from him, in the end, was how to retire. He got to a point in his career where there was nothing left to accomplish and hung it up. It baffled me when he made that decision, that is, until I found myself at the same point, and because I had seen him do it I too decided to let go of the sport I had dedicated my life to and let the next generation carry the torch." —*Mike Sandberg*

Freestyle Pioneer Mike Michigan Sandberg. Norman Kent, photographer; with permission of Norman Kent Productions.

In Bird's words

"Mike Michigan was one of the best jumpers on the team. He was one of the first to do freeflying and head down flying that nobody else could do at the time. When he would go last, he was the fastest guy and when it came to doing Sequential and Formation Flying, he could do that just as well. He could fly on his back and do barrel rolls. Michigan was just a master at it. He was one of the best trackers you would ever see—a great skydiver." —*Jerry Bird*

Jack Gregory

Jack Gregory was one of many people trained in the AFF technique when Ken Coleman was developing this novel training method in the late 70's early 80's. Ken was killed in a balloon accident shortly before the official USPA rollout of the certification program he was going to run. Gregory was then hired to assist the new Course Director Mike Johnston to conduct the first year of AFF Instructor & Jumpmaster Certification courses throughout the USA in 1981 and1982.

Jack Gregory

I started jumping in 1974 and first met Jerry at Z-hills in 1978. His was a name I had heard from my very first jumps and it was amazing to meet him. We first worked together in 1980 when a British jumper, Dave Howerski, worked a contract with the Saudi Arabian Army to develop a military demo team. He did their initial training (traditional static line, short then longer freefalls) in Saudi then brought 11 of them to Z-hills to learn RW and CRW. Jerry and Skratch Garrison were two of the RW instructors and I was the CRW instructor. I was doing a CRW team at the time that won the First World Cup of CRW shortly after. I couldn't believe that I was actually working with The Jerry Bird! Jerry had a way with words. After all the initial 2 and 3-way CRW jumps, I sent up four of the Saudis on their own to attempt their first Quadraplane. Jerry was on the ground with me as I nervously watched them begin the jump. They did a great job and built the formation fairly high. Out of nowhere

Jerry announced to everyone that we were witnessing the world's first Quadrasaud! Everyone cracked up! Maybe you had to be there but whenever I think about it I still laugh!

Z-hills first started the 40-way competition in the early 1980's during the Easter Boogie, it was decided to do it as speed formations with three different formations on three different jumps. The third jump would be the most difficult one, the 40-way round star. As the team assembled for the first time Jerry told us of his new plan on how to build the big O. In the past, speed stars were built round from the beginning with each jumper docking on wrists, shaking the arms so the person holding the grip would release and allow the new docker to spread their arms and open up the star. The downside with this method was that there was a lot of motion and waves put into the formation causing tension and dropped grips. What he wanted us to do was to start with a 4-way no contact star base. These four would start just a few feet apart. Then the next wave of eight jumpers would dock on the open and free arms of each of the base people, giving us 4 three person lines facing each other in a box shape. There were now four separate corners for everyone else to dock in waves, filling in the four open holes in each corner. These four lines would carefully move back from the center as they grew until the last four jumpers plugged the holes in each of the four corners. When the last grip was taken the formation magically transformed from four separate lines into 40 complete wrist grips, completing the star! And going back to Jerry's well-known way with words, he proclaimed that the team's name was The Hole Pluggers!

    Jerry had a unique ability to really see what everyone was doing on a jump. Before there were video cameras for instant reviews, Jerry was the guy that could tell you what you did wrong or right. It was uncanny how much he saw and how accurate he typically was in his debriefs. That was a skill many of us who organized at Z-hills tried to emulate. Having him as a role model made those of us working with him better skydivers and organizers! Having Jerry Bird around made everyone a better skydiver!
—*Jack Gregory*

Dr. Ruth

I started skydiving in the mid '80s, on a small drop zone in the Black Forest, out of a Dornier 27. (Glad it wasn't a Cessna, since one of Bird's famous sayings was, I'd rather have a sister in a whorehouse than a brother jumping out of a little Cessna.)

In those days, with no internet, it was hard to get any information, only from the skydiving magazines and a few newspaper articles. But pretty soon it was clear to me that Jerry Bird was the man to learn from and Z-hills was the place to go to become a real skydiver. He was, back then, already a living legend. I saved money, went to Florida and learned to become a good lurker. Meaning, whenever Bird's team was practicing 10, 16, 20-ways I was there with my jumpsuit in hand, ready to go in case one of the team members wouldn't show up in time.

Jerry, Dr. Ruth, and 1948 Studebaker #1.

Bird was very strict as a team boss; friendship didn't count in that moment. If a team member didn't perform well or didn't show up in time he was cut from the team. I lurked my place into the team and I was the happiest girl on the drop zone. It was a big honor to be on Bird's team, where the best of the best were part of it, and the few odd rookies. The pressure was big but the vibes were great. Bird's briefing always ended with the sentence, Don't be late, don't go low, and don't let the grip go! We girls on the team would rather have an arm ripped off than open our hands and let a grip go.

We did amazing jumps, won a lot of competitions, and had the time of our lives. We were in the right time at the right place, skydiving in paradise together with a thousand skydivers from all over the world, due to Jerry Bird. He was the wizard in the air and on the ground who attracted all those skydivers to visit Z-hills.

We became friends for life. He even performed my wedding ceremony on April 13, 2013. Hard to believe, but there I saw him for the first time being so nervous that his hands were shaking so much, he could hardly read the marriage contract. Jerry Bird, the best speaker and storyteller I know was speechless and emotionally overwhelmed. And here I am the bride, with a crying future husband on my side and my best friend having a heart attack in front of me. What a day!

Jerry officiating at Ruth's marriage ceremony.

Later, on the dance floor, Bird was back in his best form and it was a great wedding party, thanks to him and all his flowers. I forgot completely that we needed to have flowers for decoration and a bridal bouquet. It was Bird who thought about it and even had the answer. We went with five bridesmaids into the bushes and picked bunches of wildflowers. Maybe that's the reason why he was so shaky three hours later at the wedding.

There are lots of stories about Bird, everybody has different ones, but we all agree that Mr. Bird is the skydiving legend with a big heart and a great sense of humor. We all love him!

Blue skies! —*Ruth Nitsche*

Steve Woodford

Steve Woodford made his first jump with the South African Airborne in 1967. In 1969 he left for England on a mail packet and spent the next three years in Europe before emigrating to Australia where he served two years in an Infantry Regiment.

In 1975 he traveled to Canada for six months of skydiving and while there, drove an RV over a thousand miles south to Elsinore, California. Here he lived in the DZ ghetto until October of '79 when he returned to South Africa, signed up again for the Airborne, and in '81 was on combat operations in the Angolan Border Wars with Pathfinder platoon.

In 1985, footloose Woodford sailed on a homebuilt 32-foot gaff-rigged cutter from Cape Town via Brazil, then up to Fort Lauderdale. In Deland he got his AFF and Tandem Examiner ratings and went to work. Have parachute; will travel.

Steve Woodford has been on 14 world record dives. He was instrumental in presenting the proposal to USPA and then, through Kirk Verner, the USPA representative to the FAI, creating the Night World Record Large Formation and Sequential Record categories. In 1998, Woodward started organizing Night World Records at Z-hills with a 2 point 42-way, then beat that with a 2 point 49-way at The Ranch in 1999. That record stood for 16 years until the 64-way at Eloy in 2017.[83]

---

83. Photo Essay, "Night Moves—the 64-Way World Record for Largest Night Formation Skydive," *Parachutist* Magazine, January 2018, 54–56.

Steve married skydiver Maria Wijnker in 1992. Accelerated freefall jumpmasters, drop zone managers, owners, operators, load organizers, the couple has made a life together skydiving—and pursuing other adventures, such as sailing, mountain biking, hiking and canyoneering.

Here Woodford remembers his first encounter with Jerry Bird:

I had come to Elsinore at the end of '75 because for many of us, it was the skydiving mecca of the world. I remember Al Krueger and his team Captain Hook and the Sky Pirates, Don Hansen's Airfreight, Madam Sally and the Sky Hookers, and Jerry Bird were all there.

So, two years later, on September 6, 1977, I decided to organize a 30-way, never having organized something before; I had 311 jumps. I got a pen and clipboard and first went to Al Krueger who was packing and told him I was organizing a 30-way. Being Al, he said, sure. First on the list!

Then I approached Bud, his brother. He signed up. After that, it was easy. Whenever I asked somebody, they always asked first, "Who's on it?" I mentioned a few names and of course they signed up, including Jerry Bird.

Soon I had my 30-way. I approached Carl Boenish to film it. Of course he asked who was on it so I rattled off a few names. He agreed.

Ready to roll! Called everybody for a dirt dive but first cornered Jerry and asked him to organize it.

Jerry Bird is a great skydiver, mentor, and friend. —*Steve Woodford*

Kung Fu Charlie

In Bird's words

"I couldn't tell any story without talking about my friend, Kung Fu Charlie—Charle Shields. Kung Fu Charlie was one of those Denver people. He was a young jumper, probably only had 25 or 30 jumps, when I moved back to Denver form the Gulch, but he had already heard about Jerry Bird's All Stars and the Columbine Turkey Farm and he goes, How do I get on your team? I told him we were going to Orange, Massachusetts, where we are sponsored, in the spring. I suggested he go to Arizona and hook up with Jim Heydorn for instruction and jump as much as he could. Well, Kung Fu, Charlie did that over that winter.

In the spring of '74 when we moved our group to Orange, Massachusetts for our sponsored team, Wings of Orange, Kung Fu Charlie Shields came from Casa Grande and said, I have 220 jumps, Bird, I am ready. Jim Heydorn sent me. So, we put Charlie Shields on our team.

Charlie was an amazing individual. Everybody on our team could juggle, but no one had shown Charlie how to juggle. One of us picked up three objects, three apples or whatever and said, This is how it goes. You put two in one hand and one in the other hand. The hand that has two, throws a ball in the air. When it's up here in front of your forehead, you throw the ball from the hand it is going to. It took Charlie about three minutes to learn to juggle the basic pattern.

One of the things we used to do when practicing RW was to make a star and then do a back loop and make another star or make a snowflake, rather than just sit there for 30 seconds. So, Pete Gruber, who was on our team, had at one time been the California State Gymnast Champion. He showed everybody how to walk on their hands and to do back loops on the ground. He had the training belt and a guy on each side holding you and assisting you in spinning. You jumped up in the air, spun and landed on your feet. Every gymnast can do that. King Fu Charlie walks over and springs about four feet in the air, does this 360 and lands on his feet. He said, Like that? He had extraordinary body and movement control. He went to the Al Dacascos Kung Fu Academy. One of Charlie's sparring partners was Bruce Lee, the great movie actor and karate fighter. Unfortunately, Bruce Lee met a tragic death at the age of 32 in Hong Kong and he was probably poisoned by the Chinese.

I used to wear a red head band all the time. I was a hippie. Charlie could be standing eight feet away and he would say, don't move, then he would do a spinning back kick and knock the headband off without touching me. When he performed on stage he would have somebody shoot an arrow into a piece of wood, then he would put the arrow on his throat and push with both hands until the arrow broke before piercing his throat.

When Charlie and I would go to a bar, we could whip everybody. There was a big gruff, mean old man named Mike who owned a bar in Orange. He was a boxer in the Navy and he fought some professionals. He lost—but he was a boxer. When somebody played the wrong song on the jukebox or didn't do what Mike wanted, he would throw him out and maybe get a punch or two in on the way. He was the type of bartender who would sit behind the bar and drink and watch his bar.

We were there with our Wings of Orange team when Mike came out and picked on one of our smaller guys and shoved him. If I had jumped up and said, Hey you, don't do that, he would have beat me up. Charlie stood up and said, If you don't go back behind the bar, I'm going to hurt you. Mike meekly went back behind the bar and decided he didn't want to tangle with Charlie.

One time when we were in Denver we went to a Dojo where they trained black belts. We were wearing Levi's and drinking beer. These guys were in their sparring outfits with their belts on and the trainer has them hitting the heavy bag and doing spinning back kicks. They bowed to Charlie and asked him to kick the heavy bag for them. Charlie took off his shoes and his jacket and did a couple of stretches, touched the floor. The he exploded into a spinning back kick and kicked the heavy bag up to the ceiling. The trainer said, Yep, he's the only guy I've ever seen who could do that.

When we jumped in Orange that year, we jumped a small door, Beechcraft like Walt Mercer's. Charlie was the third guy out the door. We were able to put three people between the door and the wall. That meant Charlie was compressed against the wall across from the door. Well, he had the power to launch the two guys in front of him to start the exit and the guy that was following him got in the line to go out the door. Nobody else wanted to leave from that position because it would leave you almost flat with no energy going out the door. When you pick up a cat and try to drop it on its back, it flips around and lands on its feet.

Charlie could go out the door of the Beechcraft and be flat down on his belly, almost scraping the floor, then he would spring like a cat and throw his feet around and be facing the airplane and be in flight. He could tap a Twin Beech on the side and he did that just with energy. He was one of the greatest uphill people because he was a tall, lanky guy, a floater. We set that 12.76 record with Charlie Shields on our team.

Once when we went to a club in Denver, there was an incident with a bouncer. They had guys upstairs and downstairs and we got asked to leave for some reason. We were there with Stanley Brown, and he was probably slurring his words or something. We're leaving and somebody decided to mess with one of the bouncers and helped Stanley down the stairs by pushing him a little bit. All of a sudden, one of the bouncers got in the Preying Mantis position and Charlie only hit him twice. Someone commented, Was he talking to us? The guy was down and out on the floor. We went on down the steps and the bouncer at the bottom didn't want anything to do with Kung Fu Charlie. And that was the end of that.

About sparring, Charlie said, We do all the moves, but we are wearing gloves and we pull our punches. He said, I want to hit somebody. So, he entered a Thai Kickboxing contest in San Francisco, went out, and when they said Go, the fight was over. Charlie did a snap kick and broke the guy's sternum. Charlie said, They disqualified me. They said I hit him too quick so I lost, but they carried the other guy out on a stretcher. How did I lose?

When we were in South Africa, I hurt my foot. After landing, Charlie would dump his gear on the ground and run over and catch me so I didn't have to land on that 5,000 foot hard ground with my sore foot. If anybody got in his way, he knocked him out of the way. Charlie caught me two or three times.

Charlie helped me when Charmian was injured. He helped invent the Bird gear. He shared his money with us so we could compete and helped support Char in Denver. He was a rigger and one of my closest buddies. When he was still a very young man, he had a terminal speed malfunction. He was jumping a square with a different deployment system. He pulled low and deployed his reserve into the malfunction and died.

Thirty years later I got a call from some people who were writing a book on the Masters of Kung Fu and they wanted to ask me a few questions about Charlie Shields. So, even though he died at probably age 25, he still made a Who's Who of black belts.

Charlie—one of the greats and one of my buddies." —*Jerry Bird*

Late Jake

In Bird's words

"One of the most unique individuals I have ever met was Jacob C Schwan. We affectionately called him Late Jake because he was always late for the airplane, late for the dirt dive, late for a date.

Jake joined the U.S. Marines when he was 17 years old. He was a member of the 2nd Marine Battalion in World War II. Those were the guys who hit the beaches first in Guadalcanal, Tarawa, Iwo Jima. Jake got wounded but survived the war. He was a tough marine but he was the nicest man with a poetic heart.

After the war, he went back to Colorado where he lived in Leadville, which is about 7,000 feet above sea level. A mason by trade, Jake liked to hunt. He and his brother would saddle their horses and ride up to 10,000 feet in the Rocky Mountains to hunt. He was bow legged from riding horses.

Jake started jumping when he was in his fifties. He always drove a van and drove himself from Colorado to Florida and brought his little dog with him. Sometimes he dyed his dog's fur pink. Jake was a real war hero and in his later life, he wrote poetry and songs.

For his 69th birthday, his friends decided to make a 69-way. He wasn't the best jumper but they let him go last and he got in.

When he turned 80, we celebrated by making an "8" and a "0" in freefall and put them side by side. Jake wasn't really current skydiving so we put him in the base with two World Champions, Mike Michigan and Jumping Jack Jefferies, holding on to him like we do with students. The plan was to take Late Jake out and turn their exit shape into a compressed accordion to make a bar across the center of the figure "8."

Like a bucking bronco out of the gate, it took Jake about a half a second to flip clear of both of them and he was off spinning by himself.

They had to go catch him but we thought that was funny. One of the still pictures right out the door shows both World Champions upside down, like he flipped them off. Way to go Late Jake!

Jake wrote a song which he dedicated to me, called "Bird's Song."

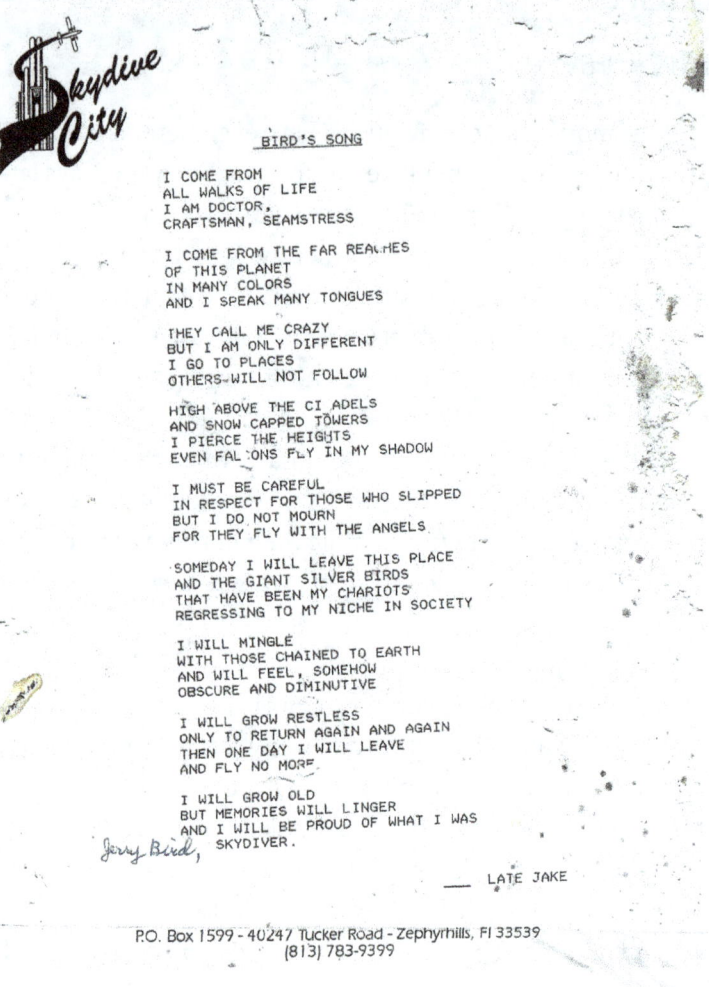

Bird's Song, a poem by Late Jake.

Bird's Song

I come from
All walks of life
I am doctor,
Craftsman, seamstress

I come from the far reaches
Of this planet
In many colors
And I speak many tongues

They call me crazy
But I am only different
I go to places
Others will not follow

High above the citadels
And snowcapped towers
I pierce the heights
Even falcons fly in my shadow

I must be careful
In respect for those who slipped
But I do not mourn
For they fly with Angels

Someday I will leave this place
And the giant silver birds
That have been my chariots
Regressing to my niche in society

I will mingle
With those chained to Earth
And will feel, somehow
Obscure and diminutive

I will grow restless
Only to return again and again
Then one day I will leave
And fly no more

I will grow old
But memories will linger
And I will be proud of what I was
Jerry Bird, skydiver

By Late Jake

Jake was a poet but he could drink like a marine. One time he came with his buddies from Colorado and Jake looked like he had been beaten up. I said, What happened to Jake? They said, He was in a bar fight. I go, What? The bar where they were hanging out had a tough guy contest. Jake was about 70 at the time and decided to enter the contest. He got in the ring with some young buck, twice as big and half his age. This guy didn't want to hit Jake but Jake knew how to box. He was a Marine. He did his little dance like Muhammad Ali and rat-a-tat-tat, he punched the guy in the nose. After that, the guy beat the hell out Jake before his friends could stop him.

Jake gave me a carving of a pair of eagles that are upside-down in the air. "To the Birdman, my mentor . . . This is the way eagles mate in the air. Try it, you'll like it."

In 2010, when I was inducted into the Skydiving Hall of Fame, the ceremony was held in Deland. That's the home of Tom Pirus, a World Champion. I believe Tommy was one of the great skydivers and organizers in the world. Before my speech I read a poem by Jacob C Schwan that I dedicated to Tom.

The Immortal
I flew with eagles in the sky. Once I saw an eagle die.
They took him to a far place back East and buried him there, they say.
But, not so, for after they had all gone, I watched and waited for a while.
Soon a giant Eagle arose, this time on great feathered wings, circling slowly.
He beckoned to me. When I could not come, he soared high above the
snowcapped tower. As he faded from sight. I heard his call. "Come back,"
I cried. I watched and waited, but he never returned.

I carry his poem in my wallet.

Jake lived to be about 90. When he died, they took him to the high mountains and scattered his ashes. Jacob C Schwan, United States Marine, I salute you, Jake." —*Jerry Bird*

28

Around the World with Jerry Bird

Venezuela

In Bird's words

"**As I traveled around the world** to the competitions in the 1970's, I met people from different countries, and one of the groups I became friendly with was from Venezuela. Pedro Luis Gonzales had come to our scrambles out in California, maybe 1969 or early '70s, and somewhere along the line the Venezuelans started coming up to Zephyrhills. Then they hired me to come down there to teach the military and to coach their 8-way team.

During one of the trips I met. Marco Straziota. His family was the South American importer of Hughes helicopters. Marco had a Hughes helicopter, 500D, sitting in his yard. That was his car.

Life got good real quick. We'd fly around in the helicopter. You could land on the beach, you could land at the hotels. We flew to the military airport, we talked to the military and Marco took me to Angel Falls for the first time. He told me, Bird, you can't bring your gear. So, I left my parachute gear and we got in the helicopter and away we went. So, now we're on Angel Falls, and he says, I didn't want you to bring your rig because you would jump and then I'd have to pick you up and I don't get to jump. But we'll get back here someday and we'll jump this.

Marco Straziota's family had a lot of power. One of the uncles was the President. They had the Get Out Of Jail Free badge. When we got stopped by the cops for speeding, Marco showed the badge to the cops and the cops stepped back and saluted. When we were going through Customs, they told the officials to get the hell out of our way and the officials got out of the way and saluted. When we landed on the military base we were surrounded by guards with machine guns and they were going to arrest us, but after we showed them the badge, they were washing the helicopter and went to get us fried chicken and cold beer. Venezuela was a lot of fun when your friends were the ruling elite.

Marco was handsome and married to a beautiful lady. He had been to the '77 World Meet on the Venezuelan 8-way team and was a boy-wonder pilot. When his company bought enough helicopters they had to get them from Culver City, California at Hughes Helicopter Corporation. These guys were the ruling elite in Venezuela, right? They sold their helicopters to their friends who were rich. Marco would say, you don't need that Ferrari, you need one of these helicopters. It's only a half million dollars, let's go get one, and they would fly to California with their instructor pilots. It's like you're getting a new car, you have to give it a test ride.

Marco could do things with their helicopter that their test pilots couldn't do. He could fly inside the envelope and on every side of the envelope, he dazzled them at Hughes. So, now, with his instructor staff and his new buyers, they would pick up their four brand new Hughes helicopters in Culver City, California and fly them back across the United States on the way back to Venezuela. On that trip the new owners learned to fly and now they have 40 or 50 hours of helicopter time going across America.

One time when I was living in Utah Marco called me and he says, Hey, we're down in Las Vegas. Do you have enough room in your backyard? Next thing I know four Hughes 500Ds from the factory landing in my backyard. Then they flew them across the country to Zephyrhills to participate in the World Meet there before heading to Venezuela.

These helicopters had floats on the skids, so if they went down over water they could at least float, they had a raft. And since Venezuela was friendly with Cuba, they could fly across Cuba without going around it. By the time their guys got home with the new toys they had bought, they were experienced helicopter pilots with formation experience in all terrains.

Unfortunately, Marco got sick and he died at a very young age. That was in 1981. I promised I would return.

In the '80's and '90's, whenever, there was a boogie, I went back to Venezuela. At first, we went to a drop zone at Higuerote. We usually had about 100 people there and Pedro Luis Gonzales was always our host. The food was great, great hospitality and we were always protected. You couldn't get into trouble while you were down there.

Later, we started to go to Margarita Island and did the helicopter boogies. Roger Ponce came down with us and we had a Russian MI-8 helicopter. We did 30-way formations. It was a private resort with a big wall around it. They had guards at the gates and once we were in the resort, your wristband covered everything. When you got up in the morning, there was a buffet and cooks who would prepare you any food any way you wanted it. You never had to pay for anything. At the booze bar you could drink as much as you wanted and you didn't have to pay for it. The staff and some other people would sometimes make 20-ways with their friends, or if there was a tandem they would do a tandem because the helicopter could hold more. They didn't want to miss this thing. We're spotting on the beach. Margarita Island used to be a Dutch possession so the Dutch airlines, maybe it was KLM, still served that island. Almost all the tourists there were from Holland. What made that extra special was, over in Europe, when they sunbathe, they are topless.

We'd land on the beach and everybody's jumping up and down and clapping and everybody is topless. Then you'd walk back up, not even 50 yards, there's a swimming pool and all the tourists there were jumping up and down topless. And as you walked by the bar, there were no rules down there, they would serve you these little beers and everybody would just take one of those Polars, a beer like Coors. One of the kids, his family owned a brewery, so they got free beer forever. You could chug one of them in between jumps. Nobody cared.

Pedro Luis was like Danny Devito. He was a little short guy. Everybody loved him. He did all the talking. They loved him at the airport. We never had to show passports or anything. He'd walk through there, wave to all the people and they just opened the gates.

We were at this Higuerote boogie and he says Bird, I don't have any packers for us. What are we going to do? At first, I packed. But there were some ice cream girls pushing a little cart and trying to make some money. It was hot and I wanted to buy some ice cream so I go talk to them for a while. I can speak enough Spanish, so I told them they were my two new packers.

By the fifth or sixth or tenth time they did it, (I always checked the important parts so they didn't route something wrong), they figured it out. By the second day, I said, I am paying you for this. They made a dollar a day selling ice cream. The fun part of this is now I have these two girls packing for me. I don't care how you pack, my parachute, it still works. If you can put the slider up, stow the brakes and get it in that fucking bag, it's going to open. I'm sitting in the shade having a Polar or something, when Luis comes over and says, Bird can I use your packers? So, now they're packing and they're getting pretty good at it.

They get paid. I left. When I went back to Venezuela two years later, I brought a girl from Zephyrhills, "Packing Kathy," as she is known. She's a rigger and she brings a crew to pack for everybody, they can pack 100 rigs a day.

Next thing I know, here comes Kathy, saying Bird, we have a problem. What's your problem?

She goes, there's some crazy Venezuelan girl here fighting with me over your parachute.

The ice cream girl came up to me and now she could speak some broken English. We talked. She said, after you taught me to pack, I went back to a place where there's a parachute club and I became their packer and then I took a course, and now I'm packing for the military. She said, I came across the country to pack for you. I have to tell you, you took my family out of poverty and now I have a real job as a parachute packer and I'm making good money, and you tell that Packing Kathy I'm going to kick her ass if she doesn't let me pack your parachute. And she wanted to do it for free, but of course I paid her."

Jumping Angel Falls

Mark III Productions Incorporated
14875 N.E. 20th Avenue
North Miami, Florida 33181
(305) 948-4336
Telex #706164

FOR IMMEDIATE RELEASE

NOVEMBER 3, 1983 - CHURÚN RIVER FALLS, VENEZUELA
CANAIMA NATIONAL FOREST, ANGEL FALLS, VENEZUELA.

ON OCTOBER 29, AN ADVENTURE FORCE OF 14 PERSONS WAS AIRLIFTED TO THE TOP OF THE HIGHEST WATERFALL IN THE WORLD. THIRTEEN LAUNCHED THEMSELVES INTO FREE-FALL INTO THE SEMI-ENCLOSED CATHEDRAL CARVED BY IONS OF FLOW OF THE ANGEL RIVER. AFTER AN APPROXIMATE FREE-FALL DELAY OF TEN SECONDS, EACH PERSON, FOLLOWING THE LEAD OF MAXIMILLIAN BOTTO OF THE VENEZUELAN AERO CLUB AND JERRY BIRD OF THE U.S.A., OPENED HIS PARACHUTE AND GLIDED TO A PREPARED JUNGLE CLEARING 150 FEET ABOVE AND ADJACENT TO THE ANGEL RIVER; SAFELY.

THIS IS THE FIRST DOCUMENTED FREE-FALL DESCENT FROM THE FAMED VENEZUELAN PRIMARY TOURIST ATTRACTION PERFORMED BY A MULTI-NATIONAL CONTINGENT OF CITIZENS FROM THE U.S.A., VENEZUELA, AND ITALY.

THIS ADVENTURE PURSUIT WAS SUBSIDIZED AND ACHIEVED BY A NEWLY FORMED HI-TECH, ADVANCED CONCEPT VIDEO SERVICE CORPORATION NAMED MARK III PRODUCTIONS, INC. BASED IN MIAMI, FLORIDA.

A FILM DOCUMENTATION WAS ACCUMULATED AND WILL BE EDITED FOR BROADCAST AFTER THE LENGTHY EXTRACTION OF PERSONNEL AND EQUIPMENT FROM THE REMOTE JUNGLE LOCATION.

MARK J. TREBLE
PRESIDENT

MJT·mih

Press Release for Mark III Productions, Angel Falls jump.

"In 1983 when I got the Bird Machine and was hooked up with Mike Scholtz as the chief pilot, one of our stockholders inquired about the possibility of jumping Angel Falls and making a movie. He owned a production company in Miami and said if he could be on the jump, he would pay for it. I got in contact with my friends in Venezuela and told them the plan. I called Carl Boenish and told him that I had an expedition going to Venezuela and that we would be the first group to go there to jump and film it. We would pay all his expenses plus a fee, whatever it took to get Carl to go. At the time, he was recovering from, I believe a broken leg, but he agreed to come. He always shot using 16-millimeter film and knew that in the jungle there would be moisture so he wanted to be in control of where the cameras were placed. We also got Tom Sanders to come.

Angel Falls. Tom Sanders, photographer.

As we were planning the logistics the person paying the expenses said he had four friends that he wanted included on the jump: Richard Pitt, Mike Scholtz, Ron Urton, Mike Color, Don Caltvedt [Moonraker[84]] and myself were the Americans. I believe we had six Venezuelans that were going to jump and a cameraman. We put this group together in America,

---

84. *Moonraker*, directed by Lewis Gilbert (1979 Beverly Hills, CA: United Artists). Don Calvedt coordinated the skydiving sequence in a scene in which Jaws pushed James Bond out of the airplane without a parachute. B.J. Worth developed the inch thick parachute pack concealed beneath the stuntman's suit. Jake Lombard eventually played Bond in the scene, BJ played the pilot and Ron Luginbill played Jaws. Both Jake and BJ became regular members of the stunt team for aerial sequences in subsequent James Bond films. *Moonraker* (film). Wikipedia https://en.wikipedia.org/wiki/Moonraker_(film)

flew to Caracas and got picked up by the Venezuelan crew. From Caracas we flew to a place called Canaima which is maybe a four-hour flight south in a 727. We got dropped off in the Orinoco River area which is almost to the Amazon basin. There is a paved runway and a little village there which we used as our base camp. We unloaded all our people, our crew along with some girlfriends and cooks. Upriver from Canaima is the river that comes in where the airport is in the plains, 50 miles from Angel Falls.

There is a tourist stop with a 20-foot waterfall and a great big pool right there and you can go paddling and do different activities. But we had the upriver camp, Ucaima, with "Jungle Rudy" Truffino.[85] He was in his 60's, a Dutch adventurer. He spoke about four languages and he had built a great place up river and lived with the native people and probably had three or four native wives, but he had a perfectly mowed camp on a really nice river with canoes. There were furnished cabins made out of rock and he had a diesel generator, so there were lamps at night and he would play music in the bar. He loved to make Bloody Marys with silver shakers and there were people there who cooked the meals. This was Jungle Rudy's Upriver Camp.

A lot of the Venezuelans wanted to be on the Angel Falls jump and this is their country, but one helicopter could carry a limited amount of people and provisions. The camp close to the bottom of the falls was very primitive with lean-tos and you had to poop in the woods. We were waiting to move but there were only certain times that we were allowed in there. Meanwhile, at the base camp we had a good time partying but we made some practice jumps. The landing area was small, like the size of my front yard, with trees all round it so I told everyone that if you jump off Angel Falls and can't land in the pea gravel so to speak, you're going to be in trouble because the trees are really tall and you could die landing. They had to show me that they had canopy control and could land in a small area or they wouldn't be allowed on the jump. Most of the quality guys from the Venezuelan group that I knew, all made it and my group, since we were paying the bill, were on automatically. But the problem was that, day after day after day, the weather was bad for filming

---

85. *Jungle Rudy*, directed by Rob Smits. (2006; Netherlands: Cinema Delicatessen) IMDB.

and for jumping. When we first arrived, the waterfall was almost dry and the river was just rock bed. The river rose and this is how close we came to being idiots. At one point when we first got there, the waterfall was almost dry. There was hardly any water falling over it and the river was just rock bed, When we first flew up river with a helicopter, there was a great big sandbar so we landed there and unloaded but fortunately somebody figured out that it was probably not a good idea to leave the helicopter there.

We flew over to the woods where the natives lived secure in the ferns and made a vertical descent into the trees and landed there. A few days later the river rose—if we had left the helicopter on the sand bar, it would have been washed away. We had a Cessna 206 there with us too but up by Jungle Rudy's; he had a real short dirt strip, if you dared. In the jungle, by the runway there were airplane bodies from the wrecks. One of the pilots landed there and we decided to do some jumps and filming at base camp.

Finally, it is time to go upriver. Some of the native people went on foot and by outboard canoe and it took them half a day. We flew the helicopter up there in 20 minutes. We set up our camp with all our provisions. At night we could hear the cougars in the jungle. Jungle Rudy had a 30-foot-long Anaconda skin on his bar so we knew we were in the jungle. From the top of Angel Falls, as far as you could see, there was nothing but swamp with trees sitting in the water. I thought, man, if the helicopter were to go down there, they might never find you.

We had to sling load 55 gallons of kerosene gas underneath the helicopter and leave them at caches to get in and out of there. The weather wasn't cooperating. David had been flying the helicopter to the top of Angel Falls, filming and dropping people off, then picking them up because the weather wasn't good enough to jump. On the last day I said, fuck it, leave us here. You don't have much gas. We will spend the night on the top of Angel Falls. I unpacked my parachute and used it as a sleeping bag. We were 5,000 feet higher than base camp and it was chilly up there and it could rain. All the water that comes off Angel Falls is from the rain up there. It's in the clouds. Over the millions of years, that's where it funnels off the wall. If you could hang under and look back, it is eroded by the wind so it's like a big amphitheater.

On the morning of our last day, the weather broke. We could see the ground; they could see us. We set Carl up at a point with his camera so he could shoot us while we were in freefall. We have somebody shooting long distance, we have people down below. I stood on the top of Angel Falls and decided that, under my canopy, under normal conditions, where I could land. I figured out the angle and radioed down on the ground and told them to go to a knoll by the river and do their best to clear it. There were rocks and stubby trees. One rock was big enough to do a stand up on. That was our landing area.

When we were at base camp doing practice jumps, Carl couldn't jump because he had a bad leg. One of the Venezuelan people was our cameraman during the fun jumps.

Back at the top of the falls, we had planned to throw rocks with streamers on them over the top as a signal to the camera people who were placed at all different angles, to start the cameras. Some were positioned 50 feet down, shooting back up. The helicopter was straight out in front of us.

Jerry at the top of Angel Falls, ready to jump. Carl Boenish and Tom Sanders, photographers.

If you drop a rock, Angel Falls is about 3000 feet off the ground, but from where you exit to where you land, it is about 5000 feet because after the rock hits, it's still so steep, it drops another 2000 feet before it levels off into the valley where we were going to land. A Wing Jumper could get probably two or three minutes of freefall. We could probably stretch it to 12 seconds so there would be time to do some RW. We were going to make a 2-way. I had made two jumps off of El Capitan when it was legal, but I was the only one in the group who had made a BASE jump.

So, we are the top, ready to go. We drop the rocks and one of the Venezuelans came out of their tent. The Venezuelans had a number people there according to a hierarchy of their country, and I assumed certain people would be the guys who would go first with us but I was wrong. Max Botto was going to be the guy. He is not wearing a helmet and I think he's wearing sandals. And on "three" he just goes. I dove off right after him so I could catch him. No sooner do I go off, I look and he's dumping. He was scared to death. So, I track off to the side and go ahead and dump. I land first, right on the place I had chosen and Max comes in and does a stand up on a rock. On that day, all 12 of the jumpers jumped and only one guy missed the landing area. He landed in a tree and he had to leave his canopy.

Angel Falls was the third and last BASE jump I ever made. After we got our gear loaded in the canoes for the Sherpas to take out of there, everybody got as skinny and as light as they could and hung onto the helicopter. It took six hours to get back to base camp by canoe and walking, and 20 minutes by helicopter. We had eight people hanging on it. We flew back to base camp where it was air conditioned and drank some margaritas. When we flew back to Miami, we were picked up by a limousine from Mark Three Studios and had a hero's welcome.

Jimmy Angel, who they named Angel Falls after, was an American gold smuggler. In 1935 he crash-landed there and walked out of the jungle a month later. Thirty years later the airplane was disassembled, brought off the mountain and put in a Museum. Angel Falls in Spanish is Salto Angel but the indigenous people who live there called it Kerepakupai Vená."

Venezuela 80-Way Formations

"In the year 2000 Venezuela celebrated the 80th anniversary of their air force. The people we knew had connections with everybody and they wanted to know if they could put together a spectacle for the air show they were going to put on in Barcelona, Venezuela. They proposed that we make an 80-way formation with the Venezuelan colors for the 80th anniversary and the Venezuelan government would pay for our transportation in country, all our food, our hotel, and give us a C-130 to jump out of. All we had to do was show up in Caracas. The people in Venezuela contacted certain people in America—Roger Nelson, Roger Ponce, Kate Cooper, BJ Worth, me—and asked us to each pick ten of our friends who can get in—and come to Venezuela for a party on us.

I'm up for that. We picked from the World Team and we show up in Venezuela. They take us to this town away from Caracas and we are put up in a plush hotel and everything is free, and I mean everything. Once a day we're supposed to make one jump and do this 80-way. We have no practice jumps but from the Venezuelan contingency, there are about 40 of them who want to be on this jump and without any practice jumps just by talking and remembering from who I knew from the past, we ended up with 20 of them to make the starting lineup and, Lyle Presse, I don't know how he ever did it, but he made a base with 12 rookies and it was there every time. We took the maximum amount of Venezuelans we could on the load. The formation we made was color coded properly with the Venezuela flag and we got free color-coded jump suits.

We went up on the day before and we got to do a practice run. Everybody was worried about the pilots and the spots and the oxygen systems, so I knew we weren't going to jump, but I wanted to see if the pilots can fly straight down the runway. So, we went up and everybody was scared. Roger Nelson was yelling, we shouldn't jump and somebody goes, Bird is just doing a practice run to see if the pilots can fly. We go on a jump run and no way Roger Ponce is going to say exit. He's my spotter, so we do the practice run, see how long it takes to get up, do this, do that, come back and land with the airplane.

During the week that this festival went on, we made seven jumps. We made seven 80-ways 100% every time with no practice jumps. But the coolest thing was we were guarded because it was a military weapon air show. You could come here and have the option to buy this anti-aircraft gun here. I thought Roger Nelson was going to buy one, you know, a machine gun to put on his airplane. And we had Americans there from Langley with all gray F-15s. And they were putting on like a factory demo. But there was military demos going on, so we had to be out on the tarmac and when we would land, it was just like we were rock-and-roll stars jumping into the crowd. We were rock stars to them. They had never seen a skydive before. You know what it's like out in Arizona when you saw a 200-way above, well we were doing this with an 80-way formation. It was always a perfect spot and when we landed, they yelled and cheered and wanted us to give them autographs and hugged us and we'd walk through the crowd and go to our area where we had armed guards and get our rigs packed. And then we just partied for the rest of the day. There were different areas to eat and all kinds of expositions going on there. But the flight line was where we hung out and our C-130 was there and we never knew when they were going to say, okay, it's time for you guys to go jump. And we would get in our C-130 and go do it.

So, one day I thought, the cockpit is open on that American gray fighter plane, an F-15 Eagle over there and I don't see anybody around. I wonder how close I can get to it. So, I go over and got my hand on that step to go up to the cockpit. I forget what they call these guys, but they're almost like a bird dog or a CIA team that travels incognito. They're protectors. They go, We've been watching you boys all week, but Mr. Bird, you shouldn't be touching our airplane. We would walk over there and turn our backs to them, like we were pissing, and pass our joints back and forth. We didn't realize there were guys in Ghillie suits with machine guns hiding in the bushes. I probably pissed on a couple of them. We told them, don't worry, we won't fuck with your airplanes.

That was another great skydiving experience. The Venezuelans would call me "pájaro" which is bird in Spanish. Roger was one of my lieutenants and so was Kate Cooper and they said by order of Pedro Luis, Bird goes last on this jump because we say so because it was easy for me to get in. I got to do all the organizing and then go to the back and load and go, Roger, spot it, go out last, swoop down and get in every time.

That was our last hurrah in Venezuela.

There's a book, *Once a Warrior King* by David Donovan.[86] Sometimes I feel that way about the places I went to when I knew the leaders of the country or the ruling elite. Venezuela was one of the countries that adopted me, so to speak. I think I went there 14 times. Venezuela and I were the Brotherhood.

When Hugo Chávez[87] took over, Venezuela turned into a Communist country. Most of my Venezuelan friends were either killed or run out of the country.

I would go out in Caracas at night by myself and go all over the city and meet people—I never had a worry. But the culture changed. Now, they would have your watch and have your arm. They would just come up, pop open a knife and slice your pants open. They don't care if they cut anything else off. They don't care. Now, you cannot go to Venezuela, you cannot jump off Angel Falls. There's no longer the sweet, street loving

---

86. David Donovan, *Once a Warrior King: Memories of an Officer in Viet Nam*, Random House Publishing Group, 1986.

87. Hugo Chávez was a Venezuelan politician, revolutionary, and military officer who served as the 52nd president of Venezuela from 1999 until 2013.

people there. So, no gringos in Venezuela now. My friend Pedro Luis said, Bird. you can't come here anymore." —*Jerry Bird*

Canadian Skies

"Jerry coached our 1975 Canadian team and we had many other adventures with the Birdman!" —*William O. Hardman*

In Bird's words

"I had a long history of going to Canada. The first time was in '73 or '74. They were having an accuracy championship sponsored by the Belvedere Cigarette Company and they wanted me to come and be the expert announcer for the Canadian Wide World of Sports. So, I went to Calgary and Regina and ended up in a place nobody ever heard of, a resort town called Fort Capelle. There was a big lake and there was a resort, and they had set up an accuracy pit. Lo and behold, the cigarette company was giving away prize money to the winners. It was a big thing. But as it turned out, it was windy as heck. You had to spot way out over the lake to land on this beach to do your accuracy.

I had it all down: *Welcome to the first annual Belvedere Cigarette World Championships of Accuracy. I'm with the Canadian Wide World of Sports, My name is Jerry Bird. I'm a world champion . . .*

I went there as an announcer. I got a free ride. I got paid. But the weather was so bad that they really didn't get to run out the meet. I don't remember how many jumps were made. There were about 50 of these guys in our sport, but I believe a Canadian guy, we called him Canadian Bill Smith, won the accuracy event and the money." —*Jerry Bird*

Bob "Greenman" Smith

The accuracy meet was at Fort Qu'Appelle, Saskatchewan and it was to include free large star attempts. The official name was the North American Open Parachute Championship, but everyone called it the Belvedere Money Meet. I flew to Regina, Saskatchewan with about half a dozen jumpers from Abbotsford, BC. Someone picked us up in a van and drove us to the site. We were put up in cabins belonging to some church girls' school summer camp. There were something like three or four bunk beds per cabin (with lots of young girls' love life dreams written on the rafters.) Bird bunked there.

And it rained. Mud all over. No jumping. Bird organized fun: Running and sliding down the muddy slopes. It was a good thing we had beer.

I had a broken foot in a cast. My logbook shows I made two jumps on the 2nd—a Saturday. The winds were howling. I was in third place in my class when I pulled out of the competition—my cast was smashed to smithereens.

The winds were even higher the next day. If I remember correctly, U.S. Accuracy champion Bill Hayes, Jimmy Lowe, and other American accuracy jumpers were there, jumping early squares, the old, longlined types. When they hit the wind shear it was almost panic with the canopies bouncing around and cells collapsing. —*Bob Greenman Smith*

In Bird's words

"Another time I went to the other end of Canada, up by Ottawa, to do a Jerry Bird Camp. That was when we had the Wings of Orange. In '75 we went there and competed in their Nationals as an invitational team with a team from Utah, our Utah version of the Migratory Bird Refuge, and we won the Canadian Nationals, but since we weren't Canadians, we were honorary winners. After that was over, they asked me to stay and be their coach and I coached the Canadian team and the next year went to the World Championships as the RW coach of the Canadian team, trying to beat Captain Hook and the American team. (They hated me.)

So, I had a connection to Canada. I've been on the East coast; I've been in the middle, and a couple other places. In the '90's, out on the West Coast in a place called the Frazier Valley near Abbotsford, there's a place called Chilliwack. Up in the air you can see Mt. Hood, Mt. Rainier, Mt. Washington, every one of them. They are snowcapped even in the summer. It's beautiful in the Chilliwack Valley. I'd go up there and do these RW camps. I always had a good time there.

It was at an airport right along the road that goes right between the mountains, in the middle of the Valley. When we jumped at the airport, we sort of interfered with their operation. Straight down the road about five miles was a little crop duster strip and that was where the club operated. If they needed a bigger airplane, they trucked us to that airport for takeoff and we landed over here like we did at Taft, where we took off at the airport and jumped out in the desert.

That year we were going to have a Pilatus Porter. A Pilatus Porter is one of those airplanes with a real long nose with a great big turbine engine and will carry up to 10 people. It has a sliding door, like a van, so you can close it in flight and when you get up to altitude you slide it open. It was a short field, short takeoff airplane so it could take off and land at this little strip right where we were. We didn't have to do any of this commuting. Everything was perfect except we had a cloud cover where we were and it's low, maybe 3,000 to 6,000 feet.

Pilatus turbo Porter before the crash. Scott Kyle, photographer.

We had about a hundred people there waiting to jump with Jerry Bird. This was in the mid '90's before GPS, so the pilot and I talked and decided that if we went to the other airport, it's clear down there and we can see the airport and we can see the mountains so we can see to hold the heading and we know that will put us right over where we're going. Let's run it on my stopwatch to see what it will take us to get over top. One minute. So, one minute out when we were over at the other airport, I could visually see the highway and the airport, so we would go over top of the clouds and then get out. We did a full load, an 8-way or 10-way. In the Porter, you always turn the copilot seat around so a jumper can sit there. That's where I sat so I could see everybody. I could look over and I spot backwards looking this way and tell him to go that way, but we were over clouds.

This Porter had been brought back from Vietnam because the Air America in Vietnam flew a lot of these aircraft that would take off at 30 miles an hour and land in 30 feet. They have a trap door in the middle to drop stuff out: bombs, mail, food, anything. It had been brought to the States and my friend in Everett, Washington, had his own airplane company and they refurbished it. It was newly licensed, newly certified and newly inspected. The pilot flew it from there to Canada to do his first boogie with me.

Everybody's tired of waiting on the ground and I said, let's try a run like in the Elsinore Valley. You see the mountains over here and the mountains over there, stay in the Valley or pull above the clouds or do whatever, but we are not going to get hurt. We go up and do this thing. By then the clouds had grown, deepened both ways, closer to the ground, closer up in the air. So, here we are and there's nothing to see but there's nothing under us. I see a mountain over here and another mountain over there. And I go, What the fuck? Let's go.

The first guy that climbs out is a floater and he's going to climb around the strut like on a Cessna. We were having a lot of people in this airplane hanging out. The biggest problem with the Porter is it's a tail dragger and the tail is real low. Well, this guy accidentally activates his main. His parachute comes out and wraps around the horizontal stabilizer and starts to open. He is jerked off the airplane as it starts to slide off at the end of the stabilizer. When they built these airplanes, they needed more air on the stabilizer. Right at each end of the horizontal stabilizer they installed caps, just a flat piece of metal that reduces the vortex around the tip and gives better directional stability. When he takes opening shock, the whole tail leaves with him (and when we recovered the stabilizer later, that cap has the piece of his canopy jammed in between it).

By now we're above the clouds. One guy has taken off the tail and it's Get out! Get out! Get out! On a plane with no tail, the stick doesn't really work. The other parts don't really work. It broke all the cables, but where the forged places were, instead of pulling the rivets out, it broke the metal arms right off, broke them in two and took them with it. And that tail landed on the ground doing a spin, so soft that after they took the broken hardware on it, they were able to use it again with no repair other than bending out the flap on the end and putting on new brackets and they did some rewiring.

Now, everybody's jumping out and I jumped out. Some people dumped right away, some were tracking, but if you tracked, you tracked into the clouds. If you dumped that high, the airplane was probably below you. But this airplane without a tail and with no control, was doing loop-de-loops and weird things in the air. Sometimes it was diving toward the ground but then it would get enough speed and it would pull out. So, we're in the clouds and there's a fucking airplane flying around you and there are people everywhere.

One guy thought he was going to stay in and help the pilot. Well, the pilot is on the other side of a wall in a seat. So, after he got flipped and flopped over a couple times, he realized it was time to get out of there. This long-haired kid jumped out too. Now there's one guy left, the pilot and it's time to get out of there.

This was a bush pilot who was a new jump pilot. He's never made a jump. Now he's sitting in a Pilates Porter which has a soft pack that you sat in. The harness on a Porter is more like a race car driver's. It's not just a lap belt. It comes over your shoulders and you lock it in. Now he has to get out. This guy, in a spinning, flopping airplane, he unhooked his shoulder harness and ditched that. The Porter does have a rip cord that you pull and that jettisons the door. That's gone.

He jumps, but the airplane is upside down, so he lands on the wing and now he has to push himself off the wing. He's jumping the NB-6 container system with no releases, and it is a cross pull. The handle is on the left side where our reserve is for us skydivers today. He finds the handle, he pulls it. But because he had never done this before and the harnesses are uncomfortable in the airplane, he didn't have the leg straps cinched up and he didn't have the harness cinched down so the leg straps slapped him real good down below. There's one big piece of iron right in the middle of your chest strap. He wasn't stable so the snap of the opening got him in the chin. But he was a bearded guy, and the Bird spot was so great, over the clouds, that he came out of the cloud, oscillating back and forth with his little round and lands right in our area. He jumps up and down yelling, I'm alive! I'm alive! I'm alive! Then he grabbed his nuts and goes, Oh, that hurts! That hurts! That hurts! He put his hand up to his face and he has blood everywhere, but it was just a little nick in the chin.

The first thing the people on the ground see is the Porter coming out of the clouds at about 2000 feet, diving to the ground and they think the pilot is showing off. He dropped them, now he's coming back. They'd never seen a Porter before and in the Chilliwack Valley, it's not very dense. There's a house about every five miles. So, they are watching and waiting and about the same time, one guy had kept tracking to go all the way through the clouds. About that time he pops out the bottom of the clouds and he dumps. They watched the airplane go in, but way over there and there's no more parachutes and they think that's the only guy that got out. Everybody on the drop zone rushed over to where the airplane went in, a couple of miles away. There was no fire, but on the drop zone in this same area, here comes to the Porter door doing a frisbee and it lands and doesn't break. There's the tail, there's the door, there's the pilot who had a round parachute. Slowly, because of their different altitudes, jumpers were coming out of the clouds and people were yelling, number six, and there's number seven, and clapping and cheering. Number ten was missing, and they thought, that's the little guy that hit the tail. He weighed about 120 pounds, and he opened at 14,000 feet. The other people dove out and tracked away. He came down a couple minutes later than everybody else. In the center cell of his square parachute, there was a round hole about the size of a cantaloupe and that piece of nylon was stuck in the horizontal stabilizer.

He wasn't hurt. But over where the airplane hit the ground, there was a two-story house with an outdoor veranda and the father was sitting on the porch and there were trees around him. Under the trees about 30 feet from him, his three small children were playing on a blanket. The airplane came straight down and hit in his front yard, between his house and his children. All the metal and diesel went forward and never touched any of them. That pilot was the happiest man in the world. He never ever got mad at the skydivers.

Lo and behold, at that place where they had the best pies and pastries, a helicopter rescue unit with first responders had been eating pies and it had just taken off. They were alerted and were hovering over the site within five minutes with an emergency Canadian Forces helicopter. But there was nobody in the airplane.

At first, the guys from the drop zone thought that everybody was in that hole in the ground. The engine was buried about 10 feet under. We later picked it all up and got it out of there. There weren't any pieces we

Crashed Porter. Scott Kyle, photographer.

couldn't pick up and just put on a trailer. We had to call Jim Perry back in Seattle and say, Hey Jim, we have a little problem.

What's that? Can I come up and fix it?

Well, the problem is that your airplane is in a lot of little pieces.

Everybody survived, the pilot jumped out, the plane crashed. Nobody died and we escaped again." —*Jerry Bird*

Skydiver William Renfroe was on that Porter. Here is what he wrote as a memorial to his friend, the pilot of the Porter, Greg MacLachlan, many years later:

William Renfroe

I don't know why but for some reason I always thought Greg MacLachlan would speak at my funeral. When I was younger, I loved meeting new friends and growing closer to them all and now that I'm older, I feel like Lt. Dan. I should have died a long time ago so I don't have to face the loss of so many people I love so much. I suppose I'll adapt and survive as always.

I met Greg at Crest Airport in Kent, Washington. I was working for Jim Perry rebuilding Pilatus Porters and doing the booking for the one airplane he had flying, taking it to skydiving events. We were scheduled to fly for the Canadian Nationals in Chilliwack, BC and we needed a pilot.

One day a longtime friend of Jim's showed up and had a buddy in tow, Greg MacLachlan. After they spoke with Jim at length, Jim said, "I think we have a pilot for your Canadian gig." I asked Jim, "What's his story?" Jim said he was an Alaskan pilot and had flown everything known to man that could be put on a dirt strip in the bush. I said, "Good because that Porter will eat his lunch if he nods off for a half second.'" Jim said, "That's no shit."

Greg showed up that Friday and hopped in the airplane with Jim. They took off into the misty skies and disappeared for an hour or so. Then, there they were on final approach. Winds were 10 to 15 and very sporadic. I looked at another mechanic and said, "That's probably Jim flying." He said, "Yeah, you're probably going to see a lot of touch-and-goes." And we did.

Eventually, you could see that Jim had turned the stick over to Greg. Poor guy was getting his ass kicked for quite a few landings and I couldn't take it anymore. I cued the mic on the hand held radio and said, "let's wrap it up since conditions are getting worse." They put it on final approach and sliced and diced in another landing to a short stop. I thought to myself, thank God it's over! NOPE. Jim bails out of the right seat and walks to me at the side of the runway and says, "tell him to take off." Glaring at me he said, "I'm serious!" I said, "Why don't we wait for better conditions? I don't want him to lose confidence and get scared off." Jim just looked at me and glared. I got on the radio and said, "'Go for it, dude!" Jim said, "That-a-boy!" and starts walking back to the house.

Greg took off just fine with all the control surfaces fluttering about while the wind socks were doing 180s left to right. Here he comes on final approach, slicing and dicing throughout the approach, and hovering above the centerline, he touches down and dances from one main to the other, eventually losing it and wipes out a runway light with the right main. Off the runway he goes, scooting across the grass parking area next to the runway, heading for someone's backyard! Yes, Crest Airpark was a live-on-the runway community and this backyard had the owner's eating breakfast on their patio. Greg brings the airplane to a halt with the prop (full throttle in reverse) in their yard and the main is on the property line. I'm sure the owners had shit their pants at this point! Greg just looked at me with his hands up, shaking his head like WTF. I promptly cued the mic and said, "'Well Squirrel, back it up and get back out there." As Greg backed the airplane out of the yard, Jim became visible to me again with his back turned. He just kept walking. Greg got back on the runway and took off. Conditions worsened and his landing got better.

The next weekend, we were off to my homeland Toledo, Washington to fly for Dave Rucker's Boogie. The weather was bad and we only flew a few loads successfully, we landed quite a few. I was on the first load that was forced to land due to weather. Of course, everyone on the plane is nervous with a new and unknown pilot. Everyone is looking at me with big round eyes. The airplane was hovering two inches off the runway, getting slower and slower, finally touching down so smoothly you couldn't feel it. Everyone was blown away how smoothly we landed, shooting the thumbs-up. Greg looked at me and said, Man, this thing sure lands nicely when it's over weight. Then everyone looked at me like, What?! I just shrugged. Every load he landed was filled with seasoned skydivers in awe.

We flew from one event to another and eventually headed to Chilliwack, BC for the Nationals. The weather was bad, we had a lot of flying to do, and a lot of people on the ground impatiently waiting. The drop zone owner, Woolsox, had arranged a world renowned skydiving organizer, Jerry Bird, to be there and organize loads with all the non-competitors to keep the airplane running.

We struggled day after day to get anything in the air. Saturday, AKA day one of competition jumps, arrived with more bad weather but eventually the weather started to break. We quickly got the first load on a call and started prepping the airplane as clouds began to break. As the first load launched, we started gearing up for the second load and I'm on this load. Jerry Bird organized a 10-way dive that we had practiced on the ground for a couple days. We boarded the airplane while it was running on the runway after successfully dropping the first load. Off we go. As we climbed, the holes in the scattered clouds started to slowly close in and eventually we were at 12,500 ft looking for a hole. I told Greg to continue to climb and loiter so we could look for a hole and a local said, 'Look. the bend in the highway,' as he pointed out the open door. After making a large heading correction, we were on jump run, 14,500 feet, and after a few minutes, the spotter called a cut. I'm in the back of the airplane and Jerry is sitting in the right seat facing the tail. Front, front float scissors out and rear, rear following along with front float, rear, door position 1, then divers 2 and 3 are moving into door positions. I'm patiently waiting in the back of the airplane, looking out the little round window, admiring the beauty of the snowcapped mountains and all of the sudden, I see a pilot chute go shooting by, followed by a taunt bridal. Someone is having a premature deployment while standing on an airplane.

Bad news! I immediately yelled, GO! GO! GO! as the bag shoots by and everyone else yells, 'OH SHIT!' I'm pushing jumpers in front of me and Jerry is like a linebacker shoving jumpers out the door. During this commotion, I heard the sound of a very large beer can getting torn in half.

As the jumpers clear the door, I fall forward and reach my arm out of the door, hugging the fuselage so I could see the condition of the tail. I was able to peek around the corner of the door jam and didn't see the horizontal stabilizer. At first it didn't register that there was nothing there. As I was trying to see the horizontal stabilizer, I was thrown against the ceiling of the cabin and was more confused. I rolled over on all fours and lifted my head to get my bearings and was immediately slammed against the floor of the cabin on my back. Again, I rolled over and grabbed the door jamb root and could see out the door far enough to see the tail was gone. We were going for another back loop as the horizon turned counterclockwise off the end of the wing tip. I yelled, GET OUT! and looked up at Greg who was flying his ass off. Feet steering on the rudder, his body hunkered down, with one hand on the stick steering his heart out, and the other hand on the throttle. I yelled again, GREG, GET OUT! He's still flying and I am getting thrown from the ceiling to the floor, on my face, back and forth. I finally got pissed off and yelled, SQUIRREL!!! At that point, he quickly sat up straight and looked over his shoulder at me and I said, Pull the door and get out!

Sitting straight up in the seat, he took his feet off of the pedals, pulled the throttle to idle, and feathered the prop. At this point the airplane was stable on its back. Greg pulled the top emergency door release and then went for the door handle to eject the door. As he pulled the door handle, the emergency door release pin fell closed because we were upside down and he realized what had happened. Then he pulled the door release again and jettisoned the door. I saw him fall on his head because he released his seat belt. At this point I was on my hands and knees heading out of the door, crawling out of the wing, as the plane was still on its back. I figured if he had made it to the point of ejecting the door and releasing his seat belt, he was on his own. As I crawled along the bottom of this inverted wing, I was thinking I wanted to get as far away from the center of the fuselage as possible, AKA the prop. In my mind, I could picture getting off of the airplane and then running into the prop at some point. As I closed in on the halfway point of the wing, I started thinking of all the possibilities of how I would depart from this wing: Stand up and run? Stand up and back flip? Crawl off and hope for a clean break? Dive for the tail that's not there?! Suddenly, I felt as if I was gently picked up and placed on heading with the airplane and in freefall. The airplane was sitting right in front of me on its back and I was looking for my buddy Greg, the guy that didn't want to wear a parachute because he would rather 'ride it in.' The pilot guy that followed checklists for decades, checklists that never said bail out. I was looking for a guy panicking in freefall who was looking for a ripcord or I was looking for a guy frozen in freefall not doing anything. The airplane started doing more back flips as I chased it, still looking for my buddy. Big backflips. Eventually it ended up zipping past me, about 20 yards away (too close), and that's when I pulled to save myself at 3500ft. I watched the airplane lay on its back and in a slow rotation disappear into the clouds with my friend.

    I looked around and saw a few canopies to my left sinking into the clouds, so I assumed that was a good direction to go. After I turned left, I reached up to stow my slider and to my surprise, I found a round pilot canopy above my head. It was Greg and he had beaten me out of the airplane! I was still sad and nervous because I was certain that the jumper that hit the tail was probably more than hurt. I was clearly not going to make it back to the drop zone so I started a slow turn because I was fairly sure I was over some open fields. As I quietly descended, I heard an odd sound behind me. Click, clack. Click, clack. As I looked behind me, I found the source of the eerie sound. It was the horizontal stabilizer that was torn from the fuselage, following me. I decided to just fly away from it and hope for the best. That was a good (lucky) decision because when I popped out of the bottom of the cloud layer, I was heading for the main road. I landed in a feedlot full of cattle and barely made it out of that, almost getting trampled by freaked out cattle. I guess they didn't like the bright pink and blue of my canopy. As I was running from stampeding cattle, I could see Greg's canopy coming down in a corn field and then a big yellow Search and Rescue helicopter circling directly over me with crewmembers huddled in the door pointing at me and where Greg was landing. That spooked the cattle worse.

    I was met at the road by a truck full of jumpers looking for people. I asked if everyone was accounted for and they said, "Yes Greg is walking to another truck now and that's it." I said, "So everyone's OK?! Thank

God!" One of the jumpers in the truck said, "We think so but not for sure." I said, What do you mean? Are all the jumpers okay or not?!"

They said, "You're not going to believe this, but the plane landed in someone's front yard where two little girls were playing." We quickly loaded up and headed to the crash site. There was a crowd of people on the road and parallel to the road, between the front yard and road, there was a ditch. Looking into the yard, with the front porch looking at me, the airplane was laying on its back in the middle of the yard. My friend Scott Kyle embraced me and said, "Thank God you're alright." I asked him about the two little girls and he pointed toward the fuselage and said, "You see that little mattress and the blankets laying three feet from the fuselage and the wing? They were on that mattress under the blanket when the airplane hit the ground. The wings ruptured and doused them with fuel. They are fine, we think. Probably in the shower now."

As I looked at the crash site, I was amazed that the power line connecting the house to the power pole was running diagonally across the yard and over the center point of the fuselage. A complete miracle it was not struck by the plane's wing! Greg showed up shortly after this and walked over with his arms wide open and a big bloody chin and shirt from the chest strap buckle hitting him when his canopy opened. He said, "WILL! My hero!" and hugged me as he told me that I saved his life. Apparently the girls were fine and all the jumpers were walking and fine. The guy that had the premature deployment was pulled from the plane and hit some jumpers on the way by, he pulled some muscles and ligaments in his arms, and he was unconscious for a moment. He also flew and landed the canopy that pulled the tail off back to the drop zone.

Greg and I were pretty banged up and could hardly move our heads from a stiff neck. William Hardman, the acupuncture god, showed up and did an electroacupuncture treatment in a little trailer at the DZ while we drank a bottle of Jack Daniels someone had given Greg for not dying, or for his first jump, not sure which. I asked Greg how he beat me out of the plain.

He said "I don't know man. I remember you ordering me out and I just knew that was it. I pulled the little lever to eject the door and then pulled the door handle. I was thinking to myself I don't know if I'm doing this in the right order but the door isn't going anywhere and I realized the sloppy little lever fell back into the closed position and when I pulled it the second time it released the door. At that point I released my seat belt and was dropped on my head and my legs just naturally fell out the door and I stood up and grabbed the wing strut. I looked in the cabin and saw my Ray-Ban sunglasses and pack of cigarettes laying on the top of the windscreen and thought man I need to get those and I really need a smoke right about now. I started to bend over and then thought wait, I need to go and pulled the ripcord."

We laughed and drank until we realized our necks had loosening up thanks to the treatment from Bill.

After the crash, the Farringtons brought up their Twin Otter and Jeff literally pointed at the Otter, said "have fun," and flew away. Greg looked at me and said, "I guess that's his idea of a check ride."

We spent lots of time together after that, just hanging out or he would take me out flying in his little Cessna 140. Over the years we would drift in and out of touch with each other, but we would always pick up right where we left off like we were never apart. I will miss you though you are still with me. —*William Renfroe*

Norway

In Bird's words

"Norway had a team of happy-go-lucky guys and one of those guys, Bent Laursson, had come to Utah to find out about Jerry Bird, where he was, and what he was doing. He found us in Cache Valley. That's where we had our DC-3, at an airport as big as Zephyrhills but in Utah. So, this guy shows up. He could hardly speak a word of English.

Bent goes, You guys accepted me and I'm on the loads. And the only words I learned to say were, *are we eating, fucking or skydiving*? That's where the "EFS" expression come from: Eat, Fuck, Skydive—the three things you need to survive. Bent Laursson learned English, he jumped with us, and then he went back to Norway to do his thing.

In '79, these guys show up at the World Meet and there's Bent on their team, the Norwegian team. The Norwegians became my friends, and they go, Hey Bird, Bent's been to Utah with you; now we want you to come to Norway.

When I was at the '79 World Meet in France, the Norway team asked me to come the next year and travel around the country to teach skydiving. In the summer of 1980, I get to Oslo and my buddies go, You're not with us this weekend. You're starting up in Stavanger. So, I get back on the train and away I went. And I'm in a country where I don't speak the language. I have nobody I know with me. In Norway they have lots of clubs and everyone pitches in. They pay for an expensive airplane and only jump on the weekend. But they had one Otter in the country and it followed wherever I went. At the club where I was teaching they would take the week off so I would have seven days of jumping with each one.

I'm there to teach skydiving to the whole country. I do my thing, I teach the people, I go to a second place and do the same thing, another drop zone with their club. And so, I'm connecting the dots and I'm the only person in the country that's jumping every day of the week. Everybody else jumps on every other weekend. If the weather's bad, they don't get to jump until next weekend. I'd move my traveling road show over here to this place 500 miles away and I do it again with a twin Otter or with whatever. Sometimes we had good weather and sometimes we had bad weather so at the end of the summer, there's going to be the Norwegian Nationals in Torp, which is a military air force base in Norway. There are a lot of cool things in Norway. Let's say they only have ten F-16 fighter planes in the whole air force. Instead of parking them on the base and have them all bombed and shot up at one time, they let their fighter pilots take them home and put them in their barns. They will be on a place where the road is straight for a mile, their crew come and open the barn doors, push the airplane out on the road, stop the traffic for a mile and the F-16 takes off and he's in the air to defend his country. They're scattered around the country like that, hidden in different places and the pilot and his crew live close by. They don't have them lined up like we did in World War II.

Bent Laurssen, Kal Amund Arneberg and Shoobi Knutson are three members of a great group of skydiving people I became part of while in Norway—the EET, *Elden Er Tænt*, which in Norse means The Flame is Lit. Many get a butterfly and flame tattoo on their left shoulder. The flame attracts beautiful people, and there are, like, 230 of us in the EET family. I was honored to be #55.

Back to my first jump in Norway: I think I'm there and they go, Oh no, we're going further north to little airport called Snåsa. This is summertime, and it's colder than hell. And they have a Cessna 206. They go, There's an instructor putting out his student on his final graduation jump so you go up with them and they'll spot. I go up and realize there's water everywhere and here's this little peninsula and the student's spotting. I finally take a little look and go, well I'd be giving some lefts. There's water forever and the land is over this way. The instructor looks and they go. I watched them jump and thought, man, maybe they know something I don't but they're landing in water.

We go around, I spot, and I land on land not far from the Jeep. The student and the instructor landed in water. The instructor S-folded the canopy around his arms and drowned. The student drug his parachute in with the waves and he was okay. They kicked us off the airport. This is my first jump ever in Norway.

So, I'm traveling around and it's the same in America. After jumping, we'd have a couple beers. And they'd go, you know, it is against the law to drink and drive in Norway so we're going to walk the five miles back to town. It's midnight, it's freezing cold and nobody had a designated driver. Well, that happened about once and I said, Give me the keys. I'll drive. And we got away with it. Not a problem anymore. One of their journalists was a parachutist and I stayed with him and his wife while I was there. He was writing an article or a book about parachuting and quoted me: The best advice I can give your country, for your jumping, is this: Remember, the beer is supposed to be cold and the skydives are supposed to be hot. So, chill your beer and put doors on your airplanes. Oh, you fucking Americans." —*Jerry Bird*

Busted in Norway

"They just took Jerry Bird!"

In Bird's words

"Now it's near the end of the summer of 1980 and I'm on Jerry Bird's Magical Mystery Tour.[88] I had been visiting drop zones all over Norway, and most of the time I didn't know anyone when I first arrived. In those days, relative work was king in the skydiving world, and every day I was teaching someone how to make their first 4-way, taking a student up and making a 2-way with them, demonstrating how to try to launch an 8-way, or whatever. Now it's my last night in Stavanger. As the day ended, someone said, hey, we're having a big party at the club tonight because you're leaving us, so don't expect to get much sleep!

And so the drinking began.

Much, much later, I told the people I'm staying with, Hey I have to catch an airplane in a few hours and so I need to go get my stuff together. By this time the jumpers have all carried their beers out of the clubhouse, because they've been kicked out. It's three in the morning or so, but the few cars and taxis that came by and saw a bunch of drunk skydivers sitting there wouldn't even slow down. I had been staying with Roar Frøiland, so I asked Roar to take his car and sneak out and leave all the drunken skydivers there—they're on their own. Three of us got into Roar's car and tried to sneak out of there, but we didn't make it very far. The car was a little Fiat, and it had a crazy weird shifter, making driving in my condition very difficult. Anyway, when we pulled out of the driveway I was in the driver's seat, but a bunch of people stopped us and climbed in the back, throwing some beers in with them. They called the cases of beers "crates."

---

88. "Magical Mystery Tour" is the title track to the 1967 album by the English rock band the Beatles and the soundtrack to the film by the same name. Paul McCartney and John Lennon wrote the song, alluding to the effects of psychedelic, consciousness expanding drugs. The film is said to be inspired by Ken Kesey's Merry Pranksters who road-tripped around the U.S. doing LSD in a psychedelic painted school bus during the summer of 1964, juxtaposed with McCartney's memories of English people on a coach bus holiday. Steven D. Stark, *Meet the Beatles: A Cultural History of the Band That Shook Youth, Gender, and the World*. New York, HarperCollins; 2005, 218.

Everybody's drunk, but I've got to get to Roar's. So, now we have two guys and two girls in the front, and one of the girls is sitting on my lap. One of us is steering, someone else is shifting, I'm playing with the girl in my lap, and the 5 extra guys are in the back. The road was divided with a cement barrier and the Fiat was sitting so low that the muffler is dragging the ground and we are sparking. Then we saw the police on the other side; they obviously see us too, and everyone goes, Oh fuck!

At that, we immediately pull over to the side of the road and get out of the car. These guys were so drunk that when they got out of the Fiat they just stacked the crates there on the ground and sat down beside them to start drinking again. Not a good first impression for the approaching cops.

Within a few minutes, here come the cops. There's nobody in the car and we're all sitting there drinking beers. And the cop comes to me, and I go, No—me not driving, no speak Norwegian and no have international driver's license, so leave me be. Then the cop starts asking questions to the group. They want to know whose car? Well, of course it's Roar's car and they're going to take the owner of the car in, but we had picked up some girls that weren't part of our little circuit and someone said, The American was driving.

They speak English. They go, here's what's going to happen: You have to go in with us and we have to question you, and we have to see your passport, but everything will be all right.

My friends go, Bird, you have to do it, it's no big deal.

So, I go to jail with this guy. And then the problems start. The first problem is they say to hand over my passport. I never carried my passport around with me when I was jumping or partying. It was hidden somewhere in my room or in my luggage. So, he goes, oh, that's a big problem. We have to know who you are first. You may be one of these wanted Americans we are looking for from Texas.

In 1980 the only way they could give you a sobriety test was to take your blood. They said, we need you to sign this release to give us your blood. And I said, absolutely not. I can't read that. It's in Norwegian and I've already told you I wasn't driving the car. There were nine people out there. You show me how you can get a driver in there with nine people. I don't know how to drive one of those cars. Nobody saw me drive it. You didn't see me driving. I'm not admitting to driving. I'm not taking your blood test. Strike one. They think about that passport. Strike two. Then I said, besides that, I'm a Jehovah's Witness and by my religion I'm not allowed to give my blood. I didn't know whether they believed that or not, but I was giving them another reason why they couldn't do that. I said that I may be a hemophiliac.

They brought another guy in dressed like us and he goes, and you have to have a doctor to draw blood, so the guy comes in this T-shirt looking like somebody woke him out of bed. He goes, I'm your doctor, and I go, I still don't give you permission. I won't sign any papers and I want to speak to the US Embassy. I'm here doing a government job so you guys have no authority over me. I haven't done anything wrong. I'm an American. I said, call the embassy.

The guy goes, Cuff him and put him on the floor. They put one of those pinch moves on me to make you go on the floor and I told the guy you can pinch as hard as you want but I'm not getting down on the ground. Well, they knocked me to the ground, they took my blood and pulled me back up. I'm handcuffed. They don't dab me off or put anything over it and I said something to the guy like, I don't believe you're a doctor and a doctor wouldn't do what you just did. And this guy backhanded me. So, he went down real fast. I just snap-kicked him in the balls. Then they beat me up.

It's been, like, 14 hours and I haven't come out of the jail. Somebody tells my friends, We need his passport. They go to my room and go through all my stuff and find my passport and bring it to the jail. Now it's the next day I've been there what seemed like 24 hours and they brought me to the front and said we have to let you go until the results of blood tests come back but we're going to charge you with assaulting an officer.

He has my passport and he kept tapping me on the nose with it and said we get to keep your passport so you can't get away. When your blood test comes back you are mine in my jail in Stavanger. And they take me out and let me go, but they said you can't leave the country without a passport.

I go ahead and get on another plane and forget about it. I don't even think about my passport. I'm supposed to be at their national championships. I'm a coach, judge, and participant. So, we'd go to Torp, an air force base. We're jumping and I'm coaching their 8-way team and they're winning. They wouldn't let me jump officially in the event, but on the 8-way one of their guys didn't do very well, so they split it to make two 4-way teams. I took the guy's name and jumped as him with the 4-way without telling the officials. They let me enter the accuracy event. I jumped a square parachute by then, and after two rounds I was in second place with a dead center and five centimeters. My 8-way team was winning, my 4-way team was in second place, I'm coaching everybody and everybody's having a great time. I think I've sold a couple of rigs I took with me over there. I'm staying in a travel trailer at the edge of the drop zone.

I land from a skydive and three detectives surround me and say, Your blood tests have come back. We're here to take you back to Stavanger. You're under arrest for drunk driving and assault, and you have five minutes to get your stuff in order.

I've been jumping in a pair of Levi's or shorts. It's summertime over there. I whisper to my group to get all my gear out of that trailer, and then I come back to these guys and they take me to Sandefjord, Norway, outside of Torp and they put me in a holding cell. I'm locked in and can't get out. You could come into the front door of the jail, and you can actually see the people that sit in the lobby right there and the lady at the front desk talked to them. But I was inside of a waiting area, not a prison, and there's other cells upstairs.

She goes, hey, you don't have to worry. I'm just waiting to sort things out here, and then she'd be back on the phone talking in Norwegian. A civilian guy comes in, John Moen, (John, I love you buddy!) John lets me know that the woman is making arrangements to ship me by prison car back to Stavanger. She's not calling the embassy and straightening this out for me. John was a Norwegian Special Forces guy that I knew. And so we're whispering through the bars and John says, if you can get upstairs, maybe you can get away. Then he leaves. And I sat there thinking about this.

At about four or five o'clock there is a shift change. I've been in a temporary cell with no toilet or anything in there. I'm invisible. It's just like being in another office but I'm locked in. So, they changed the shift and I see a new woman come in. I knock on her window and she comes to the window and I go, hey, I've been here all afternoon. I think they're getting ready to let me go, but I really have to go to the bathroom. And she goes, I can let you go upstairs. She takes me upstairs where the police officer's bathroom is.

I go in this bathroom and she's standing there by the door and I say I have to do a number two. I've been here all day, do you mind? She closes the door. I locked the door. Above the toilet there is a little window. I flap it down and the only way I'm able to go out of it is like Superman. I crawl out of it and I'm two and a half stories up and I go out and do it like the half turn. There's a little bit of an awning down there. I busted it. Somebody is at the front door of the police station yelling when they see me jump out of this window. I crawled out and I fell. But I'm okay. As soon as this happens, two guys are running down the sidewalk to where I am and they are after me. Out of nowhere a car pulls up. Just like in the movies the door swings open, a guy goes, Bird get in, and I jumped in the car and away we go.

And this is the start of the great escape."

The Great Escape

"As soon as that happened and they took me off to the drop zone, a lot of the jumpers said, oh man, there's Bird, this is very bad, he automatically goes to jail. An hour later about a dozen cop cars came crashing onto the drop zone and the rumor went around that I had escaped. The cops ran down to the trailer that I had been living in, kicked in the door and went in. It was empty. There wasn't any of my gear, clothes or my money in there and I didn't have any money or anything with me, and I still didn't have a passport. So, Bird's gone, and the people at the drop zone all know it.

The cops set up a dragnet. They know the Norwegian team was part of the escape, so they searched their parent's houses, their grandparents' houses, and they put out an Interpol alert to other Scandinavian countries in the region. The reason for this was that in those countries, the Burgomaster, the mayor, and sometimes the police chief were the same and they've held their job for 30 or 40 or 50 years. Well, in my case, the mayor/police chief of Stavanger had already called his buddy and said, we have that loud-mouth American of yours and we're going to be sending him back to you in a prison car. Then later that day he had to call him back and say, hey, he escaped. I'm the only person who ever escaped from that guy. So he was really mad and they put out a nationwide search.

I was in a third party's car. He's driving the car. He goes, Bird, you can't be in here. I can't be caught with you. They will put me in prison. Now it's jailbreak and you will go to jail for a year. As soon as you jumped out of the jailhouse window it was a totally different crime. So, he ditches the car, they find a car and they soon know who the owner of the car is. He tells them no, I'm at the airport, I wasn't the driver of that car. My car was stolen.

Now, the police have no car, no driver, and when they show up to the airport Bird is gone. The guy who picked me up drove me a couple of minutes and ditched me at a tourist beach resort. I went and mingled with the crowd of people, wearing almost nothing on the beach. I just escaped from jail and had nothing with me, so I go into the bathroom, I find toiletries, razor blades and I shaved my big beard off and cut my hair down as short as I could, like European people have. I stole some of the clothes that were hanging up so I'm no longer wearing a USA shirt, and I started sleeping in the woods right there, because this guy had said hang out, somebody will find you. But they had to put up with harassment from the police for two or three days. They searched everybody's van at the drop zone.

Finally, I got a message from somebody who walked by and said, Be by road sign 22 at midnight tonight.

I don't know who this person is and now they're gone. At midnight a little Volkswagen pulled up, the door opened, I jumped in and away we went. The driver told me they had to hide me for a while. Things are really hot and they'll get into real trouble and they're getting ready to go to the world championships with their 8-way team.

Somebody I don't even know, not one of the members of our team, takes me out in the country and says, you're going to stay with Jorgen Oesten. Jorgen doesn't have a job so I think, oh cool—I will stay with

Jorgen and drink beer, smoke pot all day and hang out. And so, after a few days of this he says that when it cools down, they'll have something. I take care of you. I say to Jorgen; you seem to be doing pretty good out here. Uh, what do you do for a living?

He goes, Me? I'm a bank robber.

Jorgen and the bank robbers were very successful at what they did. They would go to Germany in cars with machine guns and go take money and leave real quick. They would cross the borders with different names and passports and be back home and have the gold and the money and they never got caught and they never hurt anybody. Jorgan told me, you know what, I only have to work one day a year. So, I felt great. I was staying with a bank robber, and I got along good with Jorgen.

Now they had to figure out how to get me out of there. They tell me that the US embassy in Oslo has your passport but if you go there to get a new passport or if you go there and ask for asylum, the first thing they will do is call the police and say, Jerry Bird is at the US embassy trying to get his passport. So, I can't do that, I have to go to another country. My boys figure ok, the nearest country is Sweden. There are border crossings that are checked frequently and then there are the rural ones that aren't. I'm starting to think like the Steve McQueen movie, *The Great Escape*. I can't look like that guy; I can't speak with anyone with other than some Norwegian words I know or just ignore them and act weird. I put little glasses on. So, when we get to the border, they send a car across into Sweden and find that they're just doing the customary look in the car and wave them on through.

Now I'm in a Norwegian or a Swedish car going back to Sweden and I'm in the trunk. They have radio contact and they go, Right now there's only one guy in the booth and this is a real rural area. I don't know the guy who is driving the car, but they get me through and take me near Stockholm and let me out, so now I'm in Sweden with no passport. What do I do? Nobody knows where I am. I decide to go to the Stockholm Embassy. I get there and you know all the US embassies are guarded by US Marines. There is a guy on duty and I walk up and talk to him. He asks me if I need some help. I ask if I can go in there and talk to somebody, I need some help. And this guy is really pretty cool. He told me that they are looking for an American guy, and if I were you I wouldn't go in there.

Thank you. I disappeared from there and didn't go into the Stockholm Embassy.

Now, I remember that I have a friend, Mia Barnett, who moved from Casa Grande AZ to some foreign county. Mia is a skydiver and she had married a Norwegian skydiver. I found and contacted her, and she picked me up at a railroad station. Her husband is away but I know him too, so everything is good. I'm at her house and after a few hours she goes, Hey Bird, I'm getting a really bad feeling about this. You know I'm over here on an exchange program and I'm going to get in big trouble if I get caught.

She tells me I have to get out of there. She takes me down to their local train station and I get on the train to Malmo. Malmo is across the border from Copenhagen, Denmark. This was in 1980.

When I get to Malmo, I realize there is a crossing to get to Copenhagen, and in the morning, there are like 10,000 businessmen going across and there's a high-speed hydrofoil. I talked to somebody, and he said they have customs officers where the ferry comes in and maybe there's a bridge there, but on the hydrofoil, they just wave at you. So, I go and buy a newspaper, roll it up like the business guys do and try to look like them. I got on the hydrofoil and rode that over to Copenhagen, got off and walked right past customs, *Gud Dag*, and keep going and now I was in Denmark. I still didn't have a passport but now comes the fun part.

I needed to find a place to stay. Copenhagen used to be a lot like Haight Ashbury in San Francisco. There is a central park called Christiania and inside the park were all the hippies and drug users and prostitutes and other people that were living for free in buildings. It was like a city with a wall around it. I went in there and fit in just perfect, and within a day I had made friends with a bunch of people. I helped a young girl that was overdosing, and I took her to the heroin clinic. After a day or so, all the people around me knew that I was the guy who had helped her. I'd be sitting there, and somebody would come along and give me a beer or a sandwich or something. So, I'm trying to figure out my next move and I'm sitting in Christiania in Denmark at night, hiding. I don't look like Jerry Bird anymore, but a guy comes along and says, Bird, I've been looking all over for you man. I have all your money and your gear and your stuff. Your buddies from Norway have been down here and they said, Bird will find you or you'll eventually find him.

The next challenge was to find out how to get into Germany without a passport, because when you're in Denmark, you're still in the Scandinavian Interpol connection. You're still within their sphere of influence. So, I gotta get out of Scandinavia, and then I'm away from Scandinavia and Interpol. Basically, it was pretty easy. I took a train out, got off the train before the border, walked a few miles through the woods and into Germany, then went into the station and got on the train inside of Germany. I went to the US Embassy in Dusseldorf. I go in and they ask me, What's your problem?

I don't have a passport.

Did you lose it or was it stolen?

Wellll . . . really neither one of those.

Do you know where it is?

Yeah, I know exactly where it is.

They said, Well, either way, if it's lost or stolen, you have to go to the police department.

I said, Those are the guys that I'm trying to stay away from. I asked if I could see an attaché.

The attaché comes out and says, Come with me.

We go in a private room and I said, Hey, I'm an American citizen, I'm a U.S. Green Beret and I was trained by you guys. These guys assaulted me in Norway. I escaped and I need a passport.

He says, Let me check on it. When he comes back, he says, Yeah, they have your passport in Oslo. That passport is no good anymore. How did you do it?

I said I went through an escape and evasion course and I knew I was going to get in deep trouble, be put in jail for a year, get the hell beat out of me or both if I got caught. So, the idea when I left was not to get caught. The great escape for me was traveling through Norway, Sweden, Denmark, and into Germany without a passport.

The attaché says, Give me ten bucks and get your picture taken over there. Here's your new passport and don't go back to Norway.

Every year my friends in Norway would send that Burgomaster a Christmas card or call him and go na na-nanana—Bird got away!

I didn't go back to Norway after that. But my friends there didn't forget me and I didn't forget them."

Post Script:

"To finish the story, about 15 years later, I'm in Toogoolawah, Queensland, Australia. It's nighttime and we're sitting around the fire, people are playing didgeridoos, it's a great club over there, The Ramblers. A fellow walks up and says, Bird, do you remember me? It's dark and he speaks English a little bit different from the Australian English. And I go, no. He says, I'm Pauly Hansen, I was the driver of the car that got you out of Norway. I never saw him again after that.

Twenty years later I saw Mia Burnett for the first time since that, here in Zephyrhills, and she said, Bird, the police were at my house that very day because I was listed as an American skydiver living in Sweden. By then they were running down any contacts to see if I made it out of Norway. But I wasn't there, and I didn't leave any tracks.

The EET 36-way at a Herc Boogie in Sweden, about 1990. Courtesy of Karina Kaiser.

Karina's logbook diagram of that dive, signed by EET members including Jerry Bird #55. Courtesy of Karina Kaiser, pictured, and her husband Pete Reynolds, known to skydivers as Wally Gubbins, star of Leo Dickinson's copyrighted film series.

My Scandinavian friends risked a lot to help me. The EET skydiving group helped me escape and they were so generous years later in contributing to our Go Fund Me campaign for expenses related to my son's treatment and care for glioblastoma. I am grateful and humbled by their support. Elden Er Tænt, the flame is lit.

—*Jerry Bird*

Although Bird had flown the coop, many Norwegian skydivers flocked to Florida and to boogies around the world to jump with their friend Jerry Bird.

Boogies, Boogies, Boogies!

Iceland Beer Boogie

Jerry Bird is a good friend. I invited him to organize at the Beer Boogie, my home in Iceland, June 1989 . . . —*Siggi Baldursson*

In Bird's words

"I was invited to go to Iceland. One of my Icelandic friends, Runar, had a brother who was a pilot, a captain at the time, for Icelandic Air. That's the airline I flew. One time, flying to Iceland, I didn't have a seat on the Baltimore to Iceland leg. Runar's brother, the captain, says, Come with me, and I board.

Back then stewardesses were young and cute and the one on this flight was none of the above. She didn't like me sitting there in my Florida flip flops and shorts and T-shirt. But shortly the cabin filled up and she said, There's no room for you.

So, the pilot comes along and he sits me in first class. Now I'm sitting up there with the uppity ups. It takes them awhile to finish loading the airplane. Finally, the last guy comes and I'm in his first class seat. Well, to the chagrin of my favorite stewardess at the time, the pilot says, There's only one other seat left on the airplane. Come into the cockpit.

This is before 9/11, so I moved to the cockpit where they have an observer jump seat. It is raining and pouring cats and dogs and we're at Baltimore/Washington International and there are airplanes backed up everywhere, taking a real long time to take off and all the time and he's watching me getting prepared. I knew how to travel European. I've got some snacks, I've got a book and all of the amenities.

We finally get through to the taxi line, we take off and we go through this horrible rainstorm and break out of it at 30,000 feet. Now we're headed to Iceland. And he turns around and says, Up and out of there, and do you have any Tums? My stomach's not feeling good.

Of course I had some Tums, I always traveled with them. So, we switched seats. I'm in the captain's seat and he's in the jump seat. In the jump seat, you could almost lay down and take a nap. A little bit later he has my blanket and my book and my Tums and my candy and he's napping.

Now I'm in the captain's seat, so every time my favorite stewardess comes into the cockpit, I had to order something. I am a pilot, but this is a Boeing 767. We're out in the middle of the ocean, and over there to the left, there's Greenland where somebody out in some weather station or radio station, probably somebody from the Navy or Air Force sitting in a hut somewhere and they're giving air traffic control to somebody every hour or hour and a half. The pilot says, If you want to talk to the guy on the ground, he'd probably love to talk to you.

I say, Greenland One down there, how you doing today? This is Iceland 267.

And he goes, Yeah, I see you up there on my radar.

And I go, Hey, I'm on the way to Iceland and I'm going skydiving. We just carry on a regular conversation like we're in the same room.

When I start going out of his range he says, Okay, signing off. See you later. Have a good trip.

So, we crossed the Atlantic with me at the controls.

As we get close to Iceland in the morning, the sun's in my eyes coming up out of the East. The pilot says, See out there on the horizon where those clouds are? There is Iceland.

I look at the fuel gauges, and go, Yeah, what if there's one of those weather things going on in Iceland?

He goes, We land.

I go, There is an alternate airport we can be vectored to, right?

He says, No.

About five minutes out he gets up and does his stretches, washes his hands and says, Get out of my seat. He sits down and says, I like this guy, fuck the auto pilot, shut that off. I'm in charge here. Through the clouds we break out over the runway and land perfectly. And there I am in Iceland, right up there near the Arctic Circle, land of the midnight sun.

I did two boogies. The first one was a beer boogie in Fludir. Well, it's bad weather, there's always bad weather in Iceland, so we weren't jumping. But then at that time you got to meet the people and you realize, man, they live a great life here. They have geothermal heat which generates everything they need. The people sitting here on an iceberg, have a hot house, growing tomatoes and strawberries and fresh fruits and vegetables on an iceberg. Next to that, they have their hot tub or sauna and their house is heated through and through by the steam coming out of the ground. You know, if it ever got hot on the outside, they have the glacier out there for air conditioning. Open the windows. And they are very, very clean. You didn't see any litter and essentially no crime. Almost all are related to each other, it's very homogeneous. What a beautiful society.

But the reason they called it a Beer Boogie was because during prohibition they had banned alcohol in Iceland and they had never rescinded that law. Now, beer was going to be legal in Iceland again, so they called this the Beer Boogie.

We go outside of Reykjavik and into the country. Once you leave the major city, it's barren for a long way. But there was a place out there with a hotel and a restaurant, one tree and an airport. That was where we were going to have our first International Beer Boogie in Iceland. Everybody stayed at the hotel, there was nowhere else to go. We socialized in the little town there and they held events for us. But the weather was bad.

And then amazing things happened. They didn't have a jump airplane there so the airline company (which these guys had a connection to because their father was vice president of Icelandic Air and they are all captains), sends out a brand-new Twin Otter and the Twin Otter has the clam shell door for passengers to get in and out. The pilot says, You know, we have to take that door off for you to use it. So we do that.

All Otters today have inflight doors that you could open, but back then they did not. So, now we're in Iceland and we said, well, in certain places we learned for a Beechcraft you rig a piece of plywood for the door and you're blocked from the wind. (Later they built these slide up doors, like garage doors and it's made out of Plexiglass so you still see out.)

But the pilot goes, No, no, that's against the rules. I can't have a piece of plywood back there flying around after you guys exit. So, we take off flying and I realize we are over a valley where the airport is and we're flying out over what looks like the moon. And somebody tells me, oh by the way, that's where the moon vehicle, Lunar Rover was tested. And I'm going, well, shouldn't the pilot be headed back over, like stay over the airport or over the valley? And just about that time—bop bop bop bop—and one engine has a problem. The pilot, who's not a jump pilot says, Everybody out! I look out the door and I went, Not a chance. Glide this thing, descend and go back over to the valley. He does that and we all jumped out and he lands and I thought, okay, in just a little bit the airplane would be fixed. Brand new airplane, brand new engine, fried. They had to come out and swap out airplanes, then the boogie continued. But that was jump number one where they tried to put me out over the moon, and I think, okay, don't trust pilots that don't fly jumpers.

What was the best advice I could give their country about skydiving? Don't freeze to death by the time you get the altitude. Put flight doors on your airplanes.

So, now we're in Fludir and it's daylight 24 hours a day.

I thought it was a free beer boogie, but we find out that beer in Iceland turns out to cost about $7 to $9 a bottle. Siggi would walk around and hand you a beer and check you off the list to make sure you got your free beer every day. It was putting him out of business, because it turned out the beer company didn't give him the beer. But during the midst of all this, somebody said, Blue Sky and everybody quit what they're doing and went back to the airport. It was probably two o'clock in the morning, if you were using a watch. People out there don't wear watches. They come outside when the weather's good, when the sun's shining. The people and their grandmothers came out of their houses and we went to airport and started jumping, doing tandem jumps and everything. The only minor thing was that the wind was blowing. I think we had about a hundred people there and on this one day they say, Bird, this is Iceland. If we don't jump now, we don't get to jump.

So, we jumped a whole boogie and let's be conservative right now and say 20-plus mile per hour winds and nobody got hurt and some people even made their first jumps during that boogie.

Beer Boogie dive, 1989. Siggi Baldursson, photographer.

Jumping at Fludir, the airplane story, jumping in winds and a beer boogie—what a great time we had there! On the last day when it was time for me to go back to the airport to catch my flight home, Runar says, I'll fly you to the airport in my Cessna.

When you land at an international airport, you're supposed to pay a fee. Well, when we land there he gets a flat tire on his airplane which was a Cessna 180. I think, oh hell, but what he did was to stop on the international side right next to Icelandic Air. I thank him, say goodbye, get out of his airplane and get on Icelandic Airlines without even going through customs or going into the airport.

That's how I went to Iceland one time, but to put another wrinkle on all those stories, with all the love, there's always a tragedy somewhere. The people of Iceland are brothers and sisters to me and we had a great time and they took great care of me. They paid me, they flew me, they fed me. One day I was where Runar and his wife lived, and they had a daughter named Cristiana. He said she was named for his brother, who is not with us. He went away.

Later, when Runar was working and I was staying in Reykjavik, his wife and the daughter took me to a park up on the hill. Out front was this big sort of rock sculpture. We go up to look and there's a plaque on it—it was a poem in Icelandic, and the daughter interprets it for me:

This is a story about two young men who went away searching their dream and their dream was to conquer Everest. They were Icelandic and were pilots and they went to Nepal and while climbing Mount Everest, they disappeared.

The poem was very beautiful and it's about a son who went away and never returned. But the sad part of the story was the father never gave up and he went and rented all the helicopters they could and did searches. He went to South Africa and rented a 727. He spent the family fortune, so to speak, flying around Everest, looking for his son. Finally people had to tell him, Captain Runar, your son is gone. We won't rent you any more helicopters or any more aircraft.

So, the memorial is about Runar's family and his brother, Christian; a young man who went away chasing his dream, never to return. Not about death at all." —*Jerry Bird*

Stars Down Under

Brian Standring

"Brian 'Sooty' Standring is, without a doubt, an Australian skydiving legend," wrote Jo Parkinson in Australia's *Parachutist* Magazine, 2014. "If you haven't met and/or partied with Sooty in the past forty years, where have you been? He has been a constant presence at Hillman Farm Skydivers since before the World War II runway was cleared, and the club was born in 1975.

Sooty jumped as a member of the Hereford Park Club in England and after his 100th jump, joined the British Army Parachute Regiment at the age of 21. He graduated to their Red Devils Freefall Team in 1969.

Sooty moved to Australia in the early 1970s after finishing his time in the army. With a crew of like-minded skydivers he went to Darkan in 1974 to start a new club. In the process they got into some strife with the Australian Parachute Federation for not going through the proper channels to start the club (but it wouldn't be a good Sooty story without some strife).

When the Hillman Farm Skydiving Club got off the ground in 1975, Sooty became the club's first Chief Instructor. Over the past 40 years, Sooty has been Chief Instructor, Club President, Maintenance Man, Barman, and all-round larrikin. He has also won the Club's Sherman Award (awarded for the year's biggest fuck-up) on at least one occasion. Sooty loves people, loves to skydive and loves to party.

Over the course of Sooty's life, he has been a skydiver, power plant worker, caravan repairer, shearer, farrier, foster parent and carer for people with disabilities. Along the way, he has mentored and inspired so many people, including skydivers, with his wisdom and tales."

—*Jo Parkinson.*[89]

In Bird's words

"In 1977 I received an invitation from the Hillman Farm Skydiving Club in Perth, Australia. Each December, which is their summer, they would throw a big Christmas party and use their club money to pay for it and they invited me to do a Christmas camp with them. I invited Mike Hurran, my best friend at the time, to go with me. We flew to Perth, Australia and met a great group of people including Sooty Standring, the guy who was in charge.

We flew from Perth into the countryside, away from civilization, where there was an old military runway with a Quonset Hut. They had a cook to run the kitchen and the bar. I had a camper to stay in during the meet. It was a two week camp and during that time, we immersed ourselves in skydiving. Everyone jumped about five times a day and I catered to each jumper's level, whether they had 5 jumps or 500 jumps.

I broke them into the groups. There was a classroom aspect of it where I would do instruction and debriefs. I learned everyone's name and kept notes on each jumper. We did this for about a week when they said we were taking a break for Christmas. We closed down the camp

---

89. Jo Parkinson, "Sooty Standring and Hillman Farm Skydivers," *Australian Skydiver Magazine*, Issue 73 Vol. 5; 201.

and went back to Perth and stayed in a hotel but as a club, we all hung out together. The Perth Cup Horse Race was on and was one of the big events of the year, a national pastime. You could go into a cigar store or wherever and bet on the races.

There was a famous horse running that day and the odds-on favorite to win. When I bet, I don't bet on the favorite. I might win, but I wouldn't win enough money to make it worth the bet. After placing our bets, we went back to the hotel to watch the race. Part way through the race, the favorite went down, broke its leg, and everybody was bummed out. They brought the meat wagon out to the track and hauled the horse away. I had bet on the long shot and I won about $400 on my $10 bet that day.

After Christmas, we left Perth and went back to our military camp. We were trying to make the biggest formation ever made in Perth. We flew a Twin Bonanza and a Cessna in formation which are not really compatible. Our plane would take the lead and when the other plane caught up and was passing us, we jumped out. We made a 16-way and that was a record in Australia in 1977. The good jumpers were back East in Melbourne making the national championships but the Perth guys had decided to stay home and bring me there for the camp.

By the time the two weeks were up we had set a record—and most of the skydivers had made more jumps in those two weeks than they had ever made in that time period. When we finished, I gathered everyone around and gave them a personal written critique. I gave one person Rookie of the Year. He showed up here with 20 jumps and at the end of the camp I was putting him on the good loads. I made a personal written critique for everybody who was in that camp and signed it and gave it to them. It was a one page debrief about my experience jumping with them, how they did, and what they should improve on.

Two guys I remember were brothers who I nicknamed the Midget Brothers. Everybody thought that was funny because nobody else could say that, but I got away with it. I gave the "Sheepherder" my leather helmet that I wore and I was told that 30 years later it was still his most prized possession. Another guy I met was Russ Thornton who was known as the Tattoo Man. When he was growing up, his brother was learning how to do tattoos. Russ was covered from head to toe in tattoos, compliments of his brother who he now wanted to strangle. Russ was a good guy, and I ran into him again when he came to the States.

Mike Hurran was a great instructor too. A lot of people told me, Bird, your mate was a really great guy. Everybody liked Mike. He was tall, blonde and handsome—my best friend at the time. I couldn't possibly have pulled off the Camp and Boogie without him." —*Jerry Bird*

Sweden's Hercules Boogie

Anders Nyqvist

The Hercules Boogies in Sweden took place in 1982, 1985, 1987, 1989, 1991, 1993, 1995, 1997, 2000, 2002 and 2004—eleven magical and world class events. All the boogies were organized and run by the nonprofit Gothenburg Parachute Club. Load organizers varied from boogie to boogie: Jerry Bird, Jack Gregory, Derek Thomas, Roger Ponce de Leon, and others from the U.S. and of course organizers from Sweden, Norway and Finland.

Jerry at the Hercules Boogie, 1991. Jack Gregory, photographer.

The C-130 aircraft belong to the Swedish Air Force; load masters were always from the military special forces. There was very nice and smooth cooperation between civil skydivers and military forces.

Jerry Bird attended as one of the load organizers at several of these events. He also held seminars and spread good vibes in general—as always! —*Anders Nyqvist*

Kjartan Reithhaug

I had my trailer adjacent to Jerry's when we were both organizing at the 1993 Herc Boogie. Coffee together every morning. He had seen me launching 8 and 12-ways with groups of freshers and wondered how I did it. He made me demonstrate it in the hangar in the evening. "But you're Jerry Bird. How can I teach you anything?"

He replied, "If I didn't look for advice from others, I wouldn't be this good."

I was flabbergasted. We became really good friends that week. —*Kjartan Reithhaug*

Jack Gregory

I had been load organizing at the language Herc Boogies in 1985, '87, '89, and '91—the first year Jerry load organized there. And I had been working at Z-hills since the early 1980s when Jerry moved there. We worked together as DZ load organizers for years. So, it was just another day at work, albeit with a really cool jump plane and tons of wonderful Scandinavian friends—many who were regular winter jumpers at Z-hills.

At this boogie we mostly organized separate groups sent to us by manifest. The photo occurred when Jerry was ready to go up and I was on the ground with a group ready to go on the next load. I caught his attention over the noise while waving my 35mm camera. Jerry just struck that pose.

1991 was the last Herc Boogie for me because I took the job of USPA Director of Safety & Training in May 1992. —*Jack Gregory*

The North Shore of Oahu's Dillingham Field as seen under canopy, 2011. Sascha F. Schindler, photographer. Sascha Schindler made his first jump under a round canopy in 1986 with the military. He served 12 years as an Airborne Ranger before becoming a civilian skydiver. A tandem instructor and AFF instructor/examiner, Sascha has over 20,000 jumps and has been with Skydive Hawaii for more than 25 years.

Party in Paradise

"I value Jerry Bird's contribution to Party in Paradise and more importantly, his friendship over the years." —*Frank Hinshaw*

In Bird's words

"Party in Paradise was a boogie that took place on the North Shore of Oahu in January or February when it was wintertime on the mainland. This was a great opportunity to bring your wife or girlfriend, go to the North Shore to jump and vacation in Hawaii. I started going to that boogie in the '80s and had many friends there. It was a small community of jumpers and many of them were very accomplished and would come to the to the mainland to participate in the big dives.

Roger Ponce [de Leon] and I organized the meet. We jumped at Dillingham Airfield, at the point of the North Shore where the runway runs alongside the beach at sea level. It's about 12,000 feet long because in World War II, heavily loaded bombers took off from there. Skydiving

Invitation for Party in Paradise.

began there in the '60s. It was a government airfield that had an access road that went around the airport outside of the fence, so you could rent land from the government and do a through-the-fence operation. You could meet the airplane, put your jumpers on it, take off there and land at the end of the runway. Because the runway was so long, they usually took off in one direction and the planes would turn out to sea before they ever got close to the other end of the runway. They let us land inside the fence at the end of the runway and then we walked through the gate back over to where the parachute club was. It was a lucrative business and there were three parachute operations in a row.

One of my great friends there was Frank Hinshaw, the owner of Skydive Hawaii, the biggest, the best and the longest established club there. Legends on the island were Clarence Lopez, and one of their great instructors was a guy we called Papa Dopp, Richard Dopplemeyer.

I invented a game that I took with me on my travels. It involved a ring on a string. I would screw a hook into a board and swing the ring and try to hang it on the hook. I used to be able to make the hook on the first try. The guys on the North Shore liked to gamble so I would put a dollar bill in a cup. You would only get five throws. If you put the ring on the hook the first throw, everybody had to double up and pay you. But if you make it on the fourth try and nobody else made it, you would get the money. Each year when I returned, there were more guys that wanted to play the game. I had a camaraderie going at the North Shore.

One of the times I went there, I was riding in Guy Banal's Volkswagen bus and as we pulled up in front of the skydiving operation, a guy came out in the road, put up his hands and stopped the VW bus. I asked, Who's that? He goes, That's Big Bill Boyd, you'll like him.

Big Bill Boyd was a man of color, and he was a Marine Recon, probably a Master Sergeant. He was 6 foot, 6 inches, 240 pounds. He came over to me, laid a big kiss on my cheek and said, Bird, you're going to like me. He was selling flowered pants and he wanted to give me a pair because he said, If you wear them, then everybody will want a pair and buy them. So, the next day, I was out there wearing his flowered pants.

One morning, an early jump was planned for a special day of some sort—I don't remember what—with four people jumping out of a Cessna. Bill Boyd showed up, but I believe his rig wasn't packed so he used one of the student rigs. Sometimes when you jump a Cessna, they want everybody to launch at the same time and one of the positions is on the strut that we used to go out and hang on. They had Bill Boyd sit on the strut so he could dive straight off. The rig he had on was too small for him and when he was sitting there, hunched over, the reserve pin either came out or he broke the loop on the reserve and the reserve opened. It went out over the top of the wing, pulled him over the airplane, he hit the tail and streamered into the water. His son was on his surfboard in the ocean and paddled out and put his dad on the surfboard and brought him back to shore. That was how Bill Boyd died.

Bill Boyd was a warrior. Anybody who knew him said he was the guy you wanted on your team to fight alongside with. Everybody said what a great man he was and the way he died was a tragedy. Today his son is an officer in the Marines, a very fine man." —*Jerry Bird*

Bill Boyd had been Richard "Dopp" Dopplemeyer's first jump instructor. Richard recalls in 2025, that he only had five jumps when Bill Boyd died, after which he quit skydiving for a year. Later, Richard taught Bill's son to jump. He took Bill's widow on a tandem to scatter his ashes on the twenty year anniversary of his death.

"During the early years, there were some old school buses parked near the bushes and people camped out in them. GW had a bus there. He was a fun-loving guy who lived on the North Shore of Hawaii. He always wanted to jump with us. GW had been in Vietnam, Special Forces, a Green Beret officer. He was also known as "Sky" Lightning Bolt Smith. He went to helicopter flight school and became a pilot of a Special Forces Guns Ship.

GW had a prosthetic eye from being shot in the head. Those fake eyes wear out after a while, so he would give them to people as necklaces. He gave me one. GW was First Lieutenant Gerald W. Doht, Vietnam Helicopter Bronze Star Hero.

Skydive Hawaii was the largest, most successful club there and next to it was a big rock with a plaque on it. There was also a tiny cabin that was called "Switzerland." It was between two competing drop zones.

Anybody could hang out in the neutral area and not get in trouble with either drop zone.

There were a lot of great skydivers on this small island. There were three people that made Swoop Teams around the world. Clint Clausen, Shaylan Allman and JC Colclasure were world-class swoopers and really great tandem masters. You had to be a big dog to be a tandem master at Skydive Hawaii. Cruise ships came in with 120 Japanese who had made arrangements to do Tandem Jumps. They had the capability to do that there and the Japanese were very organized. The first group of twenty met outside their hotel at eight o'clock in the morning and the club bus would pick them up and take them from Honolulu to the drop zone, which was about a one hour drive. During that time, using an interpreter, they would watch a video on how to do a tandem, get a briefing and sign the waivers. When they got to the drop zone, they got off the bus, put on their tandem harness and were ready to go. The empty bus would head back to Honolulu to pick up the next group. When it got back to the drop zone, the first group had made their jumps and were shuttled back to the hotel. They shuttled back and forth all day like that. It was not unusual for Skydive Hawaii to make 100 tandem jumps in one day. These guys, these tandem masters, were really, really skilled.

During one of the boogies, it was storming. There was a partially built building, two floors high, with no roof on it. The roofing material and the sheet metal was on the ground, and we were all standing around with no shelter. I said, I'm not a professional contractor, but I am MacGyver, so we hatched a plan. We went to town and bought some 16-foot-long boards that we put bolts through. We picked up these sheets of metal and belayed them up to the roof on the leeward side of the building in the rainstorm. These were young guys who were skiers and rock climbers and carpenters, so they climbed up there and during the rainstorm we roofed their building. Not me, I just organized. it. You have to put your ceiling tape down before you overlap the tin. A guy would be on the top with somebody else holding a rope and he'd just slide down the roof, put the tape down until he got to the edge, and they'd stop him and pull him back up.

After two days, we had a roof on that building, and everybody had a dry place to go.

One of the owners of the rival drop zone was Patrick de Gayardon, a World Champion and Skydiving Hall of Fame member. One year he was named the "Skydiver of the Year." [1991 *Skydiving* Magazine.] Patrick did freefall wearing skis or riding a sky surfboard, and he designed and developed the first modern wingsuit.

Patrick was always modifying his wing. One time after he landed, he decided the flexible deflector between his legs was loose and needed adjusting, so he took out his needle and thread, and without opening his container, he restitched the flap under there between his legs to the bottom of his container and then he went back up and jumped. He didn't realize that when he was sewing, he got two lines in the loop so when this main parachute opened, those two lines were stitched to the container and consequently, his main parachute malfunctioned. When he did his cutaway, since it was sewed to his container, it didn't leave. His only other choice was to pull his reserve. He did, but his reserve entangled with the main and he died right there in the field behind the two businesses.

I was scared jumping there a couple of different times. Every once in a while, the wind switched directions and what Hawaiians call the Kona Winds blew in. When that happened, you had to jump at the opposite end of the airport because the airplanes had to take off from the end where you normally jumped from. So, you would jump and land at the other end. The locals wouldn't jump when the winds changed, but the haoles, the visiting skydivers, didn't think there was a problem. Well, if you missed, there weren't many places to land. There was a little landing area at the end of the runway and a very small area outside, or you could land on the beach. This was before the GPS spotting systems that are used today. I was told, You don't get to spot because you aren't a local. One of our instructors will spot the load for you.

The surfers in Hawaii know that if there is a cutaway and you go find the canopy that was cut away, you get a reward. If you return a main parachute from a tandem, it might be a hundred and fifty dollar reward. One lady had landed way out in the ocean and after about 30 minutes, everyone had been accounted for except for her.

She later told me, I am in my forties and I'm overweight, I'm actually a trauma nurse. I knew that in these big waves, I couldn't survive if I tried to swim to shore so I rolled over in my back and started floating. The waves would come along and put me fifteen feet under, and I had to work my way back to the surface. She had cut away her rig and two different times while she was underwater, she met her canopy again and it tried to wrap around her. She had to free herself because the current was taking her and her canopy in the same direction. It was getting late in the day, and they couldn't find her from the air. She said, My savior showed up. A kid on a big surfboard paddled up beside her, put her on and took her back to shore.

Even after I quit jumping, my friend Frank Hinshaw and his wife Mary still sponsored me to come back to the North Shore where my buddy, GW lived, even though he wasn't jumping anymore. We hung out together and he was like my patron saint. He took me to Haleiwa, the little town there, for breakfast every day. I stayed there for four months and between Frank and GW, they never let me pay for a meal, period. GW bought my breakfast every day. It was not cheap to live on the North Shore. With my pension and free housing, I still couldn't afford to live there. But we had a lot of adventures there and Frank and I always had a great time.

One of the last times I was there I became friends with Herb, who was on the staff. He wanted to buy a bus and live on the drop zone. He found a Blue Bird bus, like I have, for sale and we took a look. He bought it and he drove it back to the drop zone. He was so proud of it. A few weeks after I left, Herb did a hook turn as he was landing on the beach, he hit a palm tree and it killed him. He just cut it too close, trying to land on the beach. If you spotted long, there was a polo field that they reluctantly let you land on because you would scare the horses if they were playing polo. On one side was a little beach next to the water. If you were an expert, you could land there.

On one of my visits, JC Colclasure was getting married. At the end the day, after doing all their work jumps, the wedding party was going to jump and land on the beach by the Polo ground. All the Tandem Masters were involved in the jump. I was invited on the jump but l passed. The wedding party included JC and his pregnant wife, parents, in-laws, a grandmother and they are all jumping in wedding clothes. There were world-class Tandem Masters carrying this party. The winds were 20–30 miles per hour. Everyone landed on that little beach where there were people who grabbed them as they landed. Nobody fell down, nobody was hurt and nobody landed in the water. I said, What a demo jump! Only those Big Dogs (tandem masters) could have pulled off a jump like that.

I went there many times and knew all the regular skydivers who jumped there. I'm still great friends with my brothers at Skydive Hawaii and love them dearly. When we had a Party in Paradise Boogie, people came from around the world. I have great memories." —*Jerry Bird*

Equinox Boogie

Australia 1996 and 1998

In Bird's words

"During my travels around the world, I met Dave McEvoy—Mac the Macca. He had a drop zone in Toogoolawah, Queensland, and he invited me there, it was in the mid-'90s.

Macca at 69 years of age.

Their club, The Ramblers, had rented land in farmers' fields until they got evicted and had to move. Eventually, they bought about 100 acres in the middle of nowhere, put in a dirt air strip and set up their own version of a skydive ghetto. There were some permanent buildings and a lot of RV's and campers parked there plus two separate bars and a swimming pool. There was no reason to leave the drop zone as everything you needed was right there. The airplane they jumped from was a modern turbine aircraft, a Cessna Caravan. It was a self-contained skydiving environment with, at times, over a hundred people living there. They put on the Equinox Boogie where jumpers came from all over Australia. I met up with some skydivers from my Hillman Farm days, some of whom were now champion skydivers.

The Ramblers put on a heck of a party. There was something going on every night. In the morning I would go up to Macca's place for coffee or breakfast and he would entertain us with his saxophone. There were exotic birds, parrots and macaws all over the place. Out in the field were kangaroos jumping around. At night they liked to party and drink beer in their two bars. The cook in their restaurant would fix special meals for me. They had packers and a cameraman. The Australians are very robust and energetic. It reminded me a little bit of the Old West. They had good attitudes and if someone's car was not running, a guy would walk up and say, Excuse me, mate, I know how to fix that. Let me do that for ya.

The Ramblers were always singing and they put on a talent contest at night. There was music and juggling and a Mountain Man from New Zealand put on a one man show that had everybody in stitches. We were in the middle of nowhere and having a theater production.

One morning, I was hanging out on Dave's second floor balcony when a guy on the ground walked up. He was so tall, we were almost looking at each other eyeball to eyeball. He was a retired NFL football player by the name of Forrest Blue, an all-pro center with the San Francisco 49ers and the Baltimore Colts. Now he was a skydiver and had come to the boogie to jump with me. He was a nice man and a gentle giant. We became friends and he used to send me Christmas cards. Crazy Dave Rutger had moved to Australia and he came up to the Equinox Boogie and helped make big-ways.

Forrest Blue

Rob and Mary White and Rob Paley, who I had known from the Zephyrhills drop zone 15 years before were there. One evening we went to town for a pub crawl. It had one street and it looked like an old western town with wooden buildings and facade fronts. In one restaurant, you could order a steak that would fill your plate.

Australians loved to play games. One of the games we played had teams of two people and a glass of beer. The goal was to see how far one person could take the beer from the starting line, using the other person on your team as a bridge. Usually a big strong tall guy would be the bridge. Only his hands and feet could touch the floor. He would arch, almost like he was doing a push up and the second person, usually a small girl, crawled across the 'bridge' then leaned over as far as she could and set the beer down. Only one hand was allowed to touch the floor. Then she had to crawl backwards across the person without touching the floor. If they fell over, it didn't count. I'm not the biggest person, so when it was my turn, I used a woman who did fire and rescue as my bridge. She was stronger than I was. She knelt down and made a bridge and I climbed over her. Everybody thought that was hilarious. We didn't win.

I loved the people and I learned a little bit about the Aborigines and how they survived. They would walk across the land in a row and pick up anything that was edible—animals, snakes, berries and roots. They always carried a staff, and they would stand on one foot and rest the other one. That way they would only burn one foot on the hot sand.

Hanging out and jumping with the Ramblers at the Equinox Boogie was definitely one of the most fun Boogies I have been to. Ramblers Forever!" —*Jerry Bird*

World Boogie in Bali

In Bird's words

"I took a trip with BJ's World Team to the Island of Bali in Indonesia, the party place. There's an international airport there called Denpasar. BJ had his captains around the world sign everybody up for the big Boogie in Bali with four Hercules, and a Transall, which is a two engine Hercules, essentially performing the same. For a flat price you got all the jumps you could make while you were there—as quick as you could pack and get on an airplane.

Our group met BJ in LA and flew the Indonesian Airline, Garuda Air. We probably put 200 people on this L1011 filling up First Class and Coach. Since I was one of the organizers, I was in first class. They pumped a lot of gas because we had to fly a long way. It can stay in the air for 14 hours. After a while, the pilots got bored, everybody was bored. John Robbins was playing his sax. Everybody loved us, except for the stewardess. You know, Bring us more beer! Guys were sleeping on the floor. So, late at night I asked the stewardess to tell the pilot that I wanted to see him. I pulled out one of my old cards with a picture of the DC-3 on it and Jerry Bird, President and pilot of Pacific Utah. I asked her to give it to the captain. Next thing I know, I'm in the cockpit. A little bit later I asked for Black Val and Jim Baker, BJ's partner from Kansas City to come up front. We called him Fluke. He was Mirror Images' cameraman in '81. When they came to the cockpit, I was sitting in the captain's seat with a glass of champagne in my hand.

Black Val was a DC-3 pilot and a 25-year captain for FedEx, flying 747's. She said, I don't want to fly people; I fly boxes to Japan. She would work four days a month and make a lot of money. She and her husband were both FedEx pilots. Now they live in Belize at their fly-in airport ranch with a hundred acres and all kinds of airplanes and toys.

Her husband is Jim Slocum. During the filming of the movie, *Cast Away* [2000], starring Tom Hanks and the soccer ball, Wilson, they wanted to film an airplane crash in the Mojave Desert. They used a 727 with dummies and test equipment. There were three people on the airplane, Jim and the copilot and a tandem master. There were chase planes flying beside it. Jim lined the plane up and started the descent. There were cameras mounted all along the mountains. His co-pilot wasn't a jumper, so they had a tandem master there for him. When it was time to get out, before the plane crashed, they snapped the co-pilot in and jumped.[90]

Slocum jumped last. He set the plane to the right glide angle, the speed and put it on autopilot. He left the soccer ball, Wilson, in the copilot seat. He exited about 1800 feet and the airplane went in. When they checked out the airplane, guess what survived? Wilson. Slocum said that was more fun than anything.

By the time we got to Bali, the passengers were dancing in the aisles to John Robbins' saxophone.

I used to be known for my memory of people's names and places. I always tried to memorize as many words of the language that I could of the country I was visiting. I got off the airplane with all the sleepy Americans. When the Indonesians walked up and bowed to us they said *Selamat pagi*. I bowed and answered, *Selamat pagi*. Everybody went, Where the fuck did Bird learn Balinese? I learned at least 50 words while we were on the airplane. I always did that in every language. You need to be able to ask where the toilet is or how or where to eat. In Norway, eating is *spise*, *hoppe* is jumping. *Spise Knulle Hoppe*, that's Eat, Fuck, Skydive.

---

90. *Cast Away* (2000) directed by Robert Zemeckis, starring Tom Hanks.

In Swedish it's *Äta-Knulla-Hoppa*. Everybody learned to say that in every language. If you're a skydiver, those are the words you need.

Bali is a popular tourist island. When we landed, it was warm and beautiful. We had 700 to 800 people who came for the Boogie from all over the world. We stayed at Kuta beach which is like Waikiki with really nice hotels. The airport where we jumped was only 10 minutes away. It was like LAX. They were flying L-1011's, big airplanes, maybe 747's. The runway crossed a peninsula, and markers came out over the water and onto the other side. After two miles the runway markers were in the water again. It was probably about 12,000 feet long, so essentially two miles. When we were up in a Hercules doing a jump run, there was an exit envelope of a certain time because because you were putting people out over water. We had to have a cattle guard at the gate whose only job was to watch how long it took the groups to get out. Normally, you'd spot and say EXIT and then you let the groups out. But if somebody took too long, the last group would be two miles out at sea. The guy that was hanging over the back and over the side would hold up his hand to stop the exit and the plane would do a go around. The C-130 was flying 130 knots, enough to blow your helmet off.

The planes at the international airport would stay on the left side of the runway and we had to take off on the right side. They never shut down their operations. We never landed on their side of the runway, and we flew big airplanes at the same time they did, side by side. At the end of the day the Hercules would put the last load down the beach. First hotel, first group out. The instructors were at the last hotel, so we'd jump out last. We had a hundred people in groups of ten and we never missed once. We would land at our hotel and guys would be there to carry our parachutes and pack them and hand us a Mai Tai. It was decadence at its best. I was given my own big airplane to fill with my group, and the captains that were working with me. When I showed them my credentials, I was up in the flight deck. If I wanted to fly the airplane, I could fly it.

There was one fee for the boogie which included the hotel, food, drink and all the jumps. While the airplanes were flying, nobody cared—get on the airplane and jump. There were no tickets. One guy from Elsinore,

Dick Pedley, made 50 or 60 jumps. He said it paid for the whole trip with just the jumps he made.

One day BJ decided to make 12-way teams for anyone who wanted to do that for the day. We ended up with about twenty 12-way teams. That was probably only a third of the people that were there.

After the day was over, we would go into town. There was a place called The Tubes, which was a surfer bar. It was like an American Pizza Hut with beer. Everybody got tired of eating fish and rice so the late-night crowd went to The Tubes almost every night.

A guy from one of the establishments in town, The Pink Panther, said, Hey Bird, bring your group to Pink Panther, and I will give you free tickets, free dinner with no cover charge. But he said we probably shouldn't bring any women with us. Okay, I understood that. I went around to each team and asked how many men were on their team. If they were all men. I would go, okay, you get 12 tickets. Another team said they had 10 men. And the girls go, What the fuck's going on here, Bird? I go, I'm not allowed to tell you, this is a man thing. But I gave them ten tickets.

So, that particular night we had Bird's famous party at the Pink Panther. I told the owner that some very angry women would try to get by his security. Under no circumstance was he to let anybody's wife or girlfriend in. He said, This is a private party.

The Pink Panther was Bali's biggest whore house. We ate and drank and talked. The guards locked the doors. There were girls of every nationality, every size and color. I was there with about 250 guys and there were probably 200 girls. I sat there and drank beer with the owner and had a great time.

The next day, you can imagine who the most hated person on the drop zone was. But the owner loved it. We loved it. All the guys did. Someone gave me a shirt recently from the Pink Panther and asked if I remembered that party. I said, I'll never forget it." —*Jerry Bird*

29

Movie Stunt Work

In Bird's words

"One summer in the late '80's I got a phone call from Jake Lombard, who was working as a stunt man on a James Bond movie, *The Living Daylights*. He asked me to come out to California and help out on the movie as the stunt safety man. I got on an airplane that day and flew to California.

Jake Lombard and BJ Worth had been stuntmen on several James Bond movies. In the late '70's, BJ had written and choreographed a stunt for a James Bond movie and went with Jake to sell the studio on the idea. This was back in the day when Roger Moore was James Bond. The meeting went well and the idea was accepted. They looked at Jake Lombard and said that with a little makeup, he looked just like Roger Moore, so Jake was hired to be his stunt double. In the opening skydiving scene of *Moonraker*, Jake looked so much like Roger Moore that they were able to do close ups of him during the scene. Since they only had 60 seconds of freefall on each jump and some of the time was used for the camera people to get in place, it took 88 jumps to film the two-minute scene."
—*Jerry Bird*.

Jake Lombard

Jake Lombard made himself a long and successful career in Hollywood—his filmography on Internet Movie Data Base lists 95 titles. In the late 1970s through the '80s, Lombard and Worth worked together as stunt doubles for the talent in James Bond movies *Moonraker* (1979), *Octopussy* (1983), *The Living Daylights* (1987), *License to Kill* (1989).

Jake was involved with aerial stunt sequences in the original *Point Break*, a 1991 film that brought a big wave of new students to skydiving operations around the country after its release. Jumpers Jan Davis and Jerry Meyers are also credited with aerial stunts; Ray Cottingham and Tom Sanders are credited as camera operators.[91]

Jake Lombard, double for Patrick Swayze, (credited as aerial stunts) during the filming of Point Break (1991). Tom Sanders was a credited camera operator and his photograph was a cover of the November 1992 *Parachutist* Magazine.

In Bird's words

"Jake Lombard and I go back to the 60's. He was from Southern California, skydived at Elsinore and always showed up with the prettiest girl. He was a young skydiver at that time, but he fell in with our crowd and started skydiving with me when he could. When I left California in '72 and moved to Colorado, he came to the Turkey Meet and eventually went to Casa Grande and became a world champion skydiver. He was a very smooth jumper and jumped in the 20-way Turkey Meets at Elsinore, Perris and Z-hills and was always on the winning teams.

Jake is also a really great skier, just so smooth on his skis and was one of the first ones to endorse Snowbird in Utah. It is a very steep, difficult

---

91. *Point Break*, directed by Kathryn Bigelow (1991) Hollywood, CA: 20th Century Fox (IMDB).

course, so you better be a good skier if you ski there. He became a Heli-Ski guide and would take skiers to the Bugaboos in Canada. They would get dropped off by helicopter at the top of the peaks and ski down 15,000 feet of untracked snow. On one trip someone got run over by a Snow Cat and Jake was able to use his EMT training to help save a life. Jake has a lot of skills. He can tie every knot known to sailors. That talent was very convenient on the Bond sets.

Later, Jake Lombard and Jake Brake developed a company that made and coordinated rigging and stunt equipment for the movies. Many of the stunts required hidden rigs and Jake Brake was a master rigger, he could make and sew anything. In their equipment truck they could make harnesses that jerked Superman off a building and later edit out the harness and wire with the computer. When actors were to be blown up, they made a snatch apparatus that jerked the stunt double away from the explosion to land on a bunch of pillows. They could make almost anything in their shop. We called them the Double Jakes. Jake Brake went on to be a stunt performer in other blockbuster movies."[92] —*Jerry Bird*

BJ Worth "Filling in for 007"

The name is Worth. BJ Worth. He has made a remarkable career as a filmmaker, both of independently produced shorts and feature films.[93] His work as aerial stunt double dueling at altitude with Jake Lombard on the James Bond movies of the 1980s is legendary among skydivers.

The following is taken from his article "Filling in for 007" in which he gives a lively description of what it was like to portray the character

---

92. Jake (Jack) Brake was a stunt performer and/or stunt rigger in *Iron Man 3* (2013), *X-Men: First Class* (2011), *The Last Airbender* (2010) and many other films (IMDB).

93. BJ is credited on *The Right Stuff* (1983), *Fandango* (1985), *The Delta Force* (1986), *The Rescue* (1988), *Fire, Ice and Dynamite* (1990), *Hot Shots! Part Deux* (1993), *GoldenEye* (1995), *Terminal Velocity* (1994), *Drop Zone* (1994), *Congo* (1995), *Tomorrow Never Dies* (1997), *Firestorm* (1998), *Space Cowboys* (2000). IMDB.

James Bond in freefall, under canopy, and hanging onto a cargo net for the filming of *The Living Daylights* (1987).[94] BJ's account first appeared in *Parachutist* Magazine.[95]

On location—The Living Daylights—Tom Sanders, photographer. *Parachutist* Magazine, August 1987.

BJ Worth

... The burning debris from the explosion catches the parachute on fire but after a fast, stalling descent, he manages to land in one piece on the awning of a luxury yacht. When the beautiful and lonely damsel on board queries his identity, the audience is introduced to Timothy Dalton as the new Bond ... James Bond.

Our usual jump ship was a French Squirrel helicopter, flown by a very talented retired Royal Air Force pilot. The skydivers included Jake

---

94. *The Living Daylights*, John Glen, director (1987; Hollywood, CA: United Artists). IMDB.
95. B.J. Worth, "Filling in for 007," *Parachutist* Magazine, August 1987, 8–23.

Lombard, Dan O'Brien, Garry Carter, freefall photographer Tom Sanders and me.

Originally, the [opening] sequence finale with Bond dumping out of the Land Rover was going to be filmed in freefall with me deploying from inside the vehicle after it had been released from a helicopter. Despite a couple of successful test drops however, the powers that be decided it would be less expensive to fake it and used a dummy with an automatic opening device in a Rover propelled off a cliff.

We did the subsequent smoking parachute descent while in Gibraltar, after several tests at Perris Valley. Mike DeLuna, an ex-Golden Knight turned professional stuntman, sewed two Kevlar/Nomex pockets into the canopy to hold smoke canisters. One pocket was suspended inside the front of a cell and the other attached to the top surface. Professional exhibition jumper Chris Wentzel rigged the pyrotechnics . . .

The first test at Perris worked great, but the heat from the suspended smoke fried that cell and the "fireproof" pocket. After some emergency repairs we figured the canopy would last another jump or two. Using a static line deployment to reduce the opening shock, we ended up making three smoking parachute jumps in Gibraltar.

To get the shot I exited 2,000 feet above the top of the ridge where the camera was positioned. At 500 feet I ignited the smoke, flew toward the camera and put the canopy into a spiraling stall, sinking below the ridge right next to the vertical rock wall and toward the blue sea below. We never had to land on a yacht but on the last jump in Gibraltar I got a dead center on the beach DZ with the canopy still smoking away.

At the end of the film Bond thwarts a fifty million dollar drug deal in the remote mountains of Afghanistan and escapes with the film's heroine in a C-130 Hercules loaded with contraband. The drama begins when it's revealed that one of the villains, Necros, managed to clamber aboard on takeoff. A fight ensues in the cargo bay while Bond's beautiful lady friend tries to sort out the controls in the cockpit. The flying becomes erratic and as the nose pitches up, a cargo net full of opium bales slides into Bond and his foe, sweeping them off their feet and bulldozing them out the rear ramp of the aircraft. The net snags on the tailgate and they manage to hold on, dangling in midair and creating a new danger for both.

This mutual predicament leads to a stimulating aerial fight with the adversaries trying to dispose of each other and at the same time climb back into the aircraft. In the end, Bond wrests a knife away from Necros and cuts the net open, dumping all the bales into his rival's face. Desperate, Necros lunges onto Bond's leg and slides down to his foot, only to have Bond cut his own shoelace, thereby giving this character "the boot" and saving the day.

This was moving into uncharted territory. Not only were we supposed to devise a way to stabilize this unwieldy lump of bales with us hanging on but we then had to stage a fight on it without falling off. Hidden parachutes were in order, along with some careful research and development.

We reassembled our Gibraltar crew and added several more skydivers to our team, including Jack Brake, Jerry Bird, Bob Taylor, Harry O'Connor, Chris Worth, and Phil Pastuhov. Jake Lombard and I reversed roles from our previous fights in Bond films and I got to be the victor this time.

Jake and I were very familiar with our "regular" hidden parachutes built by Mike Zahar, but we needed some new, less detectable ones since the cameras would be so tight on us. Jack Brake and Garry Carter collaborated to design and build a thin "conventional" parachute system which was integrated into the wardrobe. Most of the main parachute packed under the armpits and the reserve spread out over the entire front torso.

When the chest-mounted main pilot chute was deployed it pulled a cable through 24 loops—splitting the back of the wardrobe—and then through eight more loops—opening the container and extracting the main in the normal manner. Using 32 closing loops may sound complicated but it was actually an extremely clean and functional system.

We substituted a C-123 for the Hercules to help reduce the air speed to 100 knots and Jake worked with the special effects crew to design a block and tackle system using winches for extending and retrieving the "bag," as it became known. Constructing the bag was a trial and error affair with everyone adding their own two cents. The end product contained 300 one-pound bales with 600 pounds of lead shot enclosed on the underside for stability in the slipstream. We laced stiffeners into the open netting which stretched between the bales and the tailgate to prevent the bag from twisting and turning upside down while we were on it.

Again, safety was our priority. Jack Brake and Jerry Bird, our loadmasters, were responsible for all activities in the cargo bay and were always in direct communication with our pilots. Garry Carter, Harry O'Connor, and Bob Taylor were our safety men. We had explosive cutters on the lines holding the bag in case of an extreme emergency situation.

The mountains around Palm Springs, California substituted for Afghanistan. To film the bag extraction from the C-123 the special effects crew used two pieces of equipment which worked like big shock absorbers. After Jerry and Harry went for a successful ride wearing standard chutes, Jake and I gave it a whirl.

The fight scenes on the bag in tow were very demanding and sometimes a bit too realistic. When Bond and Necros are trying to climb up onto the bag, Necros kicks Bond with both feet, causing him to fall and dangle by his left hand only. On two of these takes Jake was really aggressive and 007 was history.

Garry and Jerry took turns diving after me. They would open below me, land first, and signal me with wind information so I could land safely in the nasty volcanic foothills. Although we had used hidden parachutes for many films, these were the first real "saves." —BJ Worth

In Bird's words

"The movie they were working on that summer was *The Living Daylights*, starring Timothy Dalton. This was number four or five for them. I came during the middle of the shoot, replacing a stunt safety man who had left.

I was also the spotter. Their hidden rigs had about nine different cables that held a bag. It was like putting a loose bag of flour on your back and holding it in place. One pin wouldn't do it so there are loops and pins everywhere. They came up like a cat of nine tails and you took them and put a carabiner between them. Well, you better have all nine of them or the rig doesn't open. Every time Jake took one out, there was a pull up cord with it. He would say to me, Hand me the pull up cord. That's one, that's two, that's three, until you got all of them and then you hooked up the pilot chute. The pilot chute and the cutaway handle were hidden in little pockets across his chest because he was wearing clothes on top of this rig. The rig and reserve were packed around his body on the sides and flattened. To deploy the parachute, you pulled the pilot chute and it usually came out slow because it had to pull nine ripcords.

Jerry on set putting on the final touches to Jake Brake's masterpiece hidden parachute system during the filming of the James Bond movie, *The Living Daylights*. Jake on the left, BJ Worth on the right. Tom Sanders, photographer. *Parachutist*, August 1987.

On jump run, one minute out, I would hold a net bag that said Red Cross supplies on it but was supposed to be full of dope. The cameras would zoom in on me and then I would climb back in, and BJ and Jake would climb out onto the net and start their knife fight. The bag was 15 feet by 30 feet long and was moving around like a giant pillow. If something happened and they flipped off, they were out in the middle of the desert. I had all my gear on and was on the radios. If they accidentally got flipped off the netting, I had to immediately dive out after the guy and swoop him. In case the pilot chute wasn't out, I was supposed to do a pilot chute assist. But if everything worked, then I pulled lower, landed on the ground first and pulled out a little windsock on an extended fishing pole. This guy had an emergency rig, not a regular parachute and since there are no wind socks out in the desert, I needed to make sure he didn't get hurt on landing. I had a portable radio to call a helicopter to come and pick us up as we were in the middle of nowhere. We'd go back to the airport, they'd repack the rigs and go up again. We rehearsed this day after day.

During the knife fight out on the netting, Bond pulls out a knife from his boot and cuts open the netting that is holding the bags. Well, we actually had a release system through the middle of the bag so when he stabbed it, we pulled the release cord. So, BJ is gone. The net is out there jumping all over the place now. We were using an electric motor to pull the net back in and we saw Jake, hand over hand, climbing back into the airplane. He said, I don't even want to try that rig.

The studio had rented a house at the airport and craft services laid out food in buffet style, so food and drinks were always available. Somebody from the set would come around every day and give us $40 spending money. The hotel where we were staying was about ten miles away so on days when we were not working, BJ, Jake and I and a few other people hung out there. I was originally told the shoot would be for three days but it ended up being seventeen days. We probably wouldn't have stopped then, but it was getting close to Christmas, and they wanted to wrap it up before then.

During the movie my job was to line up the airplanes, make sure my guys with the hidden rigs were dressed properly and then go out and let them zoom the cameras on me. I would give the signal when the jump run was over to stop the shooting and come in off the net if they could. If somebody fell, the shooting was over anyway and that's when I made my emergency dive.

At the end of the movie shoot, the director who was on that set wanted to make a tandem jump. I had a tandem rig in Florida, so we next-day-aired it to California.

I had a tandem rating but had never made very many tandem jumps. We had a Cessna 206, a helicopter, an airplane like a C-130 painted in the Afghan colors and a few chase planes like an AT-6 where the cameraman could stand up in the back and shoot. When we were in formation, there would be three or four airplanes shooting different angles of the fight scene. I thought, well, we will take the director for a jump in one of the Cessnas. He said, Nuh uh, I want to go on the Hercules, and I want to go out on the net. So, we put the net out the back of the airplane, but during the movie shoot, I always controlled the spot and the net. Now, somebody else in our group had to control that so we put BJ in charge of spotting and running the net. I would take the director in my tandem rig and the others were going to make a star around him and take his picture. It's done all the time these days.

We go, Ready, Set, Go!

But the director didn't let go of the net and we flip over and we're hanging by his hands under this net flapping like hell. Real quickly, he loses his grip. But we ended up on our side, and we're spinning like heck. There's a thing called side spin phenomena where the tandem jumpers start to spin and can't control it or stop the spinning. That's a bad thing because you can pass out. And I look at the ground and I just dump, you know, I just dump, and I see all the other guys going by me, going down. And then I watch them dump in a clump. Like, all of a sudden they just all started dumping.

What had happened was when we were flying around the mountains and there were clouds, and somehow the plane managed to turn up a canyon. And as we flew along, the field elevation was getting higher and higher and higher. So, I opened at 3,000 feet when normally you're pulling a tandem at 5,000 feet. And now we're in the desert and we can't tell the wind direction and we landed really hard. Nobody got hurt. And then I believe he got fired for doing that stunt because it probably cost the movie company a quarter million dollars. And that ended my movie career." —*Jerry Bird*

30

Formation Records

From 10-way speed stars in the late sixties and early seventies, stars went supernova becoming "big-ways" in the 1980s, '90s, and into the 21st century.

Early Records

In Bird's words

"The first world record I was on was the 10-man baton pass in Arvin in 1965.

In 1979 we set the record in 10-way speed star, 5.16 seconds, which still stands today in the 10-way Speed Star event.

I was on the first 50-way formation after being on all the first, up to the 32-way. There was a 40-way, then there was the 50-way, then I believe it was a 64-way and it worked its way up. In about three different places, people made a 99-way but couldn't make 100.

When we were in Chicago, Roger Nelson organizing, we had a 99-way and we added a light person, a lady on the jump and she docked 100. Well, under today's rules, if you take a picture and you have a picture of it, that's the record. Back then they had a 5-second rule, so she holds on for about three seconds and now it's sort of vertical, but she's holding on to 99 people. She holds on like she's on a monkey bar. Then she tracks away and we're going, Come back, come back! We're still here, we still have time. So, that was not a 100-way record, but there is a picture of it.

I had a chance to be on the first official 100-way that was made. Tommy Piras was organizing it. I was in Oklahoma with my family. We had a new baby, and I said, no, I haven't been on any of your practice jumps. Piras said that one guy was late, they had just made a 99, so they had a slot.

"Bird, if you want to go, you're on."

I said, I know the guy who's late for practice, I don't want to take his slot.

They went up and made the first 100-way, Later, I was on the first 120-way made of twelve 10-way wedges.

At that time [mid to late 1980s] there were different groups: California doing records, Kate Cooper-Jensen doing records, Europe trying to do records, so you couldn't be on them all.

Diamond World Record

I was on the 144-way Diamond World Record with Roger Nelson.

Diamonds are squares of things. Twelve squared is 144 so our goal was to make a 144-way diamond. Roger Nelson's Freak Brother Convention in Quincy, Illinois is the event where we planned to culminate this record at the end of the summer—the eighth month—August.

So, here we are. We have 144 people. We probably have 10 airplanes in formation. A bunch of Skyvans, three of them. Otters, DC-3s—anything we can do to get that many people up in the air at once. We have a camp where everybody has paid for 25 jumps, going to 18,500 feet, wearing oxygen—so the jumps cost more than normal. Formation flights take longer to get to altitude.

At first, all the really good people, or people who think they're really good, they want to be on the outside or dock on the end or wing. They want to go out last, they want to be the hero. Well, that meant you took the intermediate-to-good fliers and say, You make the 64-way diamond base for us.

The degree of difficulty of that is hard. After about eight or ten jumps, when we hadn't made the base yet, we knew we had to change strategy.

If you have a good base, anybody can dock on a solid platform, it's not moving or floating or washing around. If the base is all over the sky or funnels, no matter how good you are, you're screwed. So, we changed the lineup, put all the real experienced people in the beginning and went up and made the 64-way for a base and it started working. We end up burning up jumps and we're down to the last day. There are probably 500 people at this boogie, maybe even 1,000. Now we have one jump left.

I wasn't really in charge. I was a captain but Roger Nelson, Tom Piras and these guys were the big captains. They asked me what I would do. I said, Hey, these two guys had 24 jumps to learn to stay above and they went below. Cut them. But they said they didn't have anybody else. One guy who was part of their circle said he'd never fall below again. And then they ask, Okay, what else? I told them that my buddy, Mike Michigan, is teaching freeflying. He is a former Mirror Image 8-way champion and he will come and jump for me if I ask him. And they go, Okay, okay, do it.

Mike said, hey, I'm real busy, I'm in the middle of a class so how about I just meet you at the airplane? I told him, great. Michigan goes, Hey Bird, I don't have a suit for this, so I told him to take mine—a Jerry Bird brand that I wear when I'm going last so I don't go below. He doesn't do any dirt diving with us. Michigan makes the jump and we make the diamond on that jump.

Diamonds are flat and we pull a diamond out the door, and the tendency is the tail wants to flip over the top. This thing is like a magic carpet ride out there in the air and at one point it gets real high. Well Michigan, because of his free flying skills, essentially stands up and pulls with all his weight back down and helps level it back out by doing the T and then levels out.

Some people thought he was just showing off, but he said he would have been flipped over the top of that thing if he hadn't done a T to pull it back down. When you put your leg down your fall faster. Anyway, we made the world record at Quincy, Illinois, on the 8th day of the 8th month, held for 8.8 seconds in 1988; chief organizer Roger Nelson.

All of a sudden there was a 200-way world record. It just kept moving up to where Roger Nelson then tried to make the first 300-way. Those didn't work out so well, but there were different attempts. The next world record for size I was on was again organized by Roger Nelson. It was a 246-way done in Chicago with about a dozen airplanes in formation at 20,000 feet. The original goal was to try for 300, but we didn't have the skill or the all the people to do that.

The last world record I was on was the 282-way with World Team 1999, in Thailand." —*Jerry Bird*

BJ's World Team

In Bird's words

"BJ formed a group called World Team. The World Team came from exactly that, all over the world, and he coordinated record attempts and boogies with skydivers from different countries. Each team had a captain from that country pick their teams. BJ trusted each captain to set the criteria and rate their jumpers. Dieter Kirsch would have an all-German team show up. Patrick Passe, one of the great skydivers and teachers, was captain of the French team and there was no question that the people he would bring could skydive as well or better than anyone else. I would bring a group and BJ would be assured that everyone would get in. If the requirement was for 20 team members, that's how many he would bring. If there were 15 captains around the world, he would tell each captain how many jumpers to bring, so without him trying to extend out to 300 people, his 15 captains would report back that they had their 20 people ready to go and here is their money. So, up front he had 300 people who had paid for their slots and jumps. Because of injuries and everything they could bring alternates who would pay their way, and they could try out there by jumping on what they call Alpha Team, which was the bench, the reserves. Our job as captains was to support the World Team.

BJ was a great organizer and manager and would delegate his captains to do the ground work but he made the final decisions.

A little Jerry Bird backstory . . .

"All the research pointed to Thailand as the most likely place to build the World Team's record attempt. I told BJ nothing gets done in Thailand without seeing ex U. S. Army colonels, like George Geczy and Jack Angel. They retired from Vietnam but stayed in Asia where they had a direct ear to the King and they were arms merchants and they spoke fluent Thai. One of them was married to Miss Thailand who was half his age. BJ later told me, Bird, I would have never gotten in the front door. I was trying to write letters to the government. So, these two guys can get you hooked up with the General that runs the Air Force by the afternoon and they pull all the strings for him.

When America was involved in the Vietnam War, they made Thailand into a little America and so what do the Americans want if you are boys and soldiers out there? Sex, drugs, rock and roll. You could go into a Thai bar and they could sing the Beatles, but they were mimicking the sounds. They couldn't speak English, but they could sing the songs. They loved Americans. They called the place The Land of Smiles.

Americans love them back. Many GI's married Thai people and brought them home. The Thais catered to Americans. They had whatever you wanted. After the war was over for 20 years, we would go back there. Now it's even bigger and there are tourists from all over the world. But when we'd go to Thailand, we had a thousand people in our entourage, so to move from the airport to a hotel that would be able to put us up was a big deal and every time we moved somewhere they had the motorcycle cops stop traffic in downtown Bangkok, open the roads and let the World Team go by, by order of the King. And so we had all these special privileges.

I was there running the bench, the alternates, so when somebody got cut, I'd have the people to move up. I was told in a private meeting room there was this one Thai guy that nobody liked, and they took me aside and said, we're worried about him that he might be doing something wrong and if he does, tell us and we'll have him arrested. And he's a Thai.

Larry, the other guy in that room, was an American citizen living in

Thailand. And I'm thinking, okay, you're in the room with me, BJ and this Air Force General and you just happen to be the guy who is a Christian missionary. (Is that sorta like the Christians in Action? The CIA?)

Larry spoke fluent Thai. He turned out to be from the Thai delegation and he was their best jumper. But I wasn't allowed to move him up and was told to keep an eye on him. And I had another guy, a Navy Seal on my team who I didn't know, but I said, you are a Navy Seal and I will recommend you to BJ just because I know if you're a Navy Seal, you can do the job. So, he was the only guy I brought out of 300 people.

When we get to Bangkok and we register, they give us a stack of free T-shirts and we have to wear a certain one every day like a uniform. So, we're loaded down with swag and somebody makes a sign to me, you know, and I got it. Other people been there for a day. I just got there. I go up, I get in my room, get rid of all my stuff and there's a party going on. This is all the party people I know, and we're drinking and everything. And boom, boom, boom. The door has a key hole in it and somebody looks out and they go, don't know who that is. And I go, what do we do? Is it cops? I look out and it's my Navy Seal. And he goes, Bird, do you think you ditched me that easy? I got two cases of beer. And he goes, I don't smoke pot, but I don't care that you guys do and I've got your six while you're here. And this was a guy as big and as bad as Harry O[96].

A little bit later there is another knock at the door. Look through the peephole and nobody knows who it is. It turns out it's the guy on my Alpha team, the bench, the Thai guy who is banned, the guy they want to arrest. Come on in. Fucking guy is named Ace. He's got two guns on, pearl-handled pistols, and he's carrying a shopping bag. He's the Bangkok Chief of Police!

And he goes, I like skydiving with you and I don't want any of your people to get in trouble, so here's a whole bag full of marijuana, Thai bud that we arrested people at the airport with today. Pass it out. Don't buy any on the street. You'd get in trouble. That's Ace.

---

96. Harry O was an American private detective television series created by Howard Rodman and starring David Janssen. It ran two seasons, from 1974-1976. Warner Brothers Television (IMDB).

So, now the World Meet is over and Ace never got into the starting lineup. By FAI rules after you make a world record—and we had just made a world record of 282—is that you have to stay alive for 24 hours. That's what I was told. They go, Don't go out and do something dangerous tonight like get killed. But now the jump is over, the teams want to go back to Bangkok and party. And BASE jump.

The main drag in Bangkok where our skyscraper hotel is, stopped traffic with cops at every end. The BASE jumpers on the World Team all got to jump off the skyscrapers in downtown Bangkok with Ace's guards in the streets. After they safely landed they started traffic again. This was all Ace. He turned out to be one of the sweethearts and our best buddy. This guy was the guy in charge of Bangkok and he gave us all his card and said if you get stopped, you give them my card. If they give you any trouble they will probably be dead by morning. We always had people covering our six."

—*Jerry Bird*

2025: The world record for freefall formation stands at 400, made by the World Team over Udon, Thani Thailand, on February 8, 2006. Skydivers, men and women from 31 countries and the Thai Royal Airforce working together—the largest multinational sports team ever assembled to pursue a common goal was organized by BJ and Bobbie Worth. In 2022 World Team was presented with the Path of Excellence Award by the International Skydiving Museum Hall of Fame.

31

Family Man

In Bird's words

"In 1983 Beth and I hooked up with Mike Schultz, got our own DC-3 and took it to the National Championships in Muskogee, Oklahoma. Now that we owned our own DC-3, we started booking our own relative work camps at other people's events, and chartering or leasing aircraft as needed.

Jerry and Beth.

On Sadie Hawkins Day, Beth asked me to marry her in a telegram and I said yes. But we were very busy and had not gotten around to it. When we were in Opa-locka, Florida, Mike suggested that since we were going to the Nationals in Oklahoma where Beth's parents lived, maybe we should get married before we went there. So, we went to Key West. We took a helicopter and a couple of airplanes with a whole bunch of people from the Mark Three Studios that Richard Pitt owned in Miami. Besides being an airline pilot, Richard had a ship captain's license and could marry people. We got married on the beach.

Richard's wife lent us a diamond that looked as big as a strawberry. She made us give it back the next day. She was the platinum blonde in the Blue Velvet Whiskey ads in the '80's. Richard had a movie studio in Miami called Mark Three and he was also the CEO of the Bird Machine Corporation.

The next day, Beth and I flew from Florida to Oklahoma for the Nationals, and I met her family for the first time. Beth was a skydiver, an artist, an athlete and a real live wire. Very shortly we had two boys, Joshua and John Brandon (JB).

Beth and Bird. Photograph taken by Jerry, about 1983. "Driving along, we saw this hawk near the side of the road and pulled over. Beth put on the gloves from the glove box, got out and the bird flew right to her. She has a way with birds." Jerry Bird, photographer.

We had an Airstream trailer and the DC-3, so we traveled around the United States, with mechanics, pilots, instructors, cameramen, and a support crew. We usually wintered in Zephyrhills. After about five years, the boys were old enough to go to school. We started them in a kindergarten at a Catholic school.

Jerry and son at the DZ. Kai Otem, photographer.

Eventually, we sold the Bird Machine and I was offered a permanent job at the old Zephyrhills drop zone as the Chief Organizer. I was on a salary but could still travel to do my own camps and boogies and seminars.

JB and Josh Bird. Laura Baker, photographer.

After a couple of years of kindergarten and first grade, we decided to homeschool our children. Between their mother, other homeschoolers, and myself, we homeschooled our children for six years. Our younger son, JB, skipped a year, so we only had to teach one grade at a time. Beth's father was a doctor. One of our good friends, Dr. Steve Groff had two sons who became famous doctors and they always gave us their second edition computers when they got a new one. My children became really good with computers at a real early age. When their mother was running the company, they were the ones who would do the graphics or print out cards. This was back when you had a tower and a console and you got your parts separately and put them together to build a computer. My kids could build them and repair them. They never learned how to write in cursive, but they can type 60 to 100 words a minute while they're talking on the phone. Eventually, JB went into internet poker, playing Texas hold'em. As soon as he started playing, he started winning.

When they were growing up we traveled to drop zones and sometimes we lived at the drop zones but I always believed that children are children and skydiving is an adult activity and not an environment for children. They spent a lot of time doing karate, playing baseball, soccer, tennis and golf. They made all the sports teams while they were in high school. They played in the band. Beth taught art class, so the homeschool parents would bring their children to our house for art. We would send our kids to the music teacher's house for music. Both of my kids are very smart and they could teach themselves independently. They could do in two hours what a high school student took all day to do. They could learn at their own pace. If they had thirty words that they needed to know the definition and how to spell, I would give them a test and the ones they didn't know would be the ones they needed to study.

By eighth grade, we decided to enroll them into a regular school. Fortunately there was a private Seventh-day Adventist school less than a mile away where children of doctors, lawyers, etc. sent their kids. They had a great math teacher. Josh took gymnastics and played in the band. The school put on a great Christmas show where everybody sang in the chorus. They got a good education there. After the tenth grade, my kids finished their junior and senior years at the public high school in Zephyrhills. They played every sport and did very well academically. Josh was such a good soccer player that he went to college on a soccer scholarship. JB went to the local university.

When JB was a senior in high school, he was usually the smallest player on every team he played on. He grew four inches and a few years later became a force in volleyball. JB was second in Little League. He could catch any ball hit to him. He made the intelligent play, throw to first, throw to home, throw to second, do a double play. He was the smallest player in the league and struck out one time when I happened to be the public announcer. The ball was probably six or eight inches outside and the umpire called strike. JB, probably 10 years old, looked at the umpire and said, That was a ball. He led the league in hitting. He couldn't hit a home run but could usually hit a single over to second or third base and then he would steal to second, then to third and then on a grounder, he would run home.

The only time he struck out was when the umpire called strike three near the end of the season, on a ball. The umpire missed the call. Almost everybody in the stands booed the ump

Both Josh and JB were great athletes, super scholars and they graduated from high school in 2002." —*Jerry Bird*

32

1990: Skydive City

Skydive City at Zephyrhills. August 6, 2021.

November 1990: Joannie Murphy and Susan Stark, with a team of supportive friends including Jerry and Beth Bird, opened Skydive City, on the southeast corner of the Zephyrhills municipal airport. Jerry was dubbed the mayor of the city. As such he influenced the drop zone culture and promoted formation skydiving, drawing skydivers from all over the world.

"Bird doing what Bird does at Z-hills." Jack Gregory, photographer.

The Big O, 1992. Bird's 40-way, 27.4 seconds. Steve Cooper, photographer.

For a few years there were two drop zones operating in close proximity to the airport. The older operation, Phoenix Parachute Center, had been involved in litigation with the city of Zephyrhills. When it was settled, the owner/operators moved their business to Lake Wales, Florida.

Skydive City, designed like an old-fashioned town square, still offers all the necessities sport skydivers have come to expect: A fleet of aircraft, covered packing, video room, training rooms, mobile homes to rent, pro shops, cafe and bar, on-site camping, mobile homes for visiting jumpers to rent. Skydive City maintains a good relationship with Zephyrhills and continues to draw teams and formation organizers from all over the world.

33

Family Matters

In Bird's words

"Beth, the artist and the skydiver and my soul mate, got sick in the late nineties and was diagnosed with Muscular Dystrophy. Over the next few years, Beth needed a caregiver, so her mother moved from Oklahoma to live with our family. The disease affected Beth and our whole family. Beth's mother was a Catholic and because I refused to join the Catholic Church, and because she thought I was keeping my boys from Catholicism, our family broke up.

I filed for divorce and forced them to give me visitation rights. Beth's father, grandfather, and great-grandfather were doctors; they had money, so they bought a nice house in a subdivision about 15 miles away. Beth, the boys and Beth's mother lived there. The boys would come home for visitation.

There came a point when Beth's health was deteriorating; she was in and out of the hospital. One day I got a call from Beth and she said, Come and get the boys, they're yours.

The boys came home and finished high school.

My job was to look after my children so I quit skydiving because my children needed me more than skydiving did. At the same time, I was having a harder time making a living skydiving. I was older, the sport was changing, there were a lot of superheroes out there. I became a taxi driver. I could pick my own hours and be my own boss. I owned my own business, and I worked in Tampa. Many times, I would get up at four in the morning and go to work to make sure that I was home when my children got home from school. They would get their own breakfast and eat their lunch at school, but I wanted to be there to take them to their practices or pick them up. As soon as they could drive, I bought them a car so they could drive themselves to school and visit their mother.

Once they graduated from high school and went away to college, my job was done, so to speak. Beth was living with her mother and we were divorced. I'd been out of skydiving for a while and was thinking of going back, but I had a heart attack. I was an outside person, very active and while I had the children, I made healthy meals so I ate pretty good. Now I was living by myself, driving a taxi, eating fast food, not exercising. I was sitting on my butt driving a taxi 12 to 14 hours a day and was stressed out because my marriage had fallen apart.

When I got up on the morning of the heart attack, my arm hurt but I had things to do. I went out to the drop zone because my friend Heidi's car had a bad battery, and I needed to change it. I opened the hood to start working on it but I told my friend, Newfie, who was there, that my arms weren't working properly and asked him to help me. He picked up the battery and we finished the job but I told Heidi that my arm hurt, and I didn't feel very good, so I went home. I was not thinking clearly but I remembered I had some aspirin on top of the refrigerator. I'm not the tallest person so I fumbled around up there but I couldn't find the aspirin bottle. This started happening about 8 AM and off and on all day long, my arm was hurting like I had a pulled muscle in my forearm. That evening, I was invited to Mary Brake's birthday party. She was married to Jake Brake, who I knew from my Utah days but now they lived here in Z-hills too. I had been part of their wedding party when they got married some twenty years before, in Utah.

There were people at the birthday party who I'd known for 10, 20, 25 years. They told me I looked ashen and gray. They found me sitting on a couch in another room, crying. They asked me what was wrong; I told them that my arm was hurting really bad. I told Mary that I was sorry, but I better go home.

They let me get in my car and I drove home. I lay down on my bed and remembered a little ditty, Go to bed, wake up dead. I got out of bed, got dressed, and got in my car. I couldn't make a decision all day because my heart was blocked, and I didn't think I was getting enough blood to my brain. I was in a daze. I drove through town and saw a Walgreens that was open 24 hours. I went in there and sat down at one of the blood pressure machines and took my blood pressure. When I looked at it, it didn't make any sense. It was 200 over something and I thought that maybe I should go to the Emergency Room.

By this time it was midnight; this had been going on for about 14 hours. I drove myself to the ER in Dade City and the first thing they did was hand me a form to fill out, I didn't know what to do with it. The lady asked me what was wrong and out of the deep recesses of my mind, I finally spit out, I'm having a heart attack. They rushed me inside and asked if I had taken aspirin. I told them I hadn't, so they gave me one. When I came home four days later, I found the aspirin bottle knocked over on top of my refrigerator.

I had a clogged artery, but I was very fortunate. They gave me blood thinners and told me I had a heart attack; I'd been having a heart attack. So, now their job was to keep me from having another one until they could figure out what was wrong. The cardiologist wanted to do a heart catheterization where he would go through my artery and up to my heart with some dye to see what was wrong with my heart. When he left the room, one of the nurses said she wanted to give me a little bit of advice. She said that he was a very good doctor, and he could do the catheterization and find out what's wrong, but he couldn't fix it there at Dade City, I would be sent to Tampa. She said I'd probably be better off going to Tampa and have the heart cath done and they could fix the problem there. They gave me oxygen and monitored me until they moved me to Tampa in an ambulance. I was taken to Pepin Heart Institute.

Joe Pepin was the owner of Bud Light Distributors in Tampa, and I had met him. He was a big-time philanthropist, a big-time sponsor, and the largest beer distributor. Anheuser Busch, who made Budweiser, was a buddy of his and they were political cronies. He sponsored a CRW Team that had Budweiser on their canopies.

Quick back story: In 1981 we tried to get them to sponsor Mirror Image. Our friends at USPA were trying to make a contract with Wide World of Sports to pay money upfront to film us. Mr. Peppin told us at that time that if we could show him we had a contract with Wide World of Sports, we could have Budweiser on everything, and we would be paid for every second we were on National TV. Well, USPA couldn't get Wide World of Sports to pay them any money, so Wide World of Sports didn't cover us.

I'm a beer drinker—or I used to be. In 1981 we went to Tampa to Mr. Pepin's headquarters, for a meeting with him about sponsorship. BJ Worth and I were there along with a USPA representative. We walked into his very nice office which was in a refrigerated hanger full of beer. His trucks were coming and going. There were plastic curtains hanging there to keep the cold air in so the whole place was refrigerated. At the front was his very beautiful office. It was about 10:30 in the morning and I noticed behind this desk there were some taps and a small refrigerator, and I thought, I like this guy already.

At one point in our conversation, he asked if anybody wanted a beer. BJ said, No sir. The second guy said, No sir. And I said, I'd love to have a beer. He swung around to the taps, pulled out a couple glasses and poured himself and me a glass of beer. I looked at BJ and thought, this is the biggest beer distributor in fucking Tampa and you're telling him you don't want a beer? So, we drank beer but we didn't get sponsorship because we weren't on TV.

So, I'm in Tampa where Mr. Pepin built the Pepin Heart Institute. I watched them do the procedure and I could see on the monitor where the artery was clogged. It was twitching like a dying snake. The catheter went through the artery like a Roto-Rooter. It had a light, a camera and a cutter on it. It cleared the blockage and left a stent that keeps it open. This used to take open heart surgery or angioplasty, They would push the plaque to the side by expanding a balloon then pull out, but six months later you needed it again. I was hoping that the stent was a permanent solution. I've had a couple more heart catheterizations to examine the stent in that way. It's what they call patent, which means open.

I walked around for 18–24 hours having a heart attack and was told that I should have been dead before I got to the ER. Fortunately, it was in the Circumflex Artery with 90% blockage so a little bit of blood was still getting through. I survived and now I'm a 14-year survivor with a stent. I get stress tests and nuclear tests. A few years ago, I quit taking all my heart medication. I don't take blood thinners. I don't take blood pressure medicine. I don't take Plavix. My heart and my blood pressure seem to be just fine. Once I started taking an antianxiety drug from my psychiatrist, I didn't need my heart medicines anymore because the anxiety and stress were causing the irregular heartbeats and high blood pressure; the psychiatric drug keeps my blood pressure under control." —*Jerry Bird*

34

21st Century Skydiving

World Team 2006 was the largest multinational sports team ever assembled to pursue a common goal: To build a freefall formation of 400 skydivers. This they completed on February 8, 2006, over Udon Thani, Thailand. Organized by BJ and Bobbie Worth, the record-breaking formation was the highlight of the Royal Sky Celebration honoring the 60th anniversary of the reign of King Bhumibol Adulyadej.

The first World Team event was held in Slovakia, 1994. The second was in Russia, followed by two in Thailand—at the first one in Thailand the team set the prior record of 357. World Team 2006 consisted of over 500 World Team Members from 30 nations including the formation skydivers, alpha team, videographers, documentation team members, ground staff, support team plus over 100 Royal Thai Air Force Flight and ground crew members. For the event, the flight line consisted of five C-130 Hercules aircraft, plus a sixth in reserve. Respect and congratulations to BJ and Bobbie Worth and all the participants and their supporters from many different nations who made this happen. The amount of planning, logistics, and cooperation, the support of the local community, and the availability of the appropriate aircraft and pilots needed to achieve this safely executed 400-way formation is hard to conceive, which is why this record may never be broken.

Jerry Bird was not on the 2006 record but he had coached many of the participants. His influence on big-way formation skydiving continues to be seen and felt. Formation dives still entice sport skydivers and they are still being organized in many different varieties. Full break sequential big-ways designed by well-known organizers attract the best formation flyers from all over the world. Full break sequential dives of any size require not only individual flying skills but discipline, teamwork and communication for success. These transitioning freefall formations are challenging and exhilarating for the fliers and visually appealing when seen from the ground or through the videographer's lens.

SOS—Skydivers Over Sixty—and JOS—Jumpers over Seventy—are active groups that regularly attempt to set new group freefall records, yet not all formation jumps are record attempts. Most of them are get-togethers in the sky and happen every weekend, all over the world.

While skydiving has diversified in the 21st century, belly flying continues to be popular and Jerry Bird's influence is an integral part of 21st century freefall formation flying. This shot, taken over Perris on August 18, 2018, by Randy Forbes, is a Wuest-way dive. "The Wuest-ways started in 1987 or '88 and are named after Doug & Marilyn Wuest. They wanted to start a regular chain of formation loads (two or more planes) that were generally in the neighborhood of 30-40 in size. Ray Cottingham and I co-shot their very first one." —*Randy Forbes*

Twenty-first century skydiving has evolved, expanded, diversified and become more highly commercialized. Parachute operations—drop zones—have changed since the early days of sport skydiving. In the 1960s and '70s, jumpers considered themselves upscale if they had a hangar and a beer 'fridge. Many of us in North America learned to jump out of single engine Cessnas, the workhorse of small DZs that carry three to five jumpers to altitude, albeit slowly. As in, you have time to take a little nap between takeoff and exit.

Those operations with access to bigger, faster aircraft—especially those DZs with year-round sunshine—grew more sophisticated throughout the 1980s and '90s, becoming destination skydiving resorts attracting teams and those weekend jumpers with the ways and means to spend on an immersive learning experience. Many DZs became tandem factories; there is more revenue generated in cranking out tandems than driving experienced jumpers to altitude. Either way, the aviation-related expenses of a parachute center are significant and there are easier ways to make a living than being a drop zone operator.

While the airplanes—and the parachutes—are faster and statistically the safety has improved, the sport has changed in other ways. Cliff Weaver was four years old in 1966 when his father started flying jumpers at Pennsylvania's York Sport Parachute Center. Cliff started jumping in 1978 and is still an active jumper and aircraft owner in 2025. Cliff reflects on the changes he has seen in the sport:

Cliff Weaver

In the 1960s it was called relative work; its definition, to fall in relativity with one another to link up in freefall. In the '70s we called it RW; it was being perfected, taught, and learned as the main reason to skydive. In the '80s it was still RW being perfected—even being used to teach a first jump student. In the '90s, still RW, being micro-tweaked and perfected, leading to the unbelievable 400-way completed in 2006, and 4 and 8-way blistering rounds that could never have been imagined in the early decades.

In the 2000s it changed to Formation Skydiving, no longer was Relativity a part of its name, and the decline started. At small DZs the lure of freeflying, wingsuiting, and swooping chiseled away at the number of people learning Relative Work. Now we are simply belly flyers, a dwindling discipline at most drop zones. Dinosaurs, mostly old people holding desperately onto our glory days. Even the name belly flyers is a little demeaning. The actual art of Relative Work has been lost at most small DZs. The hours of talking about exits, the first five seconds of the skydive, gone. The nights around the bonfire—learning, discussing, coming up with new ideas, teaching the new guy, gone. We lived during the greatest times in the sport. I'm sure there are places where people still hang around the bonfire, but falling relative, working together, and doing it in a belly to earth orientation are not the topics of conversation. We are now a minority in the sport.

Now I know how the style and accuracy people felt in the '70s and '80s. The sport is different, for many reasons, but we are all still skydivers—the most wonderful sport of them all. —*Cliff Weaver*

In Bird's words

"From the '60's to almost the '90's, relative work was the number one skill that people wanted to do in the sport. You got in every time on a fun jump, or you were on a really good team or your goal was just to get better, and it was all about RW. The RW records or size kept getting bigger and bigger. From the very first 6-way to 10-way to 20-way and the jumps in between, the 24 and 26 and 32 were all-round star records. After 32, people couldn't make big rounds pretty much anymore, so they started making geometric shapes.

Earlier, I said that if you out-practice the other teams, if you out-thought them and if you planned well, then there was a good chance you would beat them in competition. Now, teams have their own video man for every jump. Everything they do is recorded. Lots of teams have their own psychologists. They'll have their own masseuse, their own trainer, they use a wind tunnel, and of course they are sponsored.

What that has done—and I highly respect these teams like the Golden Knights, Arizona Airspeed, and the teams in Europe—is it has moved the bar so high that the recreational skydiver cannot compete on that level anymore. It's way too expensive. You can go to the Nationals and spend a lot of money, but you are not going to break into the big three at our US National competition and go walk up and win a medal. You'd better be one of the sponsored, highly trained, highly disciplined teams in the 4-way event that has made a thousand jumps during that year, plus 50 hours in the wind tunnel. Some of these teams have been doing this for five years in a row, they've taken the sport to such a high level of difficulty that the average skydiver can't compete with them, so consequently there's only three or four teams or five teams that show up that have a chance at the Nationals. Alternately, teams can enter the "B" league or the "C" League or the Left-footed Midget League and get a trophy. But competing to win against the best is really hard now, with these professional teams.

On the other hand, there are so many different things that you can do. You can be a Wing Suiter or a Swooper or an RW jumper. Many times, jumpers pick an area and specialize in that, like 4-way jumping. The USPA has 50,000 members but there are fewer than 100 or 200 people who do serious 4-way jumping.

If you want to jump by yourself, Wing Suiting or Free Flying is quite popular. If you jumped by yourself in the old days, you were kind of strange but now if you do that, you are cool because you are a free flyer. So, there are a lot of different disciplines. If you do RW, you are a belly flyer. Some jumpers only want to do big RW loads with 40 to 60 people.

To me, skydiving was about the freefall and the people. I never liked to jump by myself. The only thing in the world that matters to Wing Suiters is that wing. It's about how far and how fast they can go, how long they can stay in the sky. The important thing to the Swoopers is their canopy. They want the smallest and fastest canopy. It's not about freefall and controlling your body, it is about their gear.

We controlled our bodies as we flew through the air. What I had in my knapsack on my back didn't really matter. We loved freefall and after the canopy opened, we felt like the jump was over. The rest was just a ride to the ground. The gear I wore wasn't the reason I skydived."

—*Jerry Bird*

35

Fear

In Bird's words

"I've been asked if I was ever afraid while skydiving and the fact is, skydiving never inherently scared me but circumstances surrounding it have scared me. I have a fear of water and was afraid I would die by drowning. When I was asked if I wanted to go in the water, my answer was no. This fear was reinforced by a couple of events. I remember seeing a John Wayne movie when he found out the kid that was with them couldn't swim, he picked him up and threw him in the water.

I had a similar experience when I was growing up in West Virginia. We lived on the Ohio River and there was a big tributary called Kings Creek with a swimming hole. I was about seven or eight years old, the youngest and smallest kid there and the older kids thought it would be fun to throw me in the water to see if I could swim. While I was out there dog paddling or doing the best I could not to drown, they thought it would be fun to throw rocks at me. One rock got me right in the head and I had a cut that was bleeding. They took me home to my mother and told her I was swimming and hit my head on something. The next time they asked me to go swimming, I said, No thank you, I don't like the water.

In the summer of '88 I was in Chicago with Roger Nelson and we were trying to set a new world record—a 144-way diamond [see chapter 33, Formation Records]. One day Roger goes, Timeout, Bird; we've got a jump to make. Can you land on a tennis court? I said, Yeah, I can land on top of your head if you want. He said, We are going to do a jump for Mayor Daley of Chicago. He and Roger were buddies. One of the guys at the drop zone warned me to be careful, Roger could get me into trouble. We were going to take a cameraman on the jump and Roger, me and one other person were going to make a 3-way and land on a tennis court. Right before takeoff Roger handed me a flotation device, a vest. I said, What' that for? Well, Mayor Daley had a ship called The City of Hope and he would take sick or homeless children out on the boat for a day of fun. The tennis court we were supposed to land on was on the deck of the boat in the middle of Lake Michigan.

We flew out there over the ship and Roger threw out a streamer and we realized it was quite windy so we flew upwind and like idiots, we jumped. I thought I had it figured out. The boat was moving from the currents and I was about 20 feet above the tennis court but because of the turbulence, the boat pulled right out from under me. As I dropped below the stern I thought, Oh my God, I'm going to land in the water. I had an inflatable safety vest but I made a big mistake. I grabbed the two lanyards and jerked them. Apparently, this happens a lot. It just blows it up and the seams release and it doesn't have any air in it and now you can't take that plastic tube and blow air to inflate it.

I looked around and the other guys were a half mile away and the big boat was pulling away. The Chicago police department were out on a yacht, drinking beer and acting as the safety patrol. I was bobbing in the water and I saw their boat coming towards me and I was yelling to get their attention. They came close and saw that I had a life vest, so they threw a marker in the water next to me and kept going to rescue the other guys. I was paddling, desperately trying to stay afloat.

I had gotten my rig off but still had that stupid vest on top of me. My reserve, even in the container, had some air in it and was floating a little bit. By the time they got back to me and pulled me out of the water, I was lying there on deck, heaving. That was the second time I almost drowned.

They tried to kill me three different times that summer. We were jumping Sky Vans to try to make the world record. To start the jump, we would launch a 9-way diamond out the door. The guys on the sides had to stay in close so as not to hit the door as we went out. On one of these jumps, as we exited the airplane, a guy's rig opened and his bag was floating with the lines coming out of it. The guy next to me reached over, got the bag and pulled it off of my neck a second before it opened and that person disappeared out of the formation. I had not even been aware that the lines were wrapped around my neck, but it was all caught on video.

On another jump, they stalled one of the Sky Vans on an exit and it flipped and flopped everybody around and seven out of the nine people were injured. Fortunately, the plane didn't go upside down or dive into the ground.

While we were making the jumps, Roger always had something for me to do. One day he said, Hey, there's a little farm down the road with a crop duster strip and their family all jumps over here. On the 4th of July, we make a demo jump over there for them. So, would you and you and you go over there and make a demo jump, take your second rig, don't repack, just jump back in the airplane after you land and you'll come back and we'll be ready to go up with a hundred people again. We were making 100-way practice jumps for the 144 record world attempt later. The pilot told everybody, I'm from Alaska, I'm a bush pilot, I'm one of the best pilots, you know. I jumped in the airplane and had my rigs in my hands and am sitting in the back with my canopy wrapped around my arms. It was only an eight-minute flight back to the other drop zone and when we got there, everybody's out there dirt diving. There was one long runway which was used for the DC-3's and there's a short runway—but you've got to come over the hangar first and drop down to land on the short runway.

The Alaska bush pilot wanted to show off his short field landing. So, he came over the building, stalled the Cessna 182, hit the ground so hard on all three wheels that we bounced 20 feet up in the air and came back down. I was in the back during the landing and my butt and my back hurt like hell.

He goes, Oh, rough landing, but any landing you can walk away from is a good landing. We taxied back in.

Roger had two Cessnas that were named for his kids that were in better condition than when they came off the showroom floor. This was one of them. He usually didn't let anybody fly those; they were immaculate.

Pat taxied up, parked the airplane by the hangar and went into his office to go get his gear to be on the jump and Roger stopped everything and said, Wait a minute. The nose was hanging down, he opened the cowling and the firewalls were rippled. When he pulled up the carpet, the floorboard was rippled and the wings were hanging down. Even in the back, the tail had hit the ground and was bent. That airplane was totally destroyed. They took the engine out and the rest of the airplane was totaled.

The summer of '88 was a very exciting summer. We set the world record with the 144-way diamond. [See chapter Formation Records] In the fall of '88, Roger went to prison for five years. When he got out of prison, he started right back up where he left off. He moved to Ottawa,[Illinois] bought 500 acres of land and put in a 6,000 foot runway. He built the biggest hangar you've ever seen and it had a 300-seat movie theater in it. There were rooms underground with bunks and TV sets. They probably had 500 camper hookups and within a week of the opening, every one of them was full. Roger was an entrepreneur. He knew how to make money and he always did things in a big, big way.

So, I was afraid of water was afraid of certain pilots and some airplanes. Certain airplanes really weren't the best ones for jumping from, such as King Airs and Pilatus Porters. Twin Otters became the plane to use for jumping at almost every big drop zone. A Twin Otter is like flying a big Cessna 182 with a really strong tricycle gear. If you can fly a 182, you should be able to fly a Twin Otter. They are almost impossible to wreck. It's like a DC-3. As far as I know, nobody ever died skydiving in a DC-3 crash because either they didn't crash or they just landed again. Hundreds of people have died in smaller airplanes, like 182's. There's seems to be a 182 going down all the time now. They're 50 years old and sometimes they have pilots who just got out of flight school and they don't have many hours. Where can they get a job to build up hours? At drop zones." —*Jerry Bird*

36

What Made Jerry Bird Jerry Bird?

"Skydiving is about the relationships and the friendships that you make."
—Jerry Bird

BJ Worth inducting Jerry Bird into the International Skydiving Museum's Hall of Fame, 2010, the very first class.

"**Jerry Bird, D-3299,** stands as a pioneering figure in the evolution of formation skydiving. His journey in the sport began in the 1960s, leading to significant contributions that have left an indelible mark on skydiving history. In 2010, Jerry Bird was inducted into the International Skydiving Hall of Fame, cementing his legacy as a trailblazer in the skydiving community." International Skydiving Museum & Hall of Fame.[97]

---

97. https://skydivingmuseum.org/member/jerry-bird/

Accompanying him that first year of inductions were Lowell Bachman, Georgia "Tiny" Broadwick, Joe Crane, Colonel Joe Kittinger, Eilif Ness, Bill Ottley, Lew Sanborn, Cheryl Stearns, Ted Strong, and Gene Paul Thacker.

Teammate and friend Sam Alexander asked Jerry, "What made Jerry Bird Jerry Bird?"

In Bird's words

"I had a skill, I could skydive. But what separated me from the pack was my photographic memory and my recall.

I became skydiving's first coach, as they call it today, and I traveled the world skydiving when nobody else was doing that. I've coached the Venezuelan 8-way and 10-way teams, the German team three or four times, the Swiss team, the Norwegian team, the Iceland team. I've been to Australia and taught their teams. My schedules were like a rock and roll band. I had 16 stops in the summer: California, Arizona, Freak brothers Convention, North Carolina, Germany, Italy, Australia, North Shore of Hawaii, Venezuela, back to the States, and I did that for about ten years in a row.

There were Jerry Bird Camps where you weren't competing against anybody else. The reason this little drop zone is having a Jerry Bird Camp is because I would bring a big airplane with me and I'd bring a cameraman, and I made money doing that.

Klatovy in the Czech Republic, what a beautiful country. I go over there, the Pink Boogie, they're flying these pink Mick Jagger-with-a-tongue-hanging-out Sky Vans. The family owns the drop zone. All the Germans would cross the border because Czech was cheaper than Germany, like going to Mexico. It was the camaraderie, the friendships. When I went out of the country everybody wanted to put me up in their house. Come and meet my mother, come and meet my family. Don't leave Birdie in a hotel by himself.

In the middle of my career, I was wanted for my coaching. My thing was I could separate people, see what their weight was, how many jumps they had, put them together and make it work—even if it was just a 1-point skydive. Bird, you took 20 people up in the air and you didn't know any of them and you made a 20-way with them and that guy over there has 75 jumps. Okay, I used him in the base. But one of the things I was noted for was my recall and remembering. Remembering people's names, too. At one point I had met ten thousand skydivers around the world.

Seeing your students move from this stage to the next stage to the next stage as a skydiver was rewarding. And, later, when I see people who are famous in the sport, like BJ Worth, and I can say he was a protégé of mine, that makes me feel proud. And Dieter Kirsch in Germany, Patrick Passe in France, and Paul Berg and Sven Mortberg . . .

All these guys around the world I've left my legacy to, like Johnny Appleseed. Bird was here; we learned from him." —*Jerry Bird*

Jerry outside the Bird House at Skydive City, August 6, 2021. Wings painted by skydiver artist Lizzie Jones. Chris Johnston, photographer.

37

Life After Skydiving

After surviving the heart attack, Jerry retired from actively skydiving, though he continued to be involved in the sport as a strategist and ground coach, helping other formation organizers as a strategist and ground coach. He made a home with his grown sons and has been involved in the supportive care of John Brandon Bird, who is living with Glioblastoma Multiforme, a form of brain cancer.

In Bird's words

"I love my children. Both Josh and JB [John Brandon] are very intelligent. Josh could play music, but he became a writer. Their mother Beth was an artist. She could etch in glass; she could paint in oils. She and Rickerby were two of a kind; she painted right alongside him.[98]

Growing up, the kids played a lot of sports. Their mother was a coach or an assistant coach in their soccer league. They both started high school as juniors and JB graduated at 16. He made the sports teams, but they were 18-year-olds, and he was barely 16. That was quite a feat to hold his own. He made the All-Conference in tennis, he was a very, very good soccer player and if they had had a chess club, he would have been the school champion. Josh was also an accomplished soccer player, and he went to college on a soccer scholarship. When they graduated from high school, JB graduated third in his class. He probably should have been the

---

98. David Rickerby, an artist and skydiver known for his fantasy and surrealist paintings, including murals on jump plane bulkheads.

Valedictorian, but he didn't have enough high school credits because he had been home schooled.

During those home school times we entered the Tampa High School Chess Championships as "Bird's Homeschoolers." You were supposed to have four people on a team. We only had two, but they let us enter. Every high school has a chess club, and usually the chess club is taught by the Science teacher or some Mr. Wizard from the math department. A lot of times it's their children who are the champions. I don't know how many teams there were, but it seemed like hundreds of people were at this two day event. At the end there were three people who were undefeated. One of the guys who is running the tournament had just won the men's teachers division of the chess tournament, and his son and the other two that were undefeated were Josh and JB.

I think that rather than have a playoff system, John Brandon said, Josh, you play, or maybe they flipped a coin. I don't know how that was decided, but JB got left out. Well, JB was the best chess player, so he didn't get to play in the finals, but he was undefeated. So, Josh plays this champion high school chess player, and it gets down. I don't know that much about chess. I never play it. But you make your moves when you're playing tournament, and you write them down. After a certain number of moves, if you're not going to accomplish anything and the game's not over, it's a draw. Josh checkmates him and the kid stands up and says they were past the limit so shake hands for a draw. And Josh says, No, I win! They called a timeout and brought in the judges, and they replayed the match and counted the moves. Josh won. That was the only time we ever did that, but they wouldn't give us the team trophy because we didn't have enough team members. They were the only two people in the tournament that were undefeated. JB went to a chess tournament ten years later and beat the Master and went undefeated. He didn't play chess again and probably hasn't since then. He became a Texas hold 'em player, one of the best in the world." —*Jerry Bird*

"JB" John Brandon Bird

"A few things about me. I have demonstrated an obsessive personality throughout my life. Whenever I do something, I need to learn everything about it and do it right.

For my entire adult life. I've been a professional poker player. Not as exciting as it sounds but certainly rewarding. My real passion, however, is beach volleyball and that is as exciting as it sounds. An athletic activity at the beach and with it, in my experience, awesome people. I've also pursued some amateur comedy writing (emphasis on amateur.) Sometimes it's corny, sometimes it's dry, but it does make me laugh and, if I'm lucky. other people too. Let me give you an example of my brilliant wit: There's an idiom, no harm, no foul. Well, my version is no ham, no fowl, a vegetarian thanksgiving.

All right, that's all the time we have for comedy. In all seriousness, in my life I've been no stranger to disability. During my childhood my mother was diagnosed with muscular dystrophy. A heartbreak for her, those around her, and especially for me. I was very close to my mom and I didn't find it easy to cope with the tragedy that befell her. I was in my formative years, so the lessons I learned struck at my core and continue to resonate with me today. I learned to value and love every person and every moment in your life. It was in the aftermath of my mother's diagnosis that I first realized how much a positive mindset can reverberate with those around you. This brings me to my personal hero, my brother who spearheaded caretaker duties for our mother at a young age. It's a role he can't escape, nor would he want to.

This experience shaped who we are, dramatically teaching us both empathy and mental toughness. Fast forward to a couple of years ago. I was living a happy-go-lucky lifestyle: Poker and volleyball in Fort Lauderdale, Florida. Sand castles by day, chip castles by night, comedy in my dreams. I tried to be a genuinely good person as best I could when suddenly I was starting to feel symptoms of unknown cause. The absolute worst head and neck pain with bouts of nausea. I thought I could tough it out at first, but my condition only worsened, and the symptoms persisted. After a couple of weeks, I decided to move home so my brother and my dad could help me. An initial emergency room visit answered nothing. They didn't see anything in the CT scan. Doctors investigated further, but to no avail (the leading theory being a pinched nerve). Or, perhaps I was thinking one way or another, it was all in my head.

We never stopped trying to find answers. I continue trying to tough things out under the care of my brother who remains one of my many lifesavers, and my dad, an ever-present source of support.

After a grueling couple of months for everyone, a close family friend Natasha made sure I was admitted to the hospital for testing. She could tell my condition wasn't a joke. Within 48 hours of being admitted to the hospital, I was recovering from brain surgery. So, I'm living on borrowed time, but I think that in the most awesome way possible. Life is a gift.

Following my diagnosis of Glioblastoma and hearing the subsequent prognosis, I was in a bit of shock. My life was to look like a pineapple upside down cake, which that's sort of a nod to dad—pineapple upside down cake was always his favorite. I love pineapple. So, I made a decision to fight back.

Following surgery, I relearned the basics: Walking, feeding myself and dressing myself—very much like a toddler. Many people were—and are—doing their best to help me and when I'm in tune with the people surrounding me with support, I find we can orchestrate some civil solutions to try to manage my condition. With a positive attitude and maximum effort my functionality returned almost in full, although I currently can't juggle or drive a car. Baby steps.

I find joy anytime I'm around friends and family. Is there anything more important? I've also found a new hobby of playing board games with friends, which also appeals to my inner nerd. Speaking of which, my inner nerd isn't the worst mindset to channel while coping with many of my day-to-day maladies, a cerebral approach as it were. We've all heard it before, mind over matter, and yes, the irony isn't lost on me using my brain as a key instrument in the fight against brain cancer.

Early on in my cancer treatment, which involved radiation and chemotherapy, my doctor introduced me to the idea of another treatment called Optune. He said that Optune had been approved by the FDA for patients with newly diagnosed GBM for use in combination with the chemotherapy temozolomide TMZ. With the knowledge that there is no cure for glioblastoma and it's difficult to treat, it only made sense for me to employ a multipronged attack in my fight. I was onboard. When the time came many months later, I was given the green light to start treatment with Optune.

Keep in mind, this is just my experience. Everyone is different. That's why it's important to talk with your doctor about what's best for you, especially if you have questions or concerns about your treatment thing. Personally, I'm always delighted to respond to people. On rare occasions when a stranger enquires about the device on my head, I find that open and honest discussion about my condition and the treatment is welcome by listeners and therapeutic for me. In the event of a child being curious about what I'm wearing, I try to explain in ways that they might understand. Like, it's a device aimed at making me better. I certainly don't tell them I'm a ghostbuster.

I've found a wonderful outlet through social media to learn more about GBM, like connecting with other people and learning about their own experiences. It's been a positive experience for me because we give and receive support to each other.

I've been told I'm inspiring, which is a shameless brag. I can't imagine achieving a better goal than in some small way improving or bringing happiness to someone's life no matter how trivial. I found we're all in a fight with something in our lives and it helps us to find common ground and unity. To me, nothing is more cathartic than relating to others.

There's a wealth of positivity that can be taken from all this. I receive endless support from friends. To paraphrase a thought: When you can't walk, you crawl. When you can no longer crawl, you find someone to carry you. My brother has carried me through this. My Dad has carried me through this. All my friends and family have carried me through this. I'm fortunate to have a great team supporting me. I want for nothing except happiness for those around me

Come to think of it, okay. Yes. I really have led a charmed life."
—*JB Bird*

Let's go Tumornators!

"Everything is happening, the clouds have parted, I'm free"

As a nine-year survivor of brain cancer, I want to give a special thanks to my brother, Joshua, and my father, Dad, for keeping me going on even my worst days. Let's keep fighting brain cancer together! Woohoo!

"I get by with a little help from my friends"

Team Tumornators. brothers Josh and JB supporting the American Brain Tumor Association

Josh, JB and Jerry Bird.

2025: Jerry still travels, attending parachute industry events and skydiving reunions. Sometimes he shows up at Skydive City to see who is jumping or to meet up with a friend and swap stories. Jerry has a wealth of stories—more than one book can contain.

At home in nearby Dade City with sons Josh and JB, their two dogs Rigby and Lucy, and a cat named Luna. Jerry takes care of the house and garden and works on his vehicles. He has a real fondness for his classic Studebaker and his Bird museum on wheels—a Blue Bird bus that holds many memories and memorabilia from his skydiving years.

Jerry and his 1953 Champion Starliner coupe. JB Bird, photographer.

Coda

Nearly fifty years had passed since Bob Russell and Jory Pacht drove a thousand miles from Laramie, Wyoming, for the opportunity to jump with Jerry Bird and friends in Casa Grande, Arizona. Now it's August 2021; Bob and I and the Ground Rush crew arrive at Zephyrhills for a two-day interview with Jerry, beginning in The Bird House, Skydive City's iconic on-site museum and gathering place. Bob and I are both a little starstruck.

I started jumping out of airplanes in 1981, and while I had never jumped with Jerry or even met him, his name was legendary at the Colorado drop zone that was my nest and the place where five years later I met Bob Russell. Bob and I jumped competitively (together and separately), we became Accelerated Freefall jumpmasters, Bob got his Tandem rating and we worked for Skydive Colorado and Skydive St. Louis. I haven't made a skydive in over twenty years but once a skydiver, always a skydiver. For me, skydiving was, and is, life-affirming.

"I can't believe I'm sitting here having a beer with Jerry Bird," Bob says to me when Jerry turns to talk with Phil Mayfield. We are all enjoying beverages at Skydive City's bar after a day-long debrief with Jerry about his skydiving days and enjoying his stories. And yeah, the camera is still rolling, thanks to the dedicated film crew—our partners Chris Johnston and Bethany Baptiste—skydivers and BASE jumpers, both.

At last, the director calls it a wrap. Now the six of us are sitting on the deck of the DZ bar watching the groups of jumpers gearing up and heading to the loading area for the proverbial sunset dive. We all have our personal memories of sunset dives and we all know firsthand the camaraderie made on a drop zone and the pleasure of the day's last jump.
—*Linda Collison*

More Memories & Testimonials

A few of many...

"Jerry Bird, you rescued my main after a cutaway at Skydive City by climbing a tree!" —**Gina Amato**

"I remember Jerry at La Ferté-Gaucher in France where he came with an American 8-way team. My father, Michel Auvray, was on the French 8-way team. And I remember my mother gave Jerry a kiss on the mouth. I was furious and I told my father who reassured me, saying that wasn't a bad thing at all. That was in 1978, if my memory serves me right."
—**Pierre Auvray** (translated by the editor)

"I was so proud to be on Jerry Bird's team in Z-hills. Went from reading about him and all he had done for the sport to jumping with him. A real honor!" —**Edward Bushman Anderson**

"Skygod and very good friend at Z-hills. Remember *alors* his beautiful Corvette." —**Hugo d'Athis**

"180-degree vision. Nothing escapes. If Jerry is looking at you in freefall and shaking his head, you are wrong." —**Bill Bic**

"You taught me much. Your universal respect for all, I, for one, send deep appreciation." —**Dave Death Bellak**. ("P.S. Will never forget: "Be SAFE... have FUN... and LEARN something.")

"Brilliant skydiver!! Jerry coached us, the Endrust Skydiving Team, for the 1973 Turkey Meet 10-way speed event at Z-hills." —**Michael Bolton**

"Jerry and BJ made skydiving what it was back then." —**Max Braude**

"By the time I started jumping in 78, Jerry Bird was already a (skydiver's) household name. But it wasn't until 1987 when I was jumping with the Golden Knights did I actually meet Jerry Bird in person at the Z-hills Turkey Meet. One of the main events was Jerry's RW seminar—Jerry on a stage with a microphone, standing room only. Jerry's quick wit and sense of comedy had everyone cracking up from time to time. I was star struck like everyone else. Over the years I saw him quite a bit and made a few jumps with him. At the time he and Beth had a young family; they were an awesome couple." —**Charles Brown**

"A great boost to the jumping world." —**Betty Dawn Burkett-Ochsenschlager Coffman**

"I'm so happy I had the chance back in 1994 to be at Birdland and celebrate his 9000 jump with him." —**Gustavo Cabana**

"Jerry was better than having a photographer on the load."
—**Ken Cameron**

"I was very fortunate to jump with Jerry many times in the late '80s through early '90s. Most memorable at Bardstown, Kentucky, Richmond Boogie and Quincy where we had Canary Bird loads!"
—**Michael K. Canary**

"I was dispatched on a 15-second delay by Jerry Bird in 1981. I am from the UK. It was during the World Championships, and out of the DC-3. I came down on a reserve. Jerry signed my logbook. I had to buy a crate of beer and swallow a clam for the reserve ride." —**Ann Caswell**

MORE MEMORIES & TESTIMONIALS

"I'm grateful that I had the opportunity to jump with Jerry on multiple occasions. His skill and wisdom helped to make me the Skydiver I am today!" —**Kate Cooper-Jensen**

"One of the best ambassadors of our sport. I have made many jumps with Bird going back to the 1970s—always fun and informative. Thanks for the great and memorable times." —**Wes Colker**

"I was on a Bird Machine load in Raeford, NC with Jerry at a boogie in the '80s. On run up, before takeoff, the DC-3's left engine malfunctioned with a pop and a flame. We all hopped off on the taxiway. About an hour later they had it repaired and we reboarded. The standard command 'Scoot up front, tight!' was given. Bird added loudly, 'And cross your fingers!' We all laughed and relaxed, and just like that we were back to the business of jumping out of perfectly good airplanes." —**RL Cox**

"Among other stories with Jerry Bird, I went to Z-hills for the Christmas Boogie in 1987. He organized a 40-way wedge sunset dive which I had the honor of being invited to be part of. Bird is a legend in the business. I'm honored to know him and to have held hands in freefall with him." —**Chris Crain**

"The All Stars are the true legends and pioneers of their time. What they were able to accomplish in our sport in those times was incredible. I feel fortunate to have known some of these All Stars." —**Rick DePalma**

"Jerry coached our Canadian Speed 10 team to the 1975 World Meet in Germany." —**Manas Dichow**

"Awesome! The one and only Jerry Bird!!" —**Clifford Dobson**

"Met in Italy in an internship at Albenga, I think it was 1980 or 81. My impression was that Jerry was born not to stand on the ground, but his natural environment was the air; he flew with an impressive nature. Great person!" —**Giorgio Faina**

"Great skydiving icon. But more important, a great human being."
—**Nancy Douglas Fayard**

"He was the first person I jumped with when I arrived at Z-hills in the early '80s as an almost total beginner from Sweden. After that I did probably hundreds of jumps that he organized and it was always a blast . . . My favorite ever organizer." —**Lena Furberg**

"When I was in France in 1974, I stopped in to La Ferté Gauche, the drop zone about 40 km out of Paris, if I recall. The first question every skydiver asked me: "Do you know who Jerry Bird is?" He was a legend everywhere and probably did more for the advancement of large formation skydiving than any single other person during his prime."
—**Doug Garr**, *Between Heaven and Earth: An Adventure in Free Fall.* Greenpoint Press, 2009.

"The Wings of Orange practiced at Logan, Utah for a while. I got to meet Jerry Bird down at the laundromat. We went out to the parking lot and tossed the Frisbee waiting for our clothes to get done. I never flew a parachute with Jerry but I did fly a Frisbee, ha ha!!" —**Dave Gieber**

"I remember Jerry Bird when he was a member of the Arvin Good Guys. I was putting out students at Taft along with Eddie Armstrong and wishing I had got more involved in RW than accuracy."
—**Peter Godbold**

"Best debriefs I've been on." —**John Goscinski**

"I have jumped with Jerry many times in the '80s and '90s and I have always felt that many people in the industry never gave him the credit he deserved for advancing the sport of skydiving . . . I hope he's enjoying life." —**Joe Grant**

"Jumped with him a lot at Birdland. Awesome individual!"
—**Rick Grinder**

MORE MEMORIES & TESTIMONIALS

"There was only one Jerry Bird! He was always generous with his time."
—**Scott Harris**

"Learned a lot from The Bird-Man in the '60s, at Taft, and early '70s. Jerry was one of the few I've flown with that could, after a dive, give a total breakdown of who came in where, when and how, and then what needed to be improved on to speed it up on the next dive. The other diver that was great at this was his brother-in-law at the time, Skratch Garrison." —**Dennis Henley**

"My brother Paul, who had lost his right leg but still rode a motorcycle and was a very active skydiver, including being on Al Krueger's Pieces of Eight. Paul walked into a bar in Southern California. There were a bunch of local wannabe cowboy bikers who decided to try their luck jumping on Paul. Jerry came in and saw what was about to go down, got between Paul and his new friends and told those good old boys that 5–2 odds sounded even to him, so if they were finished exercising their jaws, it was time to get on with it. Both he and Jerry were ready to clean up a bunch of cow shit but the good old boys heard their mothers calling and split." —**Paul Henley**, as told through Dennis Henley

"Jerry Bird is one of the best ambassadors this sport had ever had. It was always fun when he was in town." —**Chad Hausman**

"I jumped with Jerry in 1973 at Casa Grande, Arizona. He lived in a trailer in the desert! I went there to have him sign my logbook for my SCR." —**William Howell**

"Jerry Bird came to our little DZ in Osceola in the late '80s and coached a few of us. Helped me fly like a rock star. I think he made every one of us feel the same way." —**Deborah Huntington**

"Bird was jumping when the low break-off and low-pulls were the norm, but after trial and error, some losing their lives, they came up with the modern-day Basic Safety Regulations. If you ever jumped with him,

you know he followed them to the T. Great guy, a jumping legend."
—**Cameron Jacques**

"Spent a whole weekend at his house with me and 12 of my friends jumping into his back yard. Such a kind and welcoming human."
—**Andrew Kennett**

"I met Jerry Bird at the ripe age of 19. Since then he has been not only a great friend but a mentor who has taught me so much. Not only about skydiving, but life. Skydiving with Jerry Bird is like playing golf with Tiger Woods. After all these decades he is one of my favorite people and best friends." —**Mark "Shoobi" Knutson**

"Jerry was an excellent competitor and a pleasure to know."
—**Al Krueger**

"Jerry is not only a great jumper but a fabulous load organizer. He has a sixth sense!" —**Nancy Kurlin**

I jumped with Jerry at Z-hills 1981–'83. I was stationed at MacDill AFB and Z-hills was my local DZ. A few of us military skydivers would jump there and Jerry took an interest in us and frequently he would organize 8-ways around our core group. A wonderful person—always helpful, kind—and a GREAT skydiver" —**Kim Langley**

"I remember being at Z-hills in 1997; Jerry Bird was organizing a 2 Otter 40-way for the sunset load. I went up to him and started doing the insecure limey-with-only-a-couple-hundred-jumps jabber . . . He let me finish and said, 'Do you want to come on the 40-way or not?' On exit I followed Brad Lambert down and got my slot. I was ecstatic! After a few beers in the bar I set off for my tent. I crossed Jerry's path and he said, 'I watched you; you did okay.' Those few words puffed my chest out. Jerry saw everything and everybody." —**Paul Ledden**

MORE MEMORIES & TESTIMONIALS

"I jumped with Jerry at Hercules Boogie-91 Sweden. Nice guy!"
—**Juha Leviakängas**

"May 1979, Jerry was on my SCS load in Pope Valley!" —**Kay Lewis**

"I'd do anything for Jerry Bird." —**Jake Lombard**

"Met Jerry Bird at the '72 World Meet in Tahlequah. First time I saw jumpers in tennis shoes and soft helmets." —**Steve Long**

"Our beloved sport owes Jerry Bird a lot . . . We have good memories of those dives from yesteryear." —**Russ Manhold**

"When you're on Bird's team you automatically perform better because he brought that out in people. There are a lot of good skydivers but there's only one Jerry Bird" —**Phil Mayfield**

"Jerry was the nicest guy in skydiving and such a great skydiver and leader. I still have a jumpsuit he gave me. It was brand new. I was really financially strapped in 1980 and he walked up and said, You need this. It meant so much to me and still does. I love this man. There are so many acts of kindness he did for people. God bless Jerry Bird." —**Ray Medley**

"I remember the first time I met him at Freeport Freak Brothers Convention. My husband said, You want to meet the sky god Jerry Bird? He's right over there. We became pretty good friends over the years."
—**Nancy McCoy**

"I met Jerry at Saint-André-Avellin Quebec where we were jumping with him at a boogie. A formation got funneled and we formed a 2-way before break-off. The next year at another boogie at St. Andre the same thing happened, and we formed a 2-way before break-off. We landed and he said, *Déja vu!* He had an excellent memory, and they were some of my most memorable jumps." —**Neil McGrath**

"We invited him as coach for our 8-way team in Italy. I tell you, it was like staying at the university of skydiving. A great man and a great time. Ciao Jerry!" —**Marcello Michi**

"Best team captain that I ever jumped with. Great team '76-'77." —**Bill Minyard**

"Early '80s at Z-hills on one of our frequent trips over from the UK, he asked me to help him with the group he was coaching. Even as a British Parachute Association Instructor/Examiner, which was an honor. The detail in his debriefs was phenomenal." —**Kerry Noble**

"Jerry Bird is the World's Most Famous Skydiver." —**Steve Noonan**

"A friendly guy, a pioneer in the art of freefall relative work, and a living legend." —**Victor Nickolich**

"Jerry gave us our briefing and was our "JM" on the first jet jump in Quincy, 1992." —**Paula Kopcik O'Malley**

"He told me in a stern voice . . . I know you didn't cause the funnel. But you drop grips when it does. You holding on to me was no good." —**James Ohare**

"I met Jerry 1985 at Z-hills. He was in the base. It was amazing how he was able to tell you what to do in freefall." —**Juan Ortiz**

"Ohio (Greene County)/Indiana (Richmond) dual state records made during the Richmond Boogie. Once Bird docked, we had the record(s). Organized by Roger Nelson, one of the early attempts had been a bit rough. One of the guys saw Jerry rushing by and called out, 'Did they give you the ax?' Without a beat, he replied, 'Yeah, and I'm swinging it!'" —**Curtis W. Pack**

MORE MEMORIES & TESTIMONIALS

"I had a great time skydiving with Jerry Bird at the Beer Boogie in Iceland 1987, organized by Siggi Baldursson. It was an honour skydiving with him! He always had his cap on and switched it magically in the plane to his frap hat. Nobody ever saw when it happened." —**Mats Pallin**

"Jerry the best skydiver in the world." —**Luis Do Pantanal**

"Jerry Bird has touched so, so many lives. He is a true legend. If you've ever had the honor of jumping with Jerry, I know he helped you become a better skydiver—he sure helped me. I was a load organizer at Z-hills in the mid to late '80s with Jerry Bird. We were like family I love this man beyond words." —**Johnny S. Parisi**

"I always had a blast with Jerry B! A good man through and through." —**John JP Patrick**

"The British Royal Marines Freefall Team trained every January to April at Z-hills, and in 1987 we brought Jerry in for our RW phase." —**Lyndon Pearce**

"Jerry was an amazing skydiver. A legend." —**Pirate**

"I was pinned by Jerry and it built to my first 8-way star. This was my 226th jump on July 12, 1974, in St. André Quebec." —**Phillip Porth**

"I got on a couple of jumps organized by the appropriately named Jerry Bird at Z-hills back in the 1980s. I was, and still am, a bit of a fast faller, shall we say. Bird slotted me into a position I could handle and I was in awe with the ease in which he made me feel welcomed and a part of the show."—**Larry Portman**

"I remember him well, jumping together at a boogie in Tanzania, Africa. What a cool dude!" —**Frederix Post**

"Jerry was my mentor in the early 90's. He taught me how to load organize and I've had a great career because of it. Proud to call him my friend." —**Lyle Presse**

"I was co-organizer with him at the Hercules Boogie in Sweden. Trailers next to each other; lots of nice chats." —**Kjartan Reithaug**

"I flew the Otter at Birdland, Bushnell Florida, winter of 1995. Good dude, Mr. Bird." —**Joshua Ruttkofsk**

"I compare Jerry Bird to baseball's Babe Ruth, what a skydiving legend! Thanks for everything, Jerry." —**Tom Sanders**

"Our Zimbabwe 4-way team got to meet Jerry Bird at the 4th World Championships of RW, at Zephyrhills, Florida U.S.A. when he was a team member of Mirror Image who went on to win the 8-way. He did so much for our sport." —**Victor Sharpe**

"Legend. I attended many a Party in Paradise, Hawaiian style. Good times and fun jumps!!!!" —**Arvel Shults**

"When I bought Chambersburg Skydiving Center we had Jerry as a load organizer. Jerry and his family were great friends. I was on his 10,000 jump as a videographer and my wife was on the skydive. Great times skydiving and many great evenings around the bonfire. The Bird is the Word!" —**J. R. Sides**

"I spent an entire summer working with Jerry at Skydive City in 1992, when I was getting serious about shooting video. Between May and Thanksgiving of 1992, I acquired the video slot at Skydive City; Jerry was the Load Organizer and the manager/Mayor. I was able to make around 300 jumps with him and I followed him to my first World Freefall Convention, and to the Barnwell Boogie. About 10 years ago I returned to Skydive City for a Turkey Meet where I filmed 10-way, and all the Turkey Meet activities. The first jump I got on was an 8-way camp and as I orbited around the formation, composing the shot with Skydive City in the center, I was overcome by emotion and started to cry in freefall as it was a full circle moment from me returning to where I had started. I don't think many people get that in their skydiving career, thank you Jerry Bird. I wish I could remember more but you know it was the '90s and Scotty was around a lot . . ." —**Justin Silva**

"I could tell a lot of stories, but I'll just say that Jerry Bird and the All Stars showed up at my drop zone, Orange, MA, in 1974. After beating all the locals in a conference meet, most of them left that DZ for the summer. I was among the few that stayed and were invited to follow Bird's 10-man team out of the twin Beech and/or jump with the alternates, including BJ Worth. Within three years all of us were jumping on Jerry's 10-man team in the Nationals." —**David B. Singer**

"A real standup man in skydiving and life." —**Dillon Smith**

"I jumped with Jerry at Orange, Massachusetts when I worked there and later at Z-hills when I was down there for the winter and living on the DZ in a rented trailer with my wife and very young daughter. Jerry was living there too. His wife had a daycare where my little one played during the workdays. I still have a picture of her pretending to feed a plastic lawn flamingo." —**David Strickland**

"Also unforgettable were Jerry's safety briefings; they were so funny that you definitely did not forget anything he said." —**Martin Stromeyer**

"Jerry Bird is to skydiving what Larry Bird was to the NBA. A legend."
—**Charles Tack**

"In 1973 most of the Midwest 10-mans were coming out of Hinkley. (James Gang, God Frogs) It was always challenging to bet the right combination of ten decent jumpers and a Beech together at the same time. But California had it all! Weather, planes, and huge talent. The All Stars were it! And I wanted to learn how to fly like them."
—**Lloyd Tosser III**

"What great things we did then . . . Jerry Bird's All Stars clocked some of the best 10-man star times in skydiving history. See that French frap hat Bird is wearing in the Boenish/Webster film of that event? I got it for him at the 1970 World Meet in Yugoslavia." —**Stan Troeller**

"I was at DeLand packing my rig. Jerry walked by and asked, 'Are you really going to jump that?' I said yes. He stopped, pulled out the main and packed it. (By the way, I was always known for my sloppy packing—13 malfunctions in about 1000 jumps)." —**Fred Walker**

"I was on the Bird 40-way speed star team for five years, from 1985-1990, and we won three of the five." —**William Weber**

"He beat everyone in his ring toss game, but I taught Jerry Bird how to front float the Pilatus Porter. Whether you had 100 jumps or a 1000, he treated you the same." —**Torsten Werner**

"Jerry used to come up to Chilliwack and load organize some of the best fun jumps of my life." —**Gordon White**

"Love my time spent and jumps with Jerry. I jumped at the Hills late 1980 and 81, then from 85 through early 1990. I was on his 40-way teams over the Easter Meet and many other jumps. He regularly passed on a lot of wisdom. I remember early on, once taking a leg grip on the inside of his leg as opposed to the leg grip on the outside. Oops! I definitely learned why that is not the best technique. I hope I have the opportunity to see Jerry again. He is one of my heroes and I would love to tell him so." —**Bob Winney**

"When I first went to Casa Grande the only thing, I knew is that it was a drop zone and Jerry Bird was there. And so, I wanted to go; I wanted to learn from this guy and hopefully if I was there long enough, he would actually talk to me. But of course, Jerry Bird is really cool, he'll talk to everybody." —**B. J. Worth**

About the Creators

Sam Alexander, creator and contributor, is a retired specialty insurance innovator, community volunteer, original member of Jerry Bird's All Stars, POV Cameraman, and hang glider pilot.

Raylene West, creator and contributor, is a retired skydiver, a hang gliding pioneer, and an enthusiastic cheerleader for Jerry Bird's All Stars.

Linda Collison, editor and contributor, is the author of *Star-Crossed* (Knopf, 2006) and other novels, short stories, articles and creative nonfiction. She is a former nurse and skydiving instructor/jumpmaster. www.lindacollison.com

Dan Brodsky-Chenfeld—Dan B.C. as he is known to many—is a world champion skydiver and large formation world record holder. Dan co-founded the professional skydiving team Arizona Airspeed. He is the General Manager of Skydive Perris, a motivational speaker, and the author of *Above All Else: A World Champion Skydiver's Story of Survival and What it Taught Him About Fear, Adversity, and Success*. Dan wrote the foreword for Jerry Bird's book.

Jerry Bird, creator and contributor, is a world champion skydiver, gear designer, coach, sports personality and the nucleus of this book.

Keep on truckin'!

Acknowledgements

It's high time a book was written about Jerry Bird, many skydivers of our generation have said. You can't do RW alone and neither can you compile a history like this by yourself. This book is a compilation of many articles, photographs, and memories shared verbally, in print, privately and on social media.

Articles from five decades of USPA's *Parachutist* Magazine are frequently referenced in this work and some have been reprinted in part, with permission. Thanks to the United States Parachute Association and in particular, Laura Sharp, Director of Communications, for her assistance and enthusiasm for this project. I'd also like to thank Melanie Greenbank of the Australian Parachute Federation for permission to reprint part of an article from their publication, *Australian Skydiver*, and for her enthusiastic support.

Each contributor has a unique perspective or personal experience to relate, or photographs to share. These many perspectives and memories combine with Jerry's to make this a shared biography, not only of the legendary Jerry Bird but a biography of the sport of which his name is an integral part. If all of us who contributed got together (living, dead, and resurrected) we could make a virtual supernova with half a dozen freefall photographers to capture it.

I want to recognize the co-creators Sam Alexander and Raylene West whose recorded interviews with Jerry instigated this book and influenced its structure, and whose written contributions add historical authenticity. Those who took the effort to put their thoughts and memories into words for this book include Rich Gernand, Charlie Wickliffe, Donna Wardean, Jim Captain, Mike Larson, Garry Carter, Siggi Baldursson, Scott Kyle, Will Renfroe, Bob Sturtivant, Cliff Weaver, Jack Gregory, Mark Knutson, William O. Hardman, Ruth Nitsche, Jake Lombard, Steve Woodford, Mike Michigan Sandberg, Jackie Smith, Jim Baker, Dieter Kirsch, Kate Cooper-Jensen, BJ Worth—thank you all for your written or spoken contributions, and thanks to Dan BC for the on-point Foreword.

I want to recognize all the photographers—amateurs and pros, living and deceased—who contributed to this work; your images are a treasured part of our sport's history. Much appreciation to those living aerial artists whose photos, film, and video have documented and inspired the evolution of our sport. Ray Cottingham, Andy Keech, Norman Kent, Luis Melendez, Tom Sanders, Randy Forbes, Dave Floyd and Mike McGowan, thank you for a lifetime of capturing us during those brief moments of freefall.

Much respect for the editorial eye and experience of Jan Works and Djan Stewart who were privy to prepublication iterations of the manuscript, and the word-for-word proof reading, fact checking and corrections of certain sections by Brendan McHugh, Mike Larson, Jim Captain, Garry Carter, Sam Alexander and Raylene West.

Skydivers are a tightly knit family. I really appreciate all of you "old school" skydivers who shared your memories, opinions, and photographs, online, via Facebook, email, telephone, and in person. These shared memories are woven into the entire works—so many we couldn't print them all. (More than enough for a Volume II if anyone wants to design and organize *that* big-way formation . . .)

This project has allowed Bob and I to meet or reconnect with so many of you, it has been personally rewarding beyond measure. For the past several years Mike Marthaller has been a good resource for the broader historical perspective of the sport—thanks Mike. Thank you Skratch for your philosophically insightful and delightful correspondence, and Clarice Rinard for lending me your collection of historical skydiving memorabilia, and for answering my questions. Mark Knutson—Shoobi—I appreciate your support of the Bird Project and for filling me in with some good details!

ACKNOWLEDGEMENTS

Our praise for filmmakers Bethany Baptiste and Chris Johnston for their hours spent recording interviews on location, their expert editing, and for designing Jerry's concept for the book cover.

I want to thank the Bird family. Bob and I had the pleasure of meeting Jerry's adult sons, Josh and JB, and learning about their unique talents and interests. Both men are handsome, gifted, gracious and supportive of each other. Our respect and gratitude to JB for sharing his journey of living with glioblastoma multiforme—and his wonderful sense of humor—with the world.

To my partner, teammate, and husband Bob Russell, thank you for your unflagging support in making this book a reality. Without you, it wouldn't have happened. And Jerry, thank you for the teaching, the stories, the friendship, and for always being Jerry Bird. —*Linda Collison*

Bibliography

Many of these books and periodicals are referenced in this work or were important to the background and subtext. Others were books Jerry recommended in his interviews.

Brodsky-Chenfeld, Dan. *Above All Else: A World Champion Skydiver's Story of Survival and What it Taught Him About Fear, Adversity, and Success.* Skyhorse Publishing, 2011.

Donovan, David. *Once a Warrior King; Memoirs of an Officer in Vietnam.* Seattle; Greenside Books, 2013.

Farmer, Matt et al. *Above Us Only Sky.* Independently published, 2023.

Garr, Doug. *Between Heaven and Earth: An Adventure in Free Fall.* New York; Greenpoint Press, 2009. Memoir.

Gunby, R.A. *Sport Parachuting, a basic handbook of sport parachuting.* Jeppesen, 1972.

Heaton, Norman. *My First 1000 Jumps; The Evolution of a Skydiver and the Organization That Became His Life.* Page Publishing, Inc., 2019.

Hooper, Jim. *Koevoet!; Experiencing South Africa's Deadly Bush War.* Helion & Company Ltd. West Midlands, England and GG Books Warwickshire; 2012.

Irwin, Lt. Col. US Army (Ret) Will. *The Jedburghs; The Secret History of the Allied Special Forces, France, 1944.* Public Affairs, New York; 2005.

Keech, Andrew C. *Skies Call.* Volumes 1, 2 and 3. Independently published; Washington D.C. and England, 1974, 1979, 1981.

Kirse Granate May, *Golden State, Golden Youth; The California Image in Popular Culture, 1955-1966.* University of North Carolina Press, 2002.

Leary, Timothy. *Flashbacks,* An Autobiography: A Personal and Cultural History of an Era. New York; G.P. Putnam's Sons, 1983.

Larson, Michael D. *Tales of the Cessna 195.* Mike Larson, 2014. Memoir.

McGowan, Michael. *Selections.* Skydiving and parachuting photography. Independently published by Mike McGowan, 2018.

Nickolich, Victor. *The Lynx; A true story of intrigue, deceit, and triumph in the midst of the Cold War.* Shreiber Press, U.S. 2016.

Poynter, Dan and Turoff, Mike. *Parachuting: The Skydiver's Handbook.* Para Publishing, 7th ed. 1998. Originally published in 1978.

Shepherd, Stan. *Skydiving; Full Flight.* Independently published, 2018.

Smith, Jackie. *Marooned.* Independently published, 2017.

Smucker, Anna Egan. *No Star Nights.* Knopf Books for Young Readers, 1989. A children's picture book about growing up in Weirton, West Virginia, the steel mill town where Jerry Bird grew up.

Stark, Steven D. *Meet the Beatles: A Cultural History of the Band that Shook Youth, Gender, and the World.* New York, HarperCollins; 2005.

Wilson, Brian with Greenman, Ben. *I am Brian Wilson, a Memoir.* Boston; Da Capo Press, 2017.

Works, Madden T. "Pat." *Parachuting: The Art of Freefall Relative Work.* RWunderground Publishing Company, 1975.

Works, Madden Travis and Works, Jan. *Parachuting: United We Fall.* RWunderground Publishing Company, 1979.

Periodicals

Parachutist Magazine. United States Parachute Association; Alexandria, Virginia. Members can access back issues online https://parachutist.com

Australian *Skydiver* Magazine, Australian Parachute Federation ; PO Box 1440, Springwood Q 4127. www.apf.com.au

Skydiver Magazine. Buena Park, California. Lyle Cameron, Editor. Out of print.

Works, Pat and Works, Jan. *RWUnderground Newsletter.* Schaumburg, Illinois and Fullerton, California. Published 1972–1976.

This collection of stories, articles, photographs and remembrances about the life and times of Jerry Bird is by no means complete—it's just a jumping off place . . .

www.ingramcontent.com/pod-product-compliance
Lightning Source LLC
Chambersburg PA
CBHW050524100526

44581CB00006B/116/J